PLEASURES AND PROBLEMS OF A ROCK GARDEN

LOUISE BEEBE WILDER

Alpines, being really noble, are the most democratic of plants, and know no distinction of rank or wealth; all they know and care for are their friends, whether from pithead or palace. Their instincts are unerring, and they have no respect of persons.

REGINALD FARRER.

PLEASURES AND PROBLEMS OF A ROCK GARDEN

LOUISE BEEBE WILDER

Illustrations by Sia Kaskamanidis

Hartley & Marks
PUBLISHERS

Published by
HARTLEY & MARKS PUBLISHERS INC.
P. O. Box 147   3661 West Broadway
Point Roberts, WA   Vancouver, BC
98281   V6R 2B8

LIBRARY OF CONGRESS CIP DATA

Wilder, Louise Beebe, 1878–1938.
Pleasures and problems of a rock garden / by Louise Beebe Wilder ;
with an introduction by Richardson Wright ; illustrations by Sia
Kaskamanidis ; nomenclature updated by Michael Boisvert.
p. cm.
Originally published : Garden City, N.Y. : Doubleday, Doran, 1928.
Includes index.
ISBN 0-88179-157-1
1. Rock gardens.   2. Rock plants.   I. Title.
SB459.W54   1998
635.9'672—dc21   97-45728

Design and composition by The Typeworks
Cover painting by Lyn Noble
Cover design by The Typeworks
Set in CENTAUR

Printed in the U.S.A.

CONTENTS

INTRODUCTION

SOME TIME ABOUT the turn of the century, the polite gardening world, which was accustomed always to hold a decorous vertical pose, began to be amused by the activities of certain men and women who insisted on reverting to the simian posture of "all fours." The cause was a new enthusiasm. It was vaguely murmured that gardening was about to merge into a Lilliputian phase.

No one took the rumour seriously, of course, since the garden was just convalescing from an operation that had removed tumorous iron stags and stiffly planted beds from its midst. It was luxuriating in the négligé of informally planted herbaceous borders and the calm green perspective of neat and unbroken lawns. Nevertheless, drop by drop, the Lilliputian tonic was administered, and before many seasons passed, began to show its effect.

In those countries that set our gardening styles (just as Paris sets our feminine fashions) this Lilliputian urge had already taken definite—and sometimes horrible—forms. It was known as rock gardening. Lordly and skycombing Alps were scaled down to the confines of an English back yard and crudely imitated in ugly piles of stones and cinders. Owners of estates that boasted rocky ledges looked upon them with kindling eyes. Gardening espoused geology as helpmeet. Leaders of floriculture and amateurs as well aspired to become minor mountaineers!

Therein a grave mistake was made. The accent had been misplaced. The word "rock" was stressed, to the confusion of many. The Germans called their endeavours "*Steingartens,*" the French "*Jardins de Rocailles.*" This new gardening threatened to become more geological than horticultural. The stones assumed greater importance than the plants that grew between them. In fact, any incidental plant capable of holding its height down to less than a foot found a home among these rocks and gave delight to boastful gardeners.

Then it was that those fastidious men and women who are ever

the leaders in gardening affairs began purging this style of its errors. For the word "rock" was substituted the word "alpine." Immediately a new vitality seized the movement. The imagination of those who had been content merely to grasp at straws instead of the substance was fired by this clear sincerity of purpose. Rock gardens were to be made for rock plants, not for stones. The rock garden should reproduce *in parvo* the environment in which these mountain plants naturally grew. Geology was dethroned and ecology assumed its place. Not until this came to pass did rock gardening deserve serious consideration.

Under this estimable influence, rock gardening has now been raised to an exacting art, wherein both the skill of the designer and the technique of the propagator are challenged. It has set hurdles that require real sporting blood to leap. Today one cannot boast that she has a complete garden unless it contain at least a few of the representative alpines set in their proper environment. Today one's gardening knowledge is limited indeed unless it includes some experience in plumbing the mysteries of alpine plants and their idiosyncrasies.

With this new phase, garden enjoyment has developed along a fresh plane. Whereas, once on a time, we had merely to stroll through a garden to reap the enjoyments of its beauty, in the rock garden we are obliged to bend, and even kneel, before all its loveliness is revealed. Humility (or at least the posture of humility) has been added to the horticultural counsels of virtue. Like workers in gems, we have patiently learned to place these glittering little plants in settings that enhance their growth and beauty. Our gardening fingers have been schooled to handle the infinitesimal.

And the study of these alpine plants has opened vast worlds to conquer. It has pointed us to the areas of wild and beautiful flowers that carpet the meadows and rocky slopes of our own mountains. No longer do we depend merely upon the continental Alps, for rock gardening has internationalized the alpine.

On this side of the Atlantic, one of the most potent factors in making rock gardening a serious matter to the horticultural world has been the work of Louise Beebe Wilder. In both her writing and her actual gardening she has been creating and teaching people how to create genuine alpine environments—the upland meadow, the glacial scree, the ledge, the mountain stream. With unflagging ardour, she has raised from seed and imported from their native habitats thousands of these tiny denizens of the mountains, and made them flourish in her own garden. Her writings, then, are based on profound knowledge and wide experience.

It has been my privilege for several years to read these writings as they came, month by month, to my desk. Through all that time they have never failed to furnish unbounded information and inspiration to thousands of readers. Now, rearranged, and brought up to date, and put between the permanent covers of this book, they constitute the most important contribution to rock gardening lore ever produced in America. May good fortune attend them!

RICHARDSON WRIGHT.

CHAPTER I

The Nature and Necessities of Rock Plants

THE ROCK GARDENER, in search of a truth to guide him in his fashioning with rocks and living green things, will find none more helpful than that proportion is beauty.

This axiom, taken to heart and acted upon, enables him to draw his little hills and vales, his jutting cliffs, his paths, pools, shrubs, and plants into such happy adjustment to each other and to the surrounding topography that the result spells reality and beauty, instead of unmeaning confusion.

And not the least significant of these adjustments has to do with the plants and shrubs chosen to clothe the bit of rugged country that a well-conceived rock garden is designed to portray. The more restricted in size and scale the small landscape, the more diminutive should be its flora and silva, for it is a fact that one great gawk of a plant in the wrong place will throw the whole scene out of scale, whereas, on the other hand, a little spruce or cedar, thoughtfully situated in regard to its surroundings, will draw the component parts together and give to the bit of landscape the look of truth and reality.

Where the construction is bold and extensive, fairly large subjects may be used, but, generally speaking, the ends of beauty and relevancy are best served when the plants chosen do not exceed a height of one foot, nor the shrubs a greater stature than three feet when full grown. Among shrubs and plants within these limitations is a wide choice, and some are fit and some are not for the purposes of the rock gardener.

Certainly, just any dwarf plant will not do. It is upon the understanding and acceptance of this premise that much of the beauty and interest of a rock garden rests.

To make of the rock garden merely a somewhat eccentric extension of the ordinary flower garden, clothing its windy heights and salubrious valleys with such as phlox and funkia, common bearded iris, salvia, and nasturtium—folk that must feel as foolish and out of place as they appear in such alien surroundings—is to pass up the opportunity for the keenest interest and enjoyment and to commit an obvious absurdity. There is no possible reason or excuse for going to the expense and great labour necessary to build a large rock garden in order merely to accommodate plants that would be far happier in the level borders. Yet up and down the country one sees magnificent sites and laboriously constructed rock work devoted to just this banal usage.

What, then, are the plants to which these very special surroundings should be dedicated? Long ago I made for myself this resolution: a rock garden should be devoted to the exclusive use of hardy plants of dwarf stature that require special conditions of soil or situation, and to those too small and fragile to hold their own or to display their charms among the strong growing occupants of the ordinary borders, yet possessing beauty of leaf or blossom in a sufficient degree to make them worthy of a special setting. This has proved a good rule. It permits a wide and catholic choice while steering us away from the incongruity of sophisticated border plants playing at being mountaineers, and saves us from the

dangers of such insatiable marauders as ground ivy, bugle, goutweed, moneywort, and creeping Jenny, freebooters too often given the character of rock plants in high standing, but which should never be allowed within the precincts set aside for the housing of choice plants.

Custom has bestowed upon the terms rock plant and alpine a somewhat broader meaning than recently obtained. An alpine, strictly speaking, is a plant growing upon a mountain *above the timber line*. Today any mountain plant—and indeed some that never saw a mountain—is credited with being an alpine. The term rock plant suggests rocky surroundings, but we now gather our "rock plants" from wood and meadow, prairie, bog, and shore, and our only restriction is that they be of dwarf stature and of a general character and disposition to look well and to thrive in a rock garden. But as I said before, just any dwarf plant will not serve. Mere dwarfness should not provide a ticket of admittance to the rock garden. For many a small plant has no beauty, and many a one is too gardenwise to appear well among the wild things that chiefly constitute our delightful company.

We might take as an example of the perfect rock plant the true alpine. This vivid creature is the product of its peculiar environment; of austere living in high places where long, snow-blanketed winters and short, blazing summers are the rule; where its roots must thrust deeply through stony detritus or insinuate themselves between narrow fissures in search of sustenance; where moisture in spring is plentiful and unfailing, and winds are ruthless and compelling.

From these exigencies has developed a type of plant possessing definite characteristics and marked personality. Briefly it may be described as of dwarf stature, often not exceeding two or three inches; of compact habit, either tufted, rosetted, or mat-making, its leaves small, close set, often hairy, leathery, or succulent, and in the majority of cases evergreen, or evergray. The flowers are clear and brilliant in colour and large for the size of the plant they adorn, prodigally borne over a short season—though sometimes giving a second blossoming in the autumn, at least in cultivation. Besides these definite characteristics, all friends of alpine plants are familiar with their peculiar cleancut sparkling brilliance of aspect, their amusing self-sufficiency, and their delight in growing and blossoming so plainly evinced where they are comfortably established that no one can behold it without experiencing a thrill. I have known many an otherwise garden-proof being stand entranced before a wildly blossoming plant of *Dianthus neglectus* [*Dianthus pavonis*] or *Campanula garganica*—the whole occupying a space that could be covered by a breakfast plate—using the most superlative language of delight and admiration.

Campanula garganica, from high rocky sections of Italy, is a typical rock plant. It accomplishes in June a veritable explosion of blue stars, beneath which its modest greenery is quite lost. *Androsace chumbyi* [*A. sarmentosa* var. *chumbyi*], from the Himalayas, is also typical, with its advancing gray rosettes and myriad pink umbrellas held a few inches above the foliage. Neither plant is taller than three inches. The mossy saxifrages form two-inch cushions of emerald verdure that are literally obliterated in May by a waving forest of slender stems bearing large, brilliantly white or pale pink blossoms.

These plants are illustrative of the type of plant which, to insure the best results, should for the most part inhabit our rock gardens. And this is the type that thrives apace and appears happy and at home in surroundings of rock and ledge and rugged contours generally. But, as will appear, the acceptance of this ideal does not by any means confine our choice to true mountain plants. One finds the same characteristics, the compactness, the freshness, the clean-cut brilliance, and the unmistakable air of being a personage in the primrose of the pasture, the orchid of the bog, in many a small wanderer on desert or prairie.

And it is to accommodate all these types and personalities and nationalities that a rock garden is designed. Here among its miniature hills and valleys, indeed within a few square feet, may be grown an incredible number and variety of plants hailing from all parts of the world. And this, I think, is the very essence of the fascination of rock gardening. Certainly no other phase of the craft gives us so wide a sense of kinship with the world of natural beauty.

A well-designed rock garden may easily have within its restricted boundaries the following topographical features: rocky hillsides, narrow ledges, windy heights, plains, sheltered valleys, a small bog, a pool, perhaps a stream, sand dunes, a beach, a heath, a bit of woodland, and, if you like, an alpine pasture. In a word, a rock garden, even a small one, may be a veritable vest-pocket world. Nor is this the difficult and complicated business it sounds. Anyone with a clear picture in his mind of these features in Nature, and possessing a little taste and ingenuity, can without difficulty conceive and construct the little landscape; and the rest is a matter of soil and exposure.

A number of plants that come rightly under the head of rock plants will grow in the ordinary soil of the garden. Of these are the common arabis and golden alyssum, hardy candytuft, some dwarf irises, cerastium, and many violas. But it is to be hoped that no rock gardener will be satisfied to stop with these amiable old friends, but will push on until his acquaintance numbers many of the small royalties of the world.

Over a large portion of the construction, a general soil mixture may be used. This must be light and free in character, sufficiently nourishing, readily pervious to moisture, so that the dread danger of winter damp is eliminated while yet a supply of drink is kept for the thirsty roots in summer. The following formula answers these requirements in a satisfactory manner, enabling the plants to withstand both drought and excess damp with equanimity and supplying a proper amount of nourishment.

It is surprising to find how many types of plants, many indeed that grow normally under quite other conditions, accept and thrive upon this unaccustomed diet:

1 part good garden loam, free from clay
1 part clean sharp sand
1 part leaf soil
1 part limestone chips

All these ingredients must be mixed and compounded thoroughly and then filled in and bedded down among the hills and valleys to a depth of at least a foot. You will then be ready to entertain a great variety of the sparkling pinks and poppies of high mountains, wee silver-leaved geraniums and erodiums, gray-tufted androsaces and mosslike saxifrages; small brilliant primroses from windy heights, fragile anemones, and a thousand more delights that never, never in a full-bodied herbaceous border will you see hide nor hair of. Gradually, it will have to be learned that some plants require less sand and grit, that some relish a diet of almost pure leaf soil, that others crave a dash of lime with their food, and that still others cannot abide it; that a few gourmands delight in old fatty manure—thus do many of the fastidious-appearing primroses —but for the most part manure has little place in the rock garden, nor has clay. Clay holds the sensitive roots in a cold and clammy embrace in winter and bakes an impervious surface over them in summer, and neither of these indignities will a proper rock plant suffer. Manure provides a too rich and stimulating diet, which causes them to lose their engaging compactness and to become leggy and without spirit. If enrichment is required, leaf mould and a little bone meal answers the purpose.

Besides the areas provided with the general soil mixture, it is delightful to incorporate a number of other features with soil to suit the plants that would naturally occupy them. Of these a little heath is easily made and is productive of much interest. Thereon may be housed the various varieties and species of heather and ling (erica and calluna). These are of a very special charm, and if a wise choice be made among them the heath will be in flower the greater part of the season. Here too will flourish our shy and lovely bird's-foot violet and intriguing *Iris verna*. The soil required is compounded of three parts peat and one of white sand, both of which may be had of nursery supply houses by the bag or barrel. The situation of the heath should lie out in the sunshine and preferably upon a windy upland slope. Various scillas may be tucked in among the little bushes.

A dampish shaded corner should be dedicated to such royalties of our own woods as the pink moccasin flower, the trailing arbutus, the chaste dalibarda, choice trilliums, shinleafs, the dwarf cornel, and the glistening wintergreen. Examine the soil in any where great oaks and evergreens abound, and provide as close a replica of it as is possible. You will need fine white sand, rotted pine or hemlock needles, rotted wood from hollow trees or old stumps, rotted oak leaves. This, well mixed, makes a highly acid soil, and in it the beauties named above and many others that require this type of soil will thrive like the proverbial bay, and out of it—in any other medium—they will promptly die.

An old stump or rotting log well placed adds a touch of reality to this portion of the rock garden. These properties also provide protection for tender plants and the gradual decomposition of the wood, especially if it be chestnut, hemlock, or oak, helps to keep up the acidity of the soil.

The soil for the meadow and hedge primulas should be composed of sticky loam—that means a clayey loam—and well-rotted manure. For these dainty creatures—the oxlip, the cowslip, and the true primrose, than which there are no more beauteous flowers—have not dainty appetites. They like a rich and heavy diet, a soil that holds them closely and retains an abundance of nourishment and moisture. Their table should be spread in a shaded, dampish corner.

Following are two lists of plants that either the tyro or the veteran may seek with almost equal confidence. It is certainly not the company commonly recommended the beginner. This eager and often highly intelligent person is always put off with such as arabis, golden alyssum, magenta *Phlox subulata* (just why the beginner never by any chance gets hold of any but the magenta type is not clear), *Cerastium*, hardy candytuft, and bugle, all well enough in their way, but great sprawling, hungry things that quickly submerge and hide his tentative bit of rock work and then start in to annihilate each other. Thus is he rather floored and confused at the outset and decides either to let the hoydens have it their own way (in which case a rock gardener is probably lost to the world), or he tears them out and begins all over again with some of the more restrained and just as lovely plants that, moreover, are no more difficult to grow.

The plants in the sunny list will, with few exceptions, thrive in the soil mixture given earlier in this chapter. Few of them, however, would hold their own in the soil of the ordinary garden borders. It must be kept in mind that "hardiness" is as contingent upon drainage as upon temperature. Therefore many a plant that would succumb in a rich and retentive soil is perfectly safe in the free and gritty mixture of the formula on page 4.

A SELECTION OF ROCK PLANTS FOR A SUNNY GARDEN
(All marked with * may be easily raised from seed)

*Achillea serbica
*Achillea tomentosa
Adonis amurensis
Adonis vernalis
*Aethionema persicum
*Aethionema Warley
  Hybrid
*Allium cyaneum
*Alyssum saxatile
  citrinum [*Aurinia
  saxatilis 'Citrinum'*]
*Alyssum montanum
Androsace sarmentosa
Androsace lanuginosa
Anemone pulsatilla
*Anthemis montana
*Anthemis aizoon
*Aquilegia flabellata
  'Nana Alba'
*Arabis albida rosea
  [*Arabis caucasica*]
*Arabis aubrietioides
*Arenaria montana
*Armeria caespitosa
*Aster alpinus
*Aster subcoeruleus

[*Aster tongolensis*]
*Aubrietia in variety
*Campanula garganica
*Campanula muralis
  [*Campanula
  portenschlagiana*]
Campanula pusilla
  [*Campanula
  cochlearifolia*]
Ceratostigma
  plumbaginoides
*Dianthus caesius
  [*Dianthus
  grationopolitanus*]
*Dianthus alpinus
*Dianthus arenarius
*Dianthus neglectus
  [*Dianthus pavonis*]
*Draba aizoon
*Erinus alpinus
*Erodium
  cheilanthifolium
*Erodium
  macradenum
*Erysimum pulchellum
Gentiana septemfida

*Geranium cinereum
*Geranium
  lancastriense
  [*Geranium
  acontifolium*]
*Gypsophila repens
*Gypsophila
  cerastioides
*Helianthemum in
  variety
Hypericum reptans
*Iberis gibraltarica
Iris gracilipes
Iris arenaria
Iris pumila caerulea
Iris cristata
*Linum alpinum [*L.
  perenne* ssp. *alpinum*]
*Linum salsoloides
Lychnis alpina alba
*Papaver alpinum
*Papaver nudicaule
*Papaver rupifragum
Phlox amoena
Phlox subulata 'G. F.
  Wilson'

Phlox subulata
  'Nelsonii'
Potentilla alba
Potentilla verna nana
*Primula cortusoides
*Primula denticulata
*Primula frondosa
*Saponaria ocymoides
Saxifraga macnabiana
Saxifraga decipiens
  [*Saxifraga hypnoides*]
Sedum dasyphyllum
Sedum sieboldii
  [*Hylotelephium
  sieboldii*]
Sempervivum
  arachnoideum
*Silene alpestris
*Silene schafta
*Tunica saxifraga
Thymus serpyllum
  'Albus'
Veronica repens
Veronica rupestris
Viola bosniaca
Viola gracilis

ROCK PLANTS FOR A SHADED GARDEN
(The soil should be largely leaf mould)

Allium moly
Anemone hepatica
  [*Hepatica americana*]
Anemone canadensis
Anemone sylvestris
*Aquilegia canadensis
Anemone sylvestris
*Aquilegia canadensis
*Arenaria balearica
Asperula odorata
*Campanula carpatica
*Campanula
  rotundifolia
Cardamine pratensis
Chimaphila maculata
*Corydalis lutea

*Corydalis
  cheilanthifolia
Cypripedium
  parviflorum
  [*Cypripedium calceolus*
  var. *parviflorum*]
Dalibarda repens
Dicentra eximia
Dicentra cucullaria
Dodecatheon meadia
Epimedium
  (in var.)
Funkia minor
  [*Hosta minor*]
Houstonia caerulea
Mertensia virginica

Mitchella repens
Mitella diphylla
*Myosotis palustris
  semperflorens
*Myosotis sylvatica
Omphalodes verna
Phlox divaricata
Podophyllum peltatum
Polygonatum biflorum
*Primula vulgaris
*Primula vulgaris
  coerulea
*Primula japonica
*Primula veris
Pulmonaria
  angustifolia

Ramondia pyrenaica
  [*Ramondia myconi*]
Sanguinaria canadensis
Soldanella alpina
Sedum ternatum
Shortia galacifolia
*Silene virginica
Silene pennsylvanica
Thalictrum minus
Tiarella cordifolia
Trillium grandiflorum
Trillium erectum
Vancouveria hexandra
Viola blanda
Viola canadensis
Viola rotundifolia

CHAPTER II

Spring Activities

Long before we have any reason to hope for flowers there have been nevertheless, expectant visits to the rock garden. Though battened down with snow, or lying snug beneath a shrouding blanket of leaves or salt hay, a mysterious sense of promise seems to float above the humped and gullied masses; a sense of stirring life and of things about to happen. And if you visit this small kingdom at almost any time during the winter and very early spring and lift a corner of the blanket, or dig a hole in the snow, you will seldom be disappointed. Quite certainly you will find something green and fresh and heartening to look upon, if only a moist, fresh primrose leaf, or a solitary snowdrop, furled and budded, biding its time.

Early in March, if this crusty month be not too bitter cold, investigation may bring to light ranks of green and white crystalline snowdrops, Christmas roses ready to blow, little heaps of green-gold nuggets that are the buds of the adonis, unnumbered points of brilliant green sent up by the little bulbs. And if the snow be not too heavy, winter crocuses are thrust through and brush the whiteness with purple shadows.

This is perhaps the most intriguing season of the year to the gardener—to the rock garden it is the most perilous. The desire to lay back the winter blanket and allow this impatient budding and blowing to go on without let or hindrance amounts to a fine frenzy. But this is exactly what must not happen. Such dire consequences follow upon a too early or too hasty uncovering that enough cannot be urged against it. I have seen a newly unblanketed rock garden, its surface sprigged with fragile bloom and freshest green, burned almost black under the cruel switching of the wild spring winds a few hours after its release.

The beating, drying winds are the scourge of this early season. The secret of safety is to remove the covering by slow degrees, thinning it day by day—one's eye on the weather—letting in those sharp breezes little by little in order that the coddled plants may become gradually hardened. If the winter blanket has been of oak leaves, a good plan is to lift the light branches that held them in place and let the wind begin the uncovering. If of salt hay, all of it should not be removed at once. Here one's wits must be the guide. No hard-and-fast rules can be laid down for the wild spring weather. No date can be set for the beginning of this task, none for its completion, for it will vary every year and in every locality. The gardener must deal rigorously with himself and feel his way. A bamboo rake is a light and handy implement to use in clearing the rock garden. It does not tear the tender growths, nor uproot the frost-loosened plants. Much of this work must be done by hand, however. Only sensitive fingers can work the last of the leaves and litter from among the matted plants. A small whisk broom may be used by those who do not like the touch of the damp earth.

And very soon the hills and valleys and little plains will be all clear, the earth giving off tingling fragrances, and hundreds of little plants preening, smiling, blossoming and all expectant of kindly ministrations.

And here let me say that the labour of caring for a rock garden is far less than that required in most other kinds of gardening. If at the outset the construction has been well carried out and the soil properly prepared, there will be little trouble. The earth will not bake and crack, and moisture will be comfortingly retained during times of drought, thus doing away with a continual stirring of the soil. Nor is there ever any heavy digging to be done, nor staking of top-heavy plants; no training of prickly climbers—hateful task—no lifting and dividing of heavy old border favourites. The barrow is seldom used, and the tools required are light.

Once in a way, indeed, one may be faced with the necessity of shifting a hundred-pound rock, or of altering the physiognomy of a mountain, but this will not be often. The task that will be ever before one is *weeding*. It is never to be neglected. One must weed as never before and with meticulous care. Let one stout-hearted weed—and they are all stout-hearted—become firmly rooted among the stones, it is there for a long stay, probably forever. Thence will its roots set out to prowl and creep, insinuating themselves under and over and around the stones, relentlessly threading themselves among the growths and tender rootlets of the choicest among our collection and eventually squeezing them to death.

Others sow their seed wildly, casting it in all directions, so that where one was, in the twinkling of an eye there will be hundreds. Grass; white clover; pussley; chickweed; a crafty yellow-flowered lady's sorrell; a wretch with the high-sounding name of *Galinsoga parviflora*, an annual possessing power to become a centenarian through its undying seeds, these are the worst, but no weed of any sort should receive the least clemency. Where they are all concerned, vigilance must become your middle name and ruthlessness your shield.

For use in the elimination of weeds from the rock garden the perfect instrument is an iron kitchen fork—or rather two kitchen forks, one long and one short. With the long one you may thrust down under the stones and gouge out long-rooted trouble makers. With it also you may go to the relief of some plant caught in the merciless grip of white clover, driving it under the sturdy crown and drawing it forth with all its white tentacles writhing and no harm done to the suffering host. With the little one you may outwit such small miscreants as chickweed, working over the fragrant mats of white thyme or creeping veronica that it delights to infest, until every vestige is finally extracted and the plant quite free of its wily enemy.

It should be said here that the tools used in the rock garden are not by any means as other tools. Secure a broad, flat basket and place in it the following articles:

A long iron kitchen fork for weeding.

A short iron kitchen fork for weeding.

A slim-jim trowel for planting small bulbs.

A very small mason's trowel for transplanting seedlings.

A larger mason's trowel for moving larger plants.

A pair of long, strong shears for clipping straggling plants.

A pair of scissors for snipping seeds and faded blossoms.

A whisk broom for clearing out litter from among plants.

A package hairpins for pegging down or layering.

A package small envelopes for holding seeds.

Wooden labels, indelible pencils, a few strawberry baskets with which to shelter newly set plants. (Do not use inverted pots for this purpose.)

The great majority of rock plants are easy enough to please. They take with amazing coolness the change from quite other conditions to garden life if something be known of their home life and an effort made to reproduce it. As soon as plants are ordered research should be made to find out what their necessities are likely to be—what soil they live in, whether moist or dry, sweet or sour, clay or sand, or whatever, whether in shade or sun or a little of each, whether the plant is quite hardy or likely to be a little tender, and its size when full grown, and you will then stand a good chance of making a rare newcomer a permanent dweller in your garden.

A well-filled larder is a great help. In an obscure place, and under cover if possible, should be boxes or barrels of the following comestibles: coarse sand, fine white sand, leaf mould, good loam, peat, crushed limestone or old mortar, stone chips such as are used to top-dress roads, and a little very old manure. All of these will be required from time to time, so it is well to have them handy that no suffering plant be kept waiting for relief.

Rock plants are subject to few or no ailments, so far as my experience goes, and few pests attack them. If a plant seems not to be thriving, try it under other conditions and it may revive, but make some effort to find out how its present surroundings differ from those to which it is accustomed.

When first you view your rock garden clear of the winter covering, quite likely you will see only loveliness and enchantment. For April is a faërie month among the hills and dales. Before you gleam breadths of early wild crocuses—so much more engaging than the fat dutchies that come later—battalions of tiny daffodils, wide gold adonis flowers, pools of sharp scilla-blue, violets and hepaticas, and primroses peeping everywhere. All the early spring flowers are so crisp and clean and lively that it seems impossible to believe that among them aught can be amiss. Yet as we stand before the lovely scene, our winterbound senses thawing slowly, we presently see that beneath the carnival there is trouble that requires immediate attention.

In all likelihood ragged gullies have been worn down the little steeps, soil displaced behind badly placed stones, earth washed from crevices which have not been securely packed. All this must be repaired and reinforced against the fury of the spring freshets. It should be seen that every stone is firmly set and wedged with earth and smaller stones, and the crevices so tightly rammed that they will not again give up the soil and so expose the roots of the plants entrusted to them.

Further scrutiny will reveal plants whose roots have washed clean of soil, and others that have arisen on their tap roots and are lying about in a most unseemly manner wholly regardless of deportment. Others will appear depleted and unenthusiastic. For these we maintain the pick-me-up basket, a close-meshed basket filled with a reviving mixture compounded of loam, sand, leaf mould, a few stone chips, and a dash of old mortar. This we work in among the growths of such as the mossy saxifrages, pinks, campanulas, and others. With it we also cover exposed roots and tuck in about any plant that appears to need it. Indeed, a top-dressing of this elixir over the entire rock garden in early spring is a consideration that will be amply repaid in blossoms and lovely greenery.

At this season the gray-leaved plants should be attended with special care. If the winter has alternated cold and warm, and damp has been much in evidence, they are probably in bad shape. They dislike, of all things, coming into contact with wet earth, and they are against excess moisture at any season, the humidity of summer as well as the thaws of winter. They should nearly all be given the highest and driest of situations and a full measure of sunshine. About them the earth should be thickly strewn with stone chips. This keeps them dry and gives them heart to display their silvered beauty.

Ragged leaves should be removed from those plants that have "felt" the winter, and others that are leggy and out of trim treated to a severe clipping with the long shears. It will be found also that some plants have not hibernated in any proper sense. They have gone on growing and spreading out beneath the snug blanket until they are endangering the lives of smaller sleepers. These must be clipped back or bodily removed.

A chief cause for activity in the early spring is discovered in the bare spaces left by plants that have not come through the winter. Sometimes these are many, sometimes few, but the cause, as I have before said, is more often damp than cold. These ragged places in the garment of the rock garden may be variously patched. One may install new plants, or divide some flourishing old ones to use in filling the gaps; or one may sow in seed of some small and attractive annual or biennial which will quickly cover the worn spot with bloom and verdure. Some useful kinds for this purpose are *Androsace coronopifolia* [*Androsace lactiflora*], *Linaria alpina* (biennials), *Gypsophila muralis*, *Asperula azurea setosa* [*Asperula orientalis*].

Plants may be lifted and divided for patching at almost any season. The time when they are in full bloom is probably the least propitious, but with care even this may be accomplished without loss. Irises, mossy saxifrages, alpine pinks, primroses, aubrietias prefer division just after they have flowered. Some authorities, indeed, contend that this is the best time to lift for transplanting or division all plants because at that time they are at the height of their vigour and push. Late April and May, late August and September, have proved very satisfactory to me for disturbing a large number of kinds. All plants growing in

tufts, rosettes, and mats are easily lifted and pulled apart. Those with long tap roots are best left in peace if they are thriving.

Planting at all times must be a matter for care and consideration. Many appear to think that, with a thing so inconsiderable as an alpine, no more is necessary than to open a slit in the earth and thrust the morsel in. This is the worst possible practice and few plants will survive it. Always a commodious hole must be dug with room at the bottom for the fragile roots to be spread out in comfort. After the first handful of soil is put in, water is added, then more earth until the excavation is full and the soil closely drawn about the neck of the plant, when a top-dressing of stone chips may be laid on as a finish. When the plant comes in a pot, and it is now possible to get them thus from numerous dealers, the ball of earth and roots must be shaken from the pot, the lower roots freed of the bits of drainage and spread out, the whole placed carefully in the excavation, and the earth drawn firmly about the neck. Loose and careless planting is responsible for the loss of many a valuable rock plant. It must feel secure before it has the courage to start growth in a new home.

A convenience is a label placed beside each newly set plant inscribed with its name, date of planting, and whence it came. When the number of one's family mounts into the hundreds, the tip of the tongue becomes decidedly overcrowded, and it is embarrassing not to be able to furnish the data sure to be called for by visitors.

This April care of the rock garden seems to

me the pleasantest work of the whole year. Not only are rock plants so charmingly responsive to every kindness, but at every turn of the way some new delight is revealed. One may go round and round the little paths, and over and over the little hills, and find each time something lovely missed before—some exquisite, fragile fern just unfolding, some jaunty bloom from a little bulb not known before, a nosegay of blue primroses, the nose of some plant we had feared would not winter. It is a pleasure to go with a bent back at this season—at least in the rock garden—for while weeding and feeding, patching and filling up crevices, we are enjoying at every step revelations of freshness and beauty, gaiety and fragrance that are a joy and a refreshment to remember throughout the year.

CHAPTER III

Crocuses, Small and Early

ALL SORTS OF crocuses are lovely and welcome wherever they will grow, but the ones best suited to the rock garden are the wild sorts, the crocus species. These, being innocent for the most part of "improvement" at the hand of man, are more in keeping with the other free spirits that inhabit this special region, and they are, speaking generally, smaller and daintier than the Dutch crocuses, and in appearance, though not in fact, more fragile and ethereal.

The Dutch crocuses are highly educated descendants of *Crocus vernus*, a species widely distributed in Europe. They are large flowered and sturdy, and rich in pure, clean colours. They are most splendidly effective when planted freely in wide drifts in the shrubbery borders, or naturalized where grass is thin and light. (No crocus will flourish and increase in heavy turf.) But the only Dutch varieties I encourage in the rock garden are the beautiful maximilian and the glowing Dutch yellow. Crocus maximilian is rather smaller as to flower than are most of the Dutch varieties, and 'tis said that the blood of an exquisite wild species, *C. tomasinianus*, courses in its veins. Its form is perfect and its colour a pure porcelain lavender. It is the best of all the dutchies, to my thinking, and deserves a show place in the rock garden and to be widely planted outside.

Very little is known of the origin of the Dutch yellow, but it has been a source of delight in gardens for more than two hundred years. It is an invaluable sort, blooming ten days before the others and creating patches of most welcome warm colour in the cold spring garden. Its constitution is of the stoutest, and it will thrive under almost any conditions save deep shade and damp. This cro-

cus is probably more often planted than any other, and in many gardens it is the first flower to show itself after the turn of the year. It does not, however, bloom as early as do many of the species, and it is a pity to wait for the Dutch yellow to know the thrill that the first crocus invariably brings. Christmas rose, snowdrop, aconite, seem always to belong to winter, a little chill and aloof, but when the first crocus is blown into the world, it makes us feel that spring has come despite the testimony of the calendar and the protestations of the weather to the contrary.

But not all crocuses belong to the late winter and spring; full as many make their appearance in the autumn and early winter. In climates less extreme than ours, it is possible to have these flowers in bloom from August throughout the winter and spring. In the neighbourhood of New York, however, we must be satisfied with much less; we must practically count out the winter months where crocuses are concerned, though I once was made exceeding proud by the flowering in my garden early in December of the fragrant yellow *Crocus vitellinus*, a species from Palestine. But only once was I allowed this pridefulness, for it never so much as appeared again. Many of the more tender winter species could be grown indoors in pots, or in coldframes in the garden, but in any case, without them, there are many species that we may enjoy during the autumn months and in the early spring, from March almost until May.

Crocuses are not generally difficult to grow.

All of them, practically, love to expand their blossoms in full sun, though many will endure light shade with a very good grace. When it comes to soil, they are not given to asceticism; they want drainage, but they also like a good deal of nourishment. The soil that grows good vegetables will grow good crocuses; they are not even total abstainers where manure is concerned, a little old and very well-rotted cow manure dug in about four inches below the bulb being much appreciated. But we do not often have so rich a diet to offer in the rock garden, and we find the crocuses do very well in the richer mixtures of loam, leaf mould, and sand, with a little bone meal stirred into the surrounding soil. As they come at both the beginning and end of the year at seasons when storms rage and mud flies, it is well to grow them under such a lightly rooting covering as is provided by the white thyme or *Veronica repens*, or to cover the ground about them with stone chips in order that the crisp freshness of their blossoms may be enjoyed unmarred.

It should be remembered that, where we plant crocuses, we must later endure untidy yellowing leaves and choose our situations for them accordingly; but on no account are the leaves to be tampered with until they turn a deep yellow, however unsightly they may be. These ripening leaves are storing up nutriment in the young corm for next season's flowers and may be removed only when fully mature.

Crocuses should be got into the ground as early as they may be procured in order that they may make roots before winter. This is especially true of the autumnal species, which for best results should be planted in August. But, alas, this is not often possible in our country. Our autumn crocuses are usually received with the other bulbs, the dear punctual things often blooming frantically in the paper bags with no roots at all. Naturally, it takes them some time to recover from such a harrowing experience, and fatalities sometimes result. Experts differ as to the proper depth for planting crocuses. I have always set them about three inches below the surface of the ground, but Mr. Bowles, the undoubted authority on these flowers, advocates "something between four and six inches" and adds that *C. aureus* [*C. flavus*] and *C. speciosus* will not object to going much deeper. In any case, they should not be near the surface, or they will be heaved out of the soil by the frost, and they are, moreover, too easily to be got at by mice. Those wretched little vandals are the only serious enemies of the crocus; they dig up the bulbs and devour them voraciously. No means by which they may be thwarted should be neglected.[1]

When plantings of crocuses become overcrowded, the corms may be lifted, the old tunics cleaned away, and the corms sorted as to size and replanted in good soil. I always count my crocus corms as if they were veritable pieces of eight!

---

[1] *I have this year seen squirrels digging up my crocuses and eating them with relish.*

Crocuses abound in the Mediterranean region of Europe and are found as well in Asia Minor, the Caucasus, and in Central Asia.

There are a hundred or more species known, though not all of them, by any means, are in cultivation at present. There is, however, much scope for making new friendships among them. I will tell of some crocuses that have lived happily in my garden and of a few that have definitely declined my hospitality.

In the spring, the first to bloom is always *C. imperati*. Rarely this species appears in late February, but always by the first week in March, unless the snow lies heavily on the ground. In the bud it is soft buff colour with purple lines, but at the magic touch of the sun it opens out showing the lovely rosy-mauve interior. The flower is large and beautiful and fragrant, and has a fragile and tender grace. It is, however, hardy and enduring and increases satisfactorily. There is a white form, also yellow in the bud, but I have not seen it.

Crocus sieberi is always a close second to *C. imperati*. It is a gay and very floriferous species, with smaller amethyst-coloured flowers, star-like when open wide. This species is easy and sturdy and is less harmed by inclement weather than some of the more fragile kinds. I have often seen it blooming cheerfully above a thick blanket of snow. It is from Greece and the islands of the Archipelago.

Yellow crocuses are very grateful to the eye during the chill spring days. They burn with a fine fire, and one's very soul is warmed by their genial glow. Of these *C. aureus* [*C. flavus*] and *C.*

susianus [C. augustifolius] are very desirable, the first, while it enjoys sunshine, will thrive and even seed itself in the shadow of deciduous trees and in the shrubbery. It begins to bloom as soon as weather permits.

In sheltered locations, C. susianus [C. augustifolius], the cloth of gold crocus, sometimes blooms here during the first week in March, but it commonly appears a little later. Its outer sepals are feathered with brown, but on sunny days it opens out wide and starlike and bright orange in colour, a small brilliant flower creating rich breadths of colour when massed. It is one of the easiest to grow and increases rapidly, and being inexpensive may be planted widely for spring cheer. C. susianus [C. augustifolius] has long been an inhabitant of Dutch and British gardens, having been sent to Clusius from Constantinople in 1587.

The Scotch crocus, C. biflorus, is often planted with the cloth of gold crocus and begins to bloom before the orange-hued blossoms are spent. The flowers of the Scotch crocus are white, lightly veined on the outer sepals with blue. It is a charming sort, a very old garden friend, asking no special kindness save a place in the sunlight where it may open wide its silvery blossoms. It increases rapidly by corm division. A native of Tuscany.

I am not sure that C. tomasinianus is not the most lovely of its kind. It blooms about March 20th here, slight and silver-gray in the bud, but opening out starrily in warm sunshine to reveal the warmer colour of the inner sepals and the hot orange stigmata. Its delicate appearance belies it, for it is in reality quite vigorous

and sows its seed about, raising up lovely young to rejoice our hearts. This precious species belongs to Dalmatia, Bosnia, and Serbia.

C. olivieri, from Greece and Romania, brings more yellow gaiety to the spring garden. Its flowers are small but make up for it by their hot orange colour. It is very free flowering and a hardy and satisfactory species that is not often seen.

C. versicolor, called by Parkinson the cloth of silver crocus, is common along the French Riviera, extending into the Maritime Alps. It is a fine sturdy species, flowering a little later than the others mentioned, with silvery white flowers richly feathered on the outer sepals with violet. All the foregoing crocuses save C. versicolor bloom before the Dutch crocuses get under way, thus greatly lengthening the period of our enjoyment of these spirited flowers of the early year. There is comforting assurance in the way their bundles of green spears are thrust through the frozen ground before there is any warmth in the air, and it is amusing to watch the way, once up, they take advantage of every relenting moment to advance their upward career in the world, and how quickly they burst into bloom. If four kinds are to be chosen to begin with, I think they should be C. sieberi, C. susianus [C. augustifolius], C. tomasinianus, and C. biflorus.

Never does one quite become accustomed to crocuses in the autumn, and their appearance is always so sudden as to be a matter of perennial astonishment; one day there is no sign of them, and the next, probably after a soaking rain, there they are—a whole troop of them, naked and exquisite, a little surprised themselves, seemingly; a delight to eyes expecting at this season only farewells, or the persistent flowering of florid late summer perennials. A warm situation should be given the autumn crocuses with the near protection of little shrubs, for they are bound to meet with much stress and strain in the way of wind and weather.

There are two crocuses that bloom in August, but these are rare species (*C. scharojani* and *C. vallicola*), and the first autumnal kind in our gardens will probably be that wondrous vase-like beauty, *C. speciosus,* as blue in colour as it is possible, seemingly, for a crocus to be, veined with deeper colour and with the fiercely burning stigmata showing finely against the rich colour of the sepals. It is the finest of the autumnal species, strong and enduring, and increasing rapidly by means of little cormlets. It flowers usually about the third week in September.

There is a splendid form of *C. speciosus* known as *Aitchisonii,* said to be the largest of autumn-flowering crocuses. It is paler in colour than the type and does not open its lovely vases until about mid-October. *C. zonatus* [*C. kokschyanus*] flowers perhaps a week later than speciosus. This is a daintier and more fragile flower, light rosy-lavender in colour, with a circle of orange dots in the throat. It is found in the mountains of Cilicia and in Palestine, and it loves a sheltered and sunny situation. *C. cancellatus,* with a wide range in Greece, Persia, and Armenia, parts of Asia

Minor and Palestine, has proved here a hardy and beautiful species, with light lilac-pink blossoms and conspicuous stigmata. It flowers in October. *C. asturicus* is also free flowering and lovely. Its colour varies somewhat among lavender and purple tones, the medium-sized blossoms appearing with the leaves. Mr. Bowles says this species is known in the Asturian mountains as the Terror of Shepherds, as its appearance after the first autumn rains proclaims the coming of winter.

C. sativus has proved with me rather a shy bloomer, but the flowers are beautiful when they do come, very large and of a bright reddish lilac colour suffused with purple at the base and veined in deep colour, with a flaming pistil, the branches of which flop over the edges of the widely expanded petals. It requires a hot situation and a rich sandy soil, and to be taken up and divided every few years. This is probably the oldest species known, having been cultivated from very ancient times "for the sake of its scented stigmata, which after careful drying provide the drug saffron."

C. iridiflorus [*C. banaticus*] is a fine sturdy species, native of Hungary and Transylvania. It grows naturally in shade among little bushes, so it should be thus considered in the rock garden. The flowers are purple and pale lilac, having something the appearance of small irises, and very effective in little patches.

C. longiflorus is a beauty, but coming from South Italy needs protection in winter in our climate. The flowers are lilac with a faint flush and very fragrant. Where it can be grown, this is one of the best of the autumnal species. I have lost it several times, but shall continue to try to get it established, giving it the warmest and most sheltered situation.

C. salzmannii has not proved hardy with me, nor has *C. hadriaticus,* but they both belong to hot countries; gardeners south of Baltimore would probably have no trouble with them. These are not many out of the great number to be had, but even a few will add immensely to the pleasure of the autumn garden.

Perhaps the best choice of four among the autumnal species would be *C. speciosus, C. speciosus 'Aitchisonii,' C. zonatus* [*C. kokschyanus*], and *C. cancellatus;* but *C. speciosus* would always come first. *C. pulchellus, C. nudiflorus, C. clusii* are as yet unknown to me, but are down on my list for trial in the near future, as they are described as hardy and satisfactory in every way.

Colchicums are superficially much like crocuses, but they do not so well fit the rock garden because of the amount of space usurped by their great leaves during the spring and early summer. These leaves appear with the first spring showers and expand to great dimensions, flopping over as they mature and smothering all smaller plants so unfortunate as to lie within their reach. Lovely and welcome as are the large crocus-like flowers in the autumn, we are apt to forget our pleasure in them when the coarse leaves—seemingly so inappropriate to the fragile flowers—make their appearance, and to resolve to put the colchicums elsewhere. And this is on the whole a wise resolve, for colchicums, or naked boys, as they were once called, because the flowers appear without leaves, do not rightfully belong in the rock garden unless it be a very large one, and they may be given a region to themselves where they need to be visited only at the time of their delightful blossoming. Various of the species do well in grass; among these are *C. autumnale, C. byzanteum,* and *C. speciosum.*

All the species are beautiful and some are fragrant. *Colchicum autumnale* is starry in form and of a soft rose-lilac throughout. Its white form is charming and most floriferous, and flowers a little later. *C. alpinum* is one of the most exquisite and is the first of the genus to make its appearance, often in August or very early in September. *C. byzanteum* is rather like autumnale, but there are botanical differences. This species is one of the most floriferous of the race. Its leaves, unfortunately, are of great size, quite spoiling it for use anywhere near small plants. The flowers of *C. speciosum* are taller than the other species and, as Mr. Bowles reminds us, resemble tulips in appearance. The flowers of this kind and its numerous varieties are pleasantly fragrant, and when well suited as to situation, will seed themselves freely.

When planted in grass [says Mr. Bowles], the increase is slow, and as with crocuses, if it is desired to obtain a stock, the roots should be planted in well-tilled ground and divided every second year. In a wild state, the corms of most of the species are found at a great depth, but in garden ground they do best with the cap of the tunic reaching the surface.

Colchicums belong to the lily family, crocuses to the irids.

A little bulb whose flower has much the appearance of a colchicum, but which blooms in early spring, is *Bulbocodium vernum*. It is a plant of the high mountains of Europe and the Caucasus, where its curious rather ragged pink flower comes out of the ground as the snows melt away. It is a very old garden plant, having been cultivated for at least three hundred years. It is not now often seen, however, which is a pity, since its promptness in making its bow to the spring world, despite storms and cold, should alone recommend it. With me, its increase has been very slow, and I read that it requires to be frequently replanted in well-drained good soil if it is to flourish and multiply.

CHAPTER IV

Miniature Daffodils

W ITH THE LIFTING of the quarantine ruling against the importation of narcissi all lovers of these lovely flowers will be devoutly thankful that they may once again come freely into our midst. We shall be especially grateful for the ability to obtain easily the miniature species which during the period of the prohibition against them have been cruelly scarce and expensive. Perhaps it is an exaggeration to say that these were, save in a narrow sense, ever really in our midst, so little were they known in this country before the ban of the quarantine fell, cutting us off from these treasures, as from others.

In pre-quarantine days, of course, here and there a curious and venturesome gardener sought out the miniatures, but it was at first thought that a rock garden was the only safe and permanent home for them, so where this convenience was lacking so were the little daffodils. And if by chance a few were planted in the crowded borders the little wild things frightened out of their wits at such a pushing crowding world, and harried by hoe and spade, as well as pressed upon by hearty bumptious neighbours, departed this life as quickly as they conveniently could.

Where there are well-built rock gardens plantations of miniature daffodils have lingered and of all the smaller bulbous plants none are so delightful for use in this special region, though with care and preparation, and protection from various perils they may, we now know, be grown elsewhere.

Now, however, with rock gardens springing into being over all the country and proving for any one with a patch of land and a little ingenuity a wholly practical and feasible venture, it is certain that the little daffodils will come into their own.

The species of miniature narcissus are found growing wild in woods and on mountain slopes of various parts of Europe and of North Africa. The Spanish Peninsula is especially rich in this buried gold, many lovely kinds making their home in the Pyrenees; France boasts several species, as does Italy, and one kind, at least, is found in the neighbourhood of Smyrna. The species from North Africa would not be hardy in the colder parts of our country, but they are enchanting for winter forcing.

Perhaps those whose eyes are filled with the inflated proportions of such giants of the race as 'King Alfred' and 'Madame Plemp' would not see a great deal to make a fuss about in the pygmies. But any who care enough for exquisite small things to make a garden solely for their accommodation will rejoice in the little daffies. They have the characteristics of the taller kinds, and they have, besides, a quaint distinction that is quite their own.

There are, for example, the wee representatives of the magnicoronati, or large trumpet daffodils, *Narcissus minimus* [*N. asturiensis*], *N. minor,* and *N. nanus* [*N. minor*], which, though so small, are made exactly in the likeness of their tall prototypes. *N. minimus* [*N. asturiensis*] grows no more than three inches tall, often not that, yet its atomic trumpet is correctly expanded and its colour as rich and stirring a yellow as is displayed by any of the race. This small being has at least two special distinctions; it is the smallest daffodil known (how could there be a smaller?), and it is the earliest to bloom. Taking an average of its flowering dates over a pe-

riod of six years, March twenty-third seems to be its most frequent time of appearance, but once it popped up considerably earlier, and again it kept us in suspense until April fifth. This quaint little individual was found by the late Mr. Peter Barr in Spain, "growing freely amongst Gorse with a south aspect." It seems in gardens to like a warm sandy peaty soil and a little shade, though not a north aspect. The bulbs are about the size of those of the common snowdrop and should be set two inches under the ground.

N. minor is also of Spanish origin, but has been known much longer in gardens than *N. minimus* [*N. asturiensis*], in fact, as Parkinson describes it, from the late Seventeenth Century at least. It grows six inches tall and is a perfect replica of *N. maximus,* its trumpet daintily expanded, a smart twist to its perianth, and its colour a full yellow. This species thrives in any good garden soil, not too heavy, and prefers shade for part of the day. There is a quaint double form for it called Rip van Winkle, and in Mr. Bowles's *My Garden in Spring* we hear of a *white* minor that was "found in an old Irish garden." What a cherished acquisition this must be to lovers of the little daffodils!

N. minor flowers with me in early April. The "great" trumpets of *N. nanus* are midway in size between those of minimus and minor; its height is about six inches, its colour rich yellow, and it is also a very early bloomer. This species has grown scarce, even in those favoured countries privileged to enjoy it, and *N. lobularis* [*N. minor*] is frequently substituted for it. The latter, however, is a native of the

Netherlands, and is what is called, in daffodil language, a bicolour, that is having a yellow trumpet surrounded by a paler perianth or petals. This grows seven inches tall and is lovely for naturalizing in grassy places about the rock garden. It is sometimes called Dutch nanus. *Narcissus* 'W. P. Milner' is also for the rock garden, though it grows eleven inches tall when well suited. It is a lovely slender variety with pale sulphur blossoms, that delights in a partially shaded situation. It has a delicate fragrance.

My fancy is greatly taken by the description of a tiny bicolour, *N. Macleaii,* said to be an old-time hybrid of unknown origin, introduced from France in 1815.* It grows robustly in ordinary soil, I read, and its flower has milk-white petals set about a golden cup-shaped crown. A pity to have missed it!

All daffodils like some shade, but the paler they are the more keenly do they crave it. There are several lovely white or very pale trumpet daffodils that belong in the shaded regions of the rock garden. The most beautiful of these is *N. moschatus* of Haworth [*N. pseudonarcissus moschatus*], the white daffodil of the Spanish Pyrenees, the whitest of all daffodils when fully open, but faintly yellow in the bud. It grows not more than six inches high, the blossoms drooping on the stems in a charming manner, and delicately fragrant. My handful of bulbs (increased from one) grow in gritty rather dampish soil with a stout rock between

---

* *This species is thought by some authorities to belong to the neighbourhood of Smyrna.*

them and the southern sun. This is one of the undoubted treasures of the race. *N. cernuus,* also of the Pyrenees, is another lovely pale daffodil. It opens a delicate lemon colour, but soon changes to white. This is called the swan's neck daffodil "from the graceful poise of the pendent flower." Sometimes confused with *N. moschatus* of Haworth [*N. pseudonarcissus moschatus*] is *N. albicans,* called Dutch *moschatus,* but it is taller by five inches than the true *moschatus* and lacks the drooping perianth so attractive in the other. This is a beautiful kind for shaded borders, but is rather large for the rock garden. These graceful white daffodils bloom from mid to late April.

N. cyclamineus is the quaintest of its kind and, save for *N. minimus* [*N. asturiensis*], the smallest and the earliest to flower. It grows not more than three or four inches tall, possesses a long tubelike trumpet, and its perianth is turned sharply back, as someone has said, like the ears of an angry mule. Its colour is bright satiny yellow throughout. Pictures of this amusing little flower appear in old French books of the early Seventeenth Century, but it was lost to cultivation for two or three hundred years. Its rediscovery in Portugal in 1887, says the late Rev. Joseph Jacob, is one of the romances of the daffodil world. Mr. Jacob relates that when the late Dean Herbert saw the plate of *N. cyclamineus* in one of these old books he exclaimed that it was an absurdity that never would be found to exist. Exist it does, nevertheless, though it is certainly a most curious little species. It is made happy in a partially shaded situation in dampish, sandy peat and once planted should be left alone for years.

Also having reflexing petals like those of a cyclamen flower, but not nearly so extreme as are those of *N. cyclamineus*, is the beautiful and graceful *N. triandrus albus*, found on the mountains of Spain and Portugal, usually in "hard gritty soil, and often emerging from some fissure in the granite and slate rocks." From a wandlike six-inch stem droop creamy white flowers, sometimes one, sometimes three or four, with bell-shaped crowns and daintily reflexed petals. It is commonly called 'Angel's Tears,' and is a most lovely species. *N. triandrus calanthus* is said to have larger flowers of a perfect snowy whiteness, but I have not seen this species. Both *N. cyclamineus* and *N. triandrus albus* have proved ready tools in the hands of the hybridists and numerous varieties have been developed from marriages with various taller species or varieties, many of which are very beautiful. A lovely wild hybrid of *triandrus*, result of a gipsy marriage in Spain, was found and introduced as 'Queen of Spain' by the late Mr. Peter Barr, who has given us so many splendid daffodils, and who was especially instrumental in introducing the small species. 'Queen of Spain' grows seven inches tall and has flowers of a fine butter yellow. It blooms, as a rule, about April twentieth, and the 'Angel's Tears' not until a week later.

A glance at the photograph of the dainty little 'Hoop-petticoat' daffodil, *N. bulbocodium*, will convince anyone of its claim to special regard. The 'Hoop-petticoats' are distinct from all other daffodils, dainty and fairylike as are no others. There are several kinds, but the only two that concern the open garden, north of Baltimore, are *N. bulbocodium citrinus* and *N. b. conspicuus*. The beautiful white *N. monophyllus*, native of North Africa, is too tender for ordinary cultivation, and would require a frame or a pot. It is said to flower in December. The other species are native of France, Spain, and Portugal.

Characteristic of these daffodils is the widely flaring trumpet, that looks for all the world like an old-fashioned crinoline, carried, or seemingly, almost blown, from the slight stems, and the very narrow rushlike foliage. The leaves make a fall growth, and keep fresh over the winter, and out from their midst in late April or early May arise the airy blossoms with delightful effect. The thick growth of their "grass" in the autumn always gives me a distinct thrill, for I well know of what pleasure it is the forerunner. These charming things are not difficult to grow; indeed, with me, they have proved the easiest of all the little daffodils asking only a gritty soil in partial shade and good drainage. *N. b. conspicuus* blooms first and is of a fine warm yellow; *N. b. citrinus* is a soft cream colour. Their height is about six inches.

Many of the sweet-scented jonquils and campernelles may be grown in clumps in fairly spacious rock gardens. These are *N. jonquilla* and *N. odorus*, with numerous forms and hybrids, having clusters of single or double fragrant yellow flowers and narrow, rushlike foliage. *N. jonquilla* comes from Spain and *N.*

odorus from Southern Europe. They are a little tall and strong-growing to be in keeping with a moderate-sized rock garden; but three of the rush-leaved species should certainly have a place. These are *N. gracilis* [*N. tenuior*] and its attractive form, *tenuior*, called the silver jonquil, and the tiniest of them all, *N. juncifolius* [*N. assoanus*]. This miniature rush-leaved daffodil grows only four inches high, its deliciously sweet flowers are about the size of a buttercup and of a rich golden yellow, and its minute trumpet is almost perfectly flat. It seems to be very scarce now. *N. juncifolius* [*N. assoanus*] is from the Pyrenees and is so small as to require a choice place in the rock garden where it may be looked after.

N. gracilis [*N. tenuior*] is the latest of the race to bloom and so of especial value. I find on consulting my notes that it has often remained in bloom as late as May twenty-seventh; beginning with *N. minimus* [*N. asturiensis*] in late March, this gives a long daffodil season. *N. gracilis* [*N. tenuior*] grows fourteen inches tall, but is very slight and graceful, carrying from three to five very sweet-scented yellow blossoms on its slender stems.

The silver jonquil blooms earlier (about April 28th), is more slender, growing not more than nine or ten inches high, and is paler in colour. It is a most charming sort, thriving and increasing in light soil and partial shade. These are very old garden flowers, having been long in cultivation, and coming originally it is said from the neighbourhood of Bordeaux, but not now often found in a wild state.

Growing daffodils from seed

For those who have time and sufficient patience, growing daffodils from seed, either that gathered from their own plants or purchased abroad, may come to be a way out of a sad difficulty. Seed of various species may often be had of the Floraire Nurseries, from Thompson and Morgan, from Perry, from the Rev. J. F. Anderson, and for the benefit of those caring to enter upon this worth-while adventure I am appending from *Daffodils,* an invaluable book by the late deeply lamented Joseph Jacob, his careful and exact directions of just how to go about it.

Daffodil seed, when fully ripe, is black and shiny. As soon as it assumes this appearance, which will probably be some time early in July, it may be sown either in the open ground or in boxes or pans. Most raisers of seedlings prefer the latter plan, although I know one or two cultivators who think the former way the best, as they contend that the plants will sooner arrive at their flowering stage. I have not tested it myself, and I am disposed to doubt it, as Mr. Engleheart, who ought to know what is the best, if anyone does, always sows the seed in boxes. Stout, wooden boxes of any convenient size may be used, provided they are from 6 to 7 inches deep, and have drainage holes at the bottom. The soil should be good, fibrous loam, with sharp sand added to make it light and porous. In filling up the boxes, care must be taken to see that the drainage is good; then enough compost may be put in to bring the level up to within an inch and a half of the top. On this the seeds must be sown at equal intervals of one-half to three-quarters of an inch, and they must be covered with soil an inch deep. It is best to put the boxes in coldframes, but the lights (sash) need not be used until frost begins, unless the weather is very wet. Then they may be put on when necessity requires; and, further, the plants may be protected by mats when the weather is particularly severe. This protection and culture in frames is not absolutely necessary; I have seen the boxes just stood out-of-doors and exposed to all weathers and the results have been good. The seed soon germinates if it is sown directly it is ripe. Everything possible should be done to promote growth by seeing the soil is kept at the right degree of moisture, and that the growing period is as long as possible, by putting on the lights when there is frost at night. The subsequent treatment consists in giving air on every suitable day, and top-dressing the boxes with cocoa fibre when the grasslike seedlings appear. This keeps down moss. At the end of two years, they may be transplanted into beds in the open, an operation which is performed, say, in June or July. They must be planted out straight from the seed pan and not in any way dried off. Attention to this matter is important, as it means very

often the saving of a year in the plant coming to its flowering stage. In planting out, enough space must be left between the bulbs (which should for convenience of cultivation be arranged in rows) to allow them to grow and flower where they are pricked off. This will be in their fourth or fifth year, although some may not flower until their sixth or seventh. Frequent hoeing between the rows is very helpful to the growth of the young plants, therefore the rows should be clearly marked when there are no leaves as a guide. The period of waiting will seem long before the first flower shows itself, but, if an annual sowing is made, once this period is passed, there will be a succession of flowering seedlings every year. It is a fact that the first flower that a young plant bears is not always a sufficient indication of what it is capable of producing. In some mysterious way, the flowers improve as the plants get older. Hence it is advisable to allow young plants that show any promise at all to bloom a second or third time before they are finally discarded. With regard to sowing out-of-doors, a similar procedure must be followed. A sheltered bed must be

chosen, and the seeds sown in drills about an inch deep. Transplanting into flowering beds should take place at the end of their second year. No protection is required, as the seedlings are perfectly hardy.

CHAPTER V

In Praise of Primroses

IT IS RATHER extraordinary, when so many plants from over-seas have found a congenial home in America, many of them running wild in the fields and disporting themselves along road-sides and watercourses, that the primrose and her sister cowslips and oxlips, plants widespread and abundant in all the counties of the British Isles and over most of Europe, should not only have gained no foothold in our wild, but have only the most meagre representation in our gardens. It is the more to be wondered at since these flowers have ever been cherished in the gardens of the Old World by high and low alike, and there can be no doubt that many roots and seeds of them were brought here by the colonists in a wistful attempt to implant in the unknown country some-thing of the remembered sweetness and friendliness of the home springtide.

What befell these early plantations of pale primroses and nod-ding cowslips, who can say! Books on early American gardening are silent concerning them. Their names, indeed, endure but fitted to American-born plants that in no wise resemble, nor are related to, those whose names they have borrowed. The marsh marigold is, in many localities, called cowslip; *Mertensia virginica*, blue and pink beauty of low grounds along the Atlantic coast, is the Virgin-ian cowslip, oenothera is the evening primrose, and often just primrose, and there are other examples that might be cited.

Just why in all the years between those early times and now this delightful race of plants should have been so neglected in this country is difficult to understand. Perhaps the first failures to es-tablish them under the more rigorous climatic conditions that prevail here resulted in a tradition of their unreliability, a tradition passed from gardener to gardener down the years but never given a thorough test. For very certain it is that we may have primroses and cowslips and oxlips, all we want of them, if we but learn and observe their necessities. And the most important of these are some degree of shade, a rich deep, moisture-retaining soil, plenty of drink during the growing season, and occasional division.

Of course, if your ground is poor and thin and porous, your situation wind-swept and sun-bitten, you will have trouble with primroses and all the tribe until you have remedied these defects. But all you who number among your possessions a strip of woodland, a little damp copse, a low meadow, or a shaded, moist corner, even a north border against the house, may plant generously, sure of a rich reward in tufts of dark, wrinkled foliage and bunches of pale blooms which, it seems to me, more than any other flowers add to the young enchantment of the spring.

To consider first the true primrose— primerole, as it used to be called in very early days, the firstling of the spring. Its botanical designation is *Primula vulgaris,* sometimes *P. acaulis.* It has the characteristic tufted growth of rough, wrinkled leaves, and the flowers, large, round, appear solitary on the stems from amid the foliage. These blossoms in the wild forms are pale yellow—the colour of fresh butter—and rarely white. But in response to the skill of enthusiasts they have been brought to assume an extraordinary array of charming hues—pink, mauve, purple, and,

wonder of wonders, a clear pure blue with a smart yellow eye. These blue primroses are quite enchanting to look upon, and amazing too, for there is no smallest hint of that old haunting magenta in their composition. Moreover, they have the most satisfactory and endearing habit of giving a second blossoming. It is November as I write, and the patch of blue primroses in the rock garden is running true to form and making ready to bloom. Clustered at the heart of the rough leaves are many buds that soon will open out into round blue flowers. I have more than once gathered them in December.

The primrose is a plant of damp shaded banks, of woodlands, of wandering streamsides. It will not endure in poor, light soils, or open sunshine. If the right sort of situation is not at hand, it is easy, however, to create with shrubs and trees a little copse, hollowing out the earth to the depth of a foot or something more, and filling in with a rich, fat mixture— well-rotted leaves, old cow manure, clay, or heavy, sticky loam, and leaving the surface slightly concave in order to catch all the moisture possible. A rotting log or old stump will add to the picture and serve also as a wind-break to the north behind which the primroses will rest safely, attentive to the south winds, and often blossoming, in the neighbourhood of New York, as early as the middle of March.

Toward winter we mulch the plants with old cow manure, or failing this, with leaf mould, working in the stuff about the tufts but not covering the crowns. When cold weather comes, a light covering of oak leaves is thrown over them and held in place by light branches.

Primroses are easy enough to raise from seed if the method described in the chapter on seeds is followed. Of first importance is it that the seed should be fresh. So do not buy seed in the spring and save it until fall before sowing. Buy it in the fall from a dealer who is willing to assure you that it has been fresh gathered, and sow it in a frame in November.

Thereafter increase may be had by division, allowing the plants, however, to grow into fine thrifty clumps before they are broken up, and carrying out this operation in the late spring soon after they have finished flowering. These divisions must be carefully looked to and kept growing strongly. They must never be allowed to dry out, and frequent waterings with weak liquid manure will help them along amazingly. Indeed, primroses of all sorts have a weakness for this soft drink and thrive upon it exceedingly.

The double primrose is a rare and lovely thing. It is less robust of constitution than its single sister and requires a very sheltered situation, an unfailing supply of moisture during the growing season, sharp and certain drainage, more coddling altogether. The rock garden is the best place for it, for therein its needs may be the more easily provided for and shelter afforded it.

The cowslips

Cowslips (*Primula veris* or *P. officinalis*) are considerably easier to grow than primroses. Al-

most any garden not utterly dry and sun-scorched will support them. Any good garden soil satisfies them, and while they like moisture and a little shadow they do not demand as much of either as do primroses and oxlips. Cowslips are quite different from the true primrose. Their leaves are smoother and not so deeply seamed and wrinkled, and the blossoms in their soft white husks are worn in little one-sided bunches, or umbels, on slender, erect stems. They are bright yellow with little red dots inside—sure mark of the cowslip—and they are deliciously and freshly fragrant. With any encouragement at all, they wax into fat clumps and send up perfect fountains of yellow bloom most lovely for the filling of certain low blue bowls indoors. There is no reason not to have a lot of cowslips, for they come easily from seed, and old plants may be divided every two or three years to increase the stock. Moreover, they self-sow quite prodigally when in congenial surroundings, and it is a great satisfaction to see young cowslips coming up along the shaded paths and pushing back beneath the shrubbery in ever-widening colonies.

Improvements have been made upon the wild cowslip to the extent that we have larger and more robust-growing plants with somewhat larger blossoms, but they do not vary readily as to colour. Only occasionally are orange or scarlet forms met with. The 'Hose-in-Hose' cowslip is a quaint old-fashioned conceit, having one blossom set within another, the name derived from a fancied resemblance to a sort of ancient footwear. Strains of 'Hose-in-Hose' seed are now to be had, and very interesting are the results to be obtained therefrom, a large percentage of the plants showing the curious variation.

The oxlip (*P. elatior*) is so closely allied to the cowslip as to be regarded in some quarters as a mere variation, though more authentically, it seems, as a separate species. It flowers just after the primrose and before the cowslip. The pale flowers are carried in a loose one-sided bunch and are larger and flatter than cowslip flowers. And quite scentless. The leaves are more like those of the primrose.

Oxlips grow naturally in moist, sunny meadows. They are thirsty. But if you cannot give them their first preference, you will meet with a good deal of success by planting them in shade and providing a rich and fatty soil that will hold what moisture there may be. Mulching with old manure or leaf mould will also help. I find that when suited they self-sow as freely as the cowslips and soon make fine thrifty clumps. There are 'Hose-in-Hose' varieties of the oxlip also that come in charming colours. One sort, a pale buff and rose combination that has been in my garden for many years, blooms almost as early as do the primroses, bursting forth into veritable bouquets of bloom most delightful for cutting.

And there is a fourth member of this group that must by no means be neglected. As a matter of fact, it is much less neglected in American gardens than any of the foregoing. The polyanthus or bunch primrose has a good deal of vogue as a spring-bedding plant. Most nurseries carry it, and it is hawked about suburban streets in the spring in company with pansies and English daisies.

The polyanthus is not known in a wild state. Its origin is in doubt, but it is probably a child of the garden. It does not appear in horticultural literature until the beginning of the Eighteenth Century, so, beside the primrose, the oxlip, and the cowslip, which appear in the very earliest records, it is a mere parvenu. But it is very grand indeed and much showier than its ancestored sisters. The polyanthus has claimed the attention of the most skilled hybridists. There are amazing and brilliant strains now to be had, with huge round bunches of blossoms on strong stems, useful alike for spring gardening and for cutting. One of the best strains is Miss Jekyll's bunch primroses running the scale from white to rich yellow, and with blossoms more than two inches across. Sutton has a fine strain also, and the Spetchley forms, exhibiting the most brilliant colours and markings, have gained a merited notoriety.

Like all their kind, these plants love comfort, rich soil, shadow, abundant moisture, but they will give some sort of response without any of these things. They are easily raised from seed, and, cared for, they are capable of the most amazing returns in growth and blossom. They are the last of the group to blossom.

With all these plants it is important that they shall be kept growing strongly throughout the open season. This means constant and generous watering in dry weather. The more lush green foliage we can induce, the more certain and splendid will be our reward in the spring. As I have said, thin liquid manure is their delight. But, failing this, just water will do.

Polyanthus primroses grow well and thrive in borders among other plants; cowslips, too, may there be made comfortable, but primroses and oxlips do not like the motley crew of the herbaceous borders, nor the drought that is liable to prevail there. They are for nicely chosen places, for moist, shaded banks, for secluded nooks in dampness, for meandering path sides in shade, for the rock garden. The latter region is a safe haven for all these charming plants of the spring. There it is easy enough to provide deposits of the rich and holding soil they so love, and there the drainage is sure while the long roots may thrust down and find their way beneath the rocks to supplies of moisture.

It is still rare to meet a primrose enthusiast in this country. But there is not now the lamentable unawareness of these flowers that once existed. A wholesome curiosity is evinced in many directions; trials are being essayed, successes delighted in. One is able to descry the faint outline of a primrose path stretching away into the future. This is destined, without doubt, to become a populous and joyous highway.

CHAPTER VI

Primulas in the Rock Garden

ONE WHO HAS had even a limited experience with growing primulas, of whatever kind, almost invariably finds himself intrigued to further investigation among them. The members of this great race appear to be gifted with a very special charm, a charm to which we become more keenly sensible with every fresh encounter with a new species. Their attraction is not to be defined in terms of splash and splurge, for they are not, generally speaking, a showy race, though certain of the Asiatics may lay claim so to be described, and some of the alpines rise to heights of quite supreme and sparkling beauty, always, however, of a refined and gentle type. But characteristic of them all, from the modest primrose of the hedgerow to the highest aloof alpine, and even of the coarser beauties of the bog, is a delicious dewy freshness that delights us and a sort of simplicity and gentleness of mien that is very appealing and seems at once to engage our best efforts in behalf of establishing them happily and healthily in our midst.

Primulas are among the earliest and most lovely of spring flowers, and a rock garden offers exceptional opportunity for enjoying a great number of the many kinds to be had. May is perhaps their festal month, but many species bloom much earlier, and *P. capitata* gives its rich purple flowers in July or August; while it is the common and most ingratiating practice of numerous of the race to vouchsafe a second blossoming in the late summer or autumn.

Primula is a vast genus whose members are scattered over most of the earth.

All the temperate zone, [writes an English admirer] is their domain. The meadows, woods and hedgerows of our own country [England], the wild precipices of the Alps, the unexplored recesses of the dark Caucasus, the Himalayas crowned with perpetual snow, the lofty plateaux of Western China and the slopes of the vast mountain ranges of North America are glorified and gladdened by their presence.

And the plants vary in character as much as do their habitats, from tight little tuffets that sit secure and serene wedged in crevices of rocks on the high mountains to stalwart plants with stems three feet tall, or more, whorled about with large lovely blossoms, and all kinds and characters between.

A veritable treasure trove is here for the rock gardener who is willing to study the needs of the species he sets out to grow and to materialize them faithfully; but let no light-hearted toiler of the soil embark upon the enterprise of growing a varied collection of primulas with the idea that he can accomplish his end with no more effort than that required in growing the common run of rock plants. While the English primrose and its neighbours, the cowslip and the oxlip, are biddable enough given fairly decent treatment, the race as a whole cannot be called one of the easiest; many of its members, indeed, will put the gardener's skill and patience to a severe test. Of the most temperamental individuals we shall have little here to say, for there are so many lovely species to be won with far less nerve strain and a very fair certainty of success if we cater to their perfectly reasonable requirements.

In the parts of our country where the summers are hot and dry, some degree of shade is necessary for all primulas. A few will grow directly under trees, others, resenting the least suggestion of dankness, will be grateful for shadow cast by distant trees or a building; for the alpines, a stone between them and the burning afternoon sun or a little slope to the north is a consideration gratefully appreciated. Nearly all primulas are lime lovers; they all detest stagnant moisture, and while they want plenty of drink during their growing season, must be absolutely assured of a dry bed in winter; drought is a deadly peril to them, and many more succumb from the heat of the sun than from winter cold or other causes. With these points clearly in mind, we may take up the special soil requirements of the various species as we go along.

To speak first of the most amiable of the alpines, there are three species that may be attempted by any careful gardener. Of these *P. marginata* is the most beautiful; it is beautiful both in leaf and flower, a small tufted thing two or three inches tall, its leaves thick and sharply notched, and edged, seemingly, with silver hoarfrost. In this becoming setting appear the lovely blossoms, many of them, wide open and of a most delicious clear amethyst colour. *P. marginata* likes to grow in a vertical crevice, and if you do not so dispose it you will be everlastingly under the necessity of digging it up and replanting it, for, as someone has said, it is a veritable stilt walker and continually hoists itself out of the ground on its small woody trunk whereupon its roots promptly perish. It likes lime but will do without it; however, it will not tolerate anything approaching a sour soil. Good loam and grit with a little lime and its face to the morning sun are all it asks for complete happiness.

P. glaucescens (*calycina*) and *P. viscosa* [*P. latifolia*] are two other minute indispensables not to be missed save for a very good reason. The former likes to be a bit more definitely shaded than *P. marginata*, and as we read that it is often found among brushwood along mountain sides, it is the part of wisdom to give it the shelter of some little bushes or to place it on the cool side of a stone, always bearing in mind its taste for lime and its need for drainage. *P. glaucescens* decorates the slopes of the Italian Alps with its dark-leaved leathery rosettes and umbels of gay rosy blossoms. *P. viscosa* [*P. latifolia*] will flourish on little ledges of the rock garden in well-drained loamy soil. Its leaves are yellowish-green and apt to be notched. All these little primulas will need at least once a year to have a top-dressing or mounding of gritty loam and chips provided for them, for they all have a tendency to work free of the soil.

There is an old children's rhyme that runs thus:

The lockety gowan an' bonny burd-een
Are the fairest flowers that ever were seen.

This couplet refers to the 'Bird's-eye' primrose, *P. farinosa*, of which Gerard wrote: "In the middle of every small flower appeereth a little yellow spot, resembling the eie of a bird, which hath mooved the people of the north parts (where it aboundeth) to call it Bird's eine." *P.*

farinosa is one of the oldest of the race in cultivation and one of the most beloved; and it has the widest distribution in nature. It claims for its playground all the Northern ranges, including our own high mountains; and varies a good deal in character according to the climatic conditions of each locality. On the heights it grows in grassy open places but again in the garden we must protect it from the relentless rays of the sun. It is a fragile, dainty, lovely thing which to see is to love. Its small rosette is softly gray by reason of a heavy coating of farina, and on a slender stem it carries a loose umbel of pink flowers with yellow eyes. *P. frondosa*, a cousin from the Balkans, is much like it, but a little larger all over.

Neither of these plants is as easy to keep in the garden as we should like, though the Balkan beauty is more steadfast than the pretty 'Bird's-eye.' Shade they must have for full half the day, and moisture during the spring, and they like lime. A little hollow filled in with loam and leaf mould and limestone chips, with the addition of some peat moss should make them happy. Mr. Farrer says that *P. farinosa* is essentially gregarious and does not like to be planted in "reverend loneliness," but to have its roots matted up sociably with other plants. Perhaps some of the little gentians might bear it company, certain of the mossy saxifrages, but any large or vigorous plant would, of course, do them to death in short order.

Some authorities make *P. mistassinica*, a minute American species, a form of farinosa. This is the smallest and most elfin of the race so far as I have seen them. It is found on wet, calcareous rocks in various parts of Maine, Vermont, and New York; it is now in the trade, and my plant came to me from a generous friend who had collected it. Thinking it wholly new to cultivation, I was amazed to find a fine coloured plate of it in Maund's *Botanic Garden*, published nearly a hundred years ago. It is always a little discouraging to realize how far we are behind British gardeners in knowledge and appreciation of the beauty and usefulness of our own plant material. Maund speaks of *P. mistassinica* as rather rare in gardens but deserving a place in every collection of the species. It is minute, forming a little huddle of very narrow leaves, and in the fullness of time materializes a loose cluster of large, starry, rosy blossoms with a delicate fragrance. This little primrose is enchanting. It came to me by way of another generous collector, from the high mountain peaks of Colorado. It is a true alpine, and likes a place in stony soil, perfectly drained, where the sun reaches it for but part of the day.

P. parryi is another native of alpine regions of the Rockies in Colorado. It is a handsome plant—much larger than those of which we have been speaking, with bright green erect leaves and large trusses of bright magenta blossoms with yellow eyes. It is a moisture lover and requires a spongy soil that does not, however, become stagnant. None of these American representatives of the race is very easy to grow, and though both *P. angustifolia* and *P. parryi* are now to be had in the trade, it is hoped that no one will acquire these rare and lovely things who is not ready to treat them with intelligent care and solicitude.[1]

P. cortusoides and its allies from the Far East present a much easier problem in the garden than do the shy Americans. They all enjoy a loamy soil, rich in humus and thoroughly well drained, and a situation in partial shade. *P. cortusoides* itself, long cultivated in gardens, is a most attractive little plant with a loose tuft of soft wrinkled leaves and six-inch stems carrying heads of pretty rose-coloured blossoms. It is a native of western Siberia, from the Ural to the Altai Mountains; but comes all the long distance and settles down in our gardens with no fuss whatever, so long as the sun does not burn it, nor stagnant moisture cause it to sicken and die. The difference between it and *P. saxatilis* is discerned only by botanists; to the lay eye they are one and the same thing. But *P. sieboldii* (syns. *P. patens, P. cortusoides amoena*) is quite individual. Its leaves are larger and softer and more wrinkled and its trusses of flowers are larger, too, and more showy, and varying from pure white (some with delicately fluted petals) to a fairly bright crimson. It has the unusual property in a primula of a creeping rootstock, which runs about just under the surface of the earth and keeps cropping out in little soft tufts of leaves and so forming new plants.

P. sieboldii is a Japanese, and one hears doubts expressed of its hardiness; but it has lived and prospered in my cold New York gar-

---

[1] *The Rocky Mountains are granite formation, which means that plants native to them are independent of lime, some, indeed, resenting its presence.*

den for a good many years. Its nook is a sheltered one, however, and it is given a covering of leaves in winter. The soil for it should be light and loamy and fibrous with decomposed vegetable matter. Of the same group is *P. lichiangensis* [*P. polyneura*], a fairly recent introduction of Mr. Forrest's from the shady limestone cliffs and ledges of the Lichiang range in western China. It is a newcomer to my garden, but looks flourishing and is apparently no more capricious than the other members of its particular group.

And now to say a word about the bog beauties, many of which have been introduced from the Far East during the last twenty-five years. At the outset let us make it clear that a bog is not the invariable price of their glory. Indeed, in those parts of our country cursed by what might be termed a freeze-and-thaw winter programme, a bog provides far from safe cold weather quarters for these plants, however much they might enjoy it in summer. The constant heave and throw of the earth caused by the unstable temper of the weather plays havoc with the roots and crowns of the primulas, tearing and wrenching them, and not infrequently plants are thrown bodily out of the ground. What these plants absolutely require is plenty of moisture and nourishment during the growing season (and that means all summer) and a guarantee against disturbance during what should be a period of complete rest.

The ideal situation for growing most of the especially thirsty primulas is along the banks of a stream where the roots may find their way down to moisture and the crowns remain high and dry. It is rarely possible to make this luxurious provision for them, streams not being among the common run of garden blessings; but no one need lose heart on this account. To grow the majority of the bog primulas with complete success, all that is necessary is a shaded situation and a deep bed of rather heavy loam well enriched with cow manure, and copious watering during periods of dry weather in spring and summer. A light mulch of peat moss would probably further insure their comfort by helping to conserve moisture.

In such a bed, all the so-called candelabra section will flourish. These primulas are characterized by great lush tufts of leaves and tall, strong stems bearing many whorls of blossoms in various colours. *P. japonica* is the oldest and best known of them and a good plant, though some may object to its magenta livery. It has, however, a finer form of splendid colour and an albino which is lovely and floriferous. *P. pulverulenta* resembles japonica, but is a more noble plant with taller stems covered with farina and rich crimson blossoms. This plant married to the vermilion flowered *P. cockburniana* has given life to some superb hybrids with colours entrancingly ranging from scarlet through many tones of apricot, salmon, and vermilion. *P. cockburniana* is, unfortunately, a biennial, but like all this section of primulas is easily raised from seed and so kept on hand.

P. bessiana and *P. bulleyana* are also splendid bog primulas, the one with rich purple flowers, the other of a lovely orange-apricot colour. *P.*

CHAPTER VII

The Fascination of the Wild Tulips

M ID-SPRING FINDS most gardens quite gorgeously decorated with tulips—the aesthetic darwins, the graceful cottagers, the prim and shining earlies—beds and borders filled with them, the shrubbery alight with them, and colonies of them thrusting up among the lusty perennials. They are lovely, indispensable, we would not do without them, yet what of the wholly engaging little wild species that inimitably adorn various far places of the earth?

It is strange that those who so admire the almost too sumptuous and sophisticated garden varieties do not more often seek out for very curiosity, if for nothing else, some of the wild species. Not until they have had some of these little wildings under their eye, have seen them in bud and in flower, shining in the sun, drooping in the rain, can they be said to know the best that tulips have to tell. Their wayward grace is unknown to the garden beauties, and no two of them are shaped alike. Their colours are immaculately clean and fresh, and, if various of the species are planted, we may have tulips in the garden from March until well into June—and no small boon, this.

Of course, these wild things are no use for bedding or for anything that has to do with uniformity or smugness. These free spirits refuse to march in battalions or to edge the borders trimly. The rock garden is the best place for them, particularly for the dwarfs, but a sunny shrub border where they may be scattered in free groups and will not be subject to overmuch grubbing and cultivating suits them well.

The late Mr. Dykes, of iris fame confessed as his second love the wild tulips. He advises for them a sweet soil well impregnated with lime, light and sandy and well-drained, which has been well manured the previous season. Note this qualification and heed it, for fresh manure is a deadly menace to tulips as to all bulbs. Mr. Dykes also considered it advisable to take up the bulbs as soon as the stems have withered to a point where they may be bent without snapping, storing them until the following autumn, when they should again be planted. This is a good deal more trouble than many of us are willing or able to take, and for our encouragement we have Mr. Farrer stating that all that is necessary for success with the wild tulips is to plant them on some sunny slope of the rock garden and there forever leave them alone to continue and increase. If this method is possible in England, so much more so must it be in parts of our country where long ripening summers and snow-blanketed winters are the rule. In my own garden, I do not take up the tulip bulbs, as I find that all of them continue from year to year, and a number increase appreciably.

Seeding is a strain upon the wild tulips, especially when grown in captivity, so the faded blossoms should be invariably removed. Unless this is done, we are apt to suffer from few blossoms the following spring. In planting, the bulbs should be set from three to five inches below the surface of the ground, according to the size of the bulb. When the leaves appear in spring, it is made quite plain to us whether or not we are to enjoy flowers. If the bulb sends up one leaf, there will be no

flowers, but, if two appear, we may rejoice. There is no reason to be discouraged if all the bulbs of a planting do not bloom the first year. It must be remembered that they are often collected bulbs, taken from the wild and not from nursery-grown stock, and may not all be of blossoming size.

There are a great number of these tulip species, but space permits me to offer only an enchanting handful that have grown in my garden and have given me infinite pleasure from year to year as well as an occasional disappointment.

Usually the first to bloom is the beautiful species from the steppes of Turkestan, *T. kaufmanniana*, commonly called the waterlily tulip. It is dwarf in stature, but the blossoms are large goblets, glistening white, the outer segments flashed with brilliant carmine or bright yellow. In a good year, this tulip may come into bloom late in March, but it varies with the season's vagaries. The waterlily tulip makes a splendid show either in border or rock garden and may be relied upon as one of those that will endure and increase as the years pass.

Almost, if not quite, as early, a small sprightly species, *T. biflora*, from the Caucasus, makes its appearance on a warm ledge and is not always recognized by visitors as a tulip at all. Its height here is about six inches, though it is said to attain a greater, and it not only bears two flowers on a stem, but occasionally is so generous as to produce three or four. The blossoms, which are about the size of a five-cent piece, are pale green-blue without and white inside with a dark eye. This dainty creature is said to be an ardent lime lover.

While April is still young, *T. dasystemon* and *T. polychroma* fairly astonish the world with the unusual character of their beauty. The leaves of the first make a dark little splash upon the ground from which arise large starry blossoms, golden at the heart in a gleaming white setting, on stems only about three inches tall. From strong bulbs, several blossoms are forthcoming, and I know of no more joyous spring manifestation than a clump of these little shining flowers. It is said that, if the seedpods be not removed, *T. dasystemon* will seed itself.

T. polychroma, a Persian, is upstanding in habit. Its blossoms are cup-shaped on stems perhaps six inches tall, a charming tone of mauve without and much paler within, lighted by a yellow stain. It is a most lovely species.

T. greigi is a magnificent scarlet-flowered species (occasionally marked with yellow) with light-coloured leaves stained with a dull purplish colour. It is for the border rather than the rock garden, for, though dwarf as to stature, the blossoms are so large as to be out of scale with the smaller species. Scarlet one delights in, however, when dealing with tulips, and there are a number of most engaging species flaunting that challenging colour and suitable in size for the rock garden.

The dwarfest and most vivid of these is a little slender species, *T. linifolia*, with narrow wavy leaves that lie flat on the ground and intense scarlet blossoms. It is said to enjoy growing among other plants such as *Aubrietia deltoidea* and *Arenaria montana* through which it thrusts its leaves and blossoms strongly. It is

from Central Asia. *T. montana*, another small beauty, has a bulb coated with "wool" but this covering does not sufficiently protect it from even a slight degree of standing moisture in the soil, from which it suffers much. A handful of sand should be placed around the bulbs of this mountain species and a well-drained situation given it. The blossoms are a fine blood red, and the leaves are curiously waved or crimped. My favourite among the red tulips, however, is *T. praestans*, from Bokhara, that wears the most amazing high, thin scarlet colour known, I believe, to the kingdom of flowers. The stems and leaves are slightly downy, and often there are several of these dazzling blossoms on the wandlike stems. It is a May-flowering species, and the height is something over a foot.

T. sprengeri is the last of all the tulips to bloom, sending up its pointed sealing-wax red blossoms often as late as the middle of June on stems about eight inches high. It is an Armenian species, hardy, and under satisfactory conditions increases with fair rapidity. It ripens plenty of seed, and blooming bulbs may be raised in four years.

The interesting slashed blossoms of *T. acuminata* present a most striking blend of red and yellow—a sort of suffusion. Many do not care for this bizarre type, but others are enchanted with it, and of these I am one of the most enthusiastic. The stems are long and slender and the blossoms rather small; on a little height in the rock garden they are most effective. It is said not to be a true species but of obscure garden origin.

Yellow ever plays a conspicuous part in the colour scheme of the spring, and it is worn by no prettier flowers than the little wild yellow tulips. There are a number of these, but three of them are particularly lovely. *T. silvestris* grows wild in orchards and other pleasant places in various parts of Great Britain. It is one of the most fragrant and gayest of flowers with butter-yellow blossoms, opening out wide, carried on lissom stems a foot tall. It makes a charming interplanting for clumps of *Phlox divaricata*. *T. silvestris* has a fault, however. While it increases with great rapidity, it is apt under certain conditions to blossom sparsely. The finest I ever had were growing in a south border under a wall where the soil was very rich and where they enjoyed a light shelter provided by a great Scotch brier rose. Here they bloomed almost unfailingly. But in the poor soil of the rock garden they have not done so well. There is a form, however, called *silvestris major*, that is quite reliable in the matter of a yearly display. It is a little taller and heavier all through than the type.

T. persica, from Persia, blooms almost as late as the scarlet *T. sprengeri*, and is one of the most amiable and reliable of all. It is very dwarf and its leaves at their first coming forth twist and curl about upon the ground in a very curious manner. The stems are only a few inches tall, and the blossoms, sometimes two or more to a stem, open out flat and starry from a bronze bud. They are sweet-scented. *T. batalini*, with pale yellow pointed flowers, deliciously fragrant, is a fine sort but seems to have grown scarce and expensive of late.

Two more species remain to be mentioned, the sprightly little lady tulip, *T. clusiana*, and *T. primulina*, a most desirable kind from North Africa. *T. clusiana* is fairly well-known as it is forced in great quantity for the winter flower shows. But in this climate, at any rate, it is an uncertainty, though so lovely that one must be continually trying to suit it. It comes originally, I read, from the northwest frontier of India, but has been widely naturalized in northern Italy and in southern France, where it must indeed present a charming show, growing in grassy places and perhaps among the olives. We may conclude, I think, that it is not really hardy in the neighbourhood of New York. A few bulbs come through, but these in time disappear, worn out probably by the strain of our severe winters. But nothing could be more sparklingly fresh and gay than the blossoms of the lady tulip. The pointed bud carried on a slender stem is bright cherry red; as it opens, the gleaming white interior with a dark stain at the heart is disclosed.

T. primulina is olive green in the bud and opens out pure white. It is about eight inches tall and seems to be one of the most willing and reliable species. With me it has not only remained for several years but increased appreciably. The blossoms have the curious habit—unique so far as I know with tulips—of remaining closed during the heat of the day.

When the time for making up the bulb order comes round, give yourself the pleasure of knowing some of these little wild tulips. A choice of six that are bound to please is the following: *T. kaufmanniana, T. dasystemon, T. persica, T. sylvestris major, T. linifolia,* and *T. sprengeri.*

CHAPTER VIII

Miscellaneous Bulbs

Besides the crocuses, daffodils, and tulips that have been spoken of in earlier chapters, there are many other bulbs of a size to fit the rock garden which should be given a place there if only in little groups of a dozen or so of a kind. They all add immeasurably to the gaiety of the nations represented in this special area and to the interest and delight of the early spring days.

Earliest come the snowdrops, pale children of the snows, that carry within their frosted bells the first faint fragrance of the year. In sheltered places in my own garden they bloom early in February if not buried beneath heavy snow, and I have more than once known them take advantage of an "amazing interlude" of mild weather in January to slip out of the half-frozen muck and flower serenely. *Galanthus nivalis* is the little snowdrop most often planted, and where it is made happy seeds itself freely. But its great relative, *G. elwesii,* is even more valuable, not only because it makes more show—and show is at a premium in the February garden—but because it comes into bloom a little earlier than the smaller species. A form of *G. elwesii,* called *robustus,* is said to make its appearance even a little earlier, and, of course, the earlier the better when it comes to flowers after the turn of the year. But, if the snow lies deep, they and we must possess our impatient souls with patience. The double form of *G. nivalis* is rather pretty, and there is a little green-tipped form, *G. virid-apice,* offered by Barr and Sons, that is said to be attractive. Other snowdrops are *G. fosteri,* the giant *G. plicatus, G. cilicicus,* and, while they do not differ greatly from each other, it is pleasant, where there is space, to include the different species for the sake of their early appearance.

Snowdrops like shade, though if it be very dense or the exposure toward the north, they naturally will not bloom so early. For soil, an ordinary garden loam suits them, but they do not object to moderate acidity and they will thrive beneath evergreen or other trees. They are never more lovely than when planted broadcast in thin woodland where the nodding white flowers push their way upward through brown leaves and freshening mosses. In the rock garden, they may be given the shelter of little bushes or planted where small ferns and mosses are allowed to dwell. Set the little bulbs an inch apart and three deep and get them into the ground as early as possible. The earliness has a good deal to do with our success with snowdrops as well as with the winter aconite and the snowflake (leucojum), so when the bulb order arrives, deal first with these, for every day out of the ground means a loss of vitality for which we must pay when spring comes round in a loss of beauty and vigour.

Closely related to the snowdrop and precious beyond words in the early garden are the snowflakes. To the superficial eye, *Leucojum vernum* might appear to be a giant snowdrop. It begins to bloom before the snowdrops have wholly gone, bearing large, snowy, white bell-like blossoms, the petals smartly tipped with green, nodding on stems six to eight inches tall. The blossoms are fragrant and usually nod solitary on the stems, but there is a form called *vagneri*, that has always two flowers to a stem. *L. vernum carpathicum* has also two flowers on each stem, and the petals are tipped with

yellow. The summer snowflake, *L. aestivum*, is a more vigorous and leafy plant, growing a foot or more in height, with lush leaves much like those of a narcissus and tall stems carrying clusters of white, nodding flowers. This species, blooming toward the end of May, is delightful to have, but it is not as beautiful as *L. vernum*. The snowflakes like a light rather sandy soil in either sun or shade, and to show their full effectiveness should be planted in colonies of at least a dozen bulbs.

Blooming with the snowdrops, that is, appearing in time to make a gay show with them, though not starting so early, is the winter aconite, *Eranthis hyemalis* that grows from a tiny tuber. It is a small but very punctual visitor, humping up a green back while the weather is still cold and then quickly lifting a round yellow head which opens out into a flower about the size of a buttercup above a bright green ruff, the finished product about three inches tall and very quaint and prim. *E. cilicica* [a variety of *E. hyemalis*] is a more recently introduced species which to my eye differs little from *E. hyemalis* save that its blossoms are slightly larger and its blossoming a few days earlier. There is a third kind, *E. tubergeni*, said to be a hybrid of the two, and soft primrose in colour; but of them all I like best the little old green-gold *hyemalis* that grew in Gerard's garden at Holborn in 1589; long has this prim small flower kept faith with gardeners.

The winter aconite will grow under trees and where suited will seed and increase freely. It should be planted in little close masses among snowdrops with a few bright blue scillas to blossom forth before the last of them take their departure.

Happily, the blue-flowered bulbs of spring are many and of an especially lovely blueness. The first to make its bow to the rejuvenated world is one of the prettiest, *Hyacinthus azureus* [*Muscari azureum*], often sent out as *Muscari azureum;* but the difference between hyacinthus and muscari is plain, the bells of the former being always open while those of the latter are closed at the neck like a little sack. *H. azureus* [*M. azureum*] flowers not long after the snowdrops, indeed, sometimes with them, and it is one of the most lovely and indispensable of spring flowers. It colour is pure azure, growing darker as the wedge-shaped inflorescence fades. Another little hyacinthus blooms a good deal later. This is *H. amethystinus,* whose stems are very slender and droop with the weight of many little bells, soft blue in colour. It is a very old flower in gardens, but has never been a best seller, for the reason, I suppose, that it takes many of the graceful slender things to make any show at all. In the rock garden, however, where small things have a chance to show their charms, this species makes a dainty display when twenty-five or more are set closely together in a half-shaded situation. It blooms toward the end of May, when flowers from bulbs are getting scarce.

Of the muscaris, the old grape hyacinth, *M. botryoides,* which is a very ancient garden friend, is the one most often planted. In certain sections of our country, it has escaped from cultivation and is often to be found staining a neglected meadow or stretch of roadside with its glorious colour. It is a free seeder and so must be planted in some spot where this capacity for reproduction will be an advantage and not a nuisance. And in the rock garden it does sometimes become a nuisance, as I have found to my cost. I plant only small colonies of grape hyacinths in the rock garden save in outlying parts where they will not thrust up among small fragile plants. The white form is less pervasive and a very lovely thing, the inflorescence appearing like a spike of small pearls.

The well known 'Heavenly Blue' grape hyacinth is a form of *M. conicum,* the starch hyacinth, found at Trebizond, larger than the common grape hyacinth and, with me, blooming a little later. It is also quite heavenly fragrant and should be planted in large patches wherever there is room for it, but not among small plants in the choicer regions of the rock garden, for it, too, is a wild seeder and a strong grower, and soon usurps more space than may be allotted it in restricted quarters. It, moreover, makes a late summer growth which lies about untidily until the blossoms appear in spring, and afterward until it is matured. The fragrance of 'Heavenly Blue,' Mr. Joseph Jacob says, is like a mixture of the spicy scent of the real old clove carnation and the "ecclesiastical" odour of the night-scented stock. Anyway, with the sunshine full upon them, few scents are more delicious. These three among the muscari are the most important for general planting, but those like myself who are bitten with the urge to collect may like to tuck in about the rock garden a number of others.

There is *M. argaei* (*atlanticum*) [*Muscari armeniacum 'Argaei'*] not greatly differing from *M. botryoides* but more purple in colour; *M. moschatum* [*M. macrocarpum*] (the musk hyacinth), not very conspicuous but richly scented, with blunt little flower spikes of grayish blue; *M. paradoxum* [*M. bellevia pycanthium*] with very dark blue flowers on stems nine to twelve inches high; *M. plumosum*, the feather hyacinth, a curious form with light violet thready blossoms; *M. comosum*, the tassel hyacinth, with a tuft of sterile blossoms at the top which give it a curious tumble-headed appearance.

Chionodoxas flower in March and are highly prized in the rock garden, both because of their small size and for their lovely cerulean blossoms. This is a small genus of only two or three species, natives of the mountains of Asia Minor and Crete, "where they flower in profusion amid the melting snow." Hence their vernacular name, glory of the snow. The flowers of *C. sardensis* are bright gentian-blue throughout and appear a little earlier than the blue and white blossoms of *C. luciliae*. Both of these small things will bear generous planting in the rock garden, where, if safe from disturbance, they will sow their seed and also increase by offsets. *C. timol*, I do not know, but it is said to resemble *C. luciliae*, blooming later, however. *C. gigantea* is described as having larger and flatter flowers, variable in colour, sometimes being soft lavender.

Much additional blue garniture is brought into the spring garden by the scillas. Earliest to flower among them is *Scilla bifolia*, bright blue and floriferous, delightful when planted in little close masses. It usually makes its appearance in mid-March, and is but three inches tall.

S. sibirica, a piercing blue in colour, blooms during the last weeks of March and in early April, and is the best known of its family. It increases rapidly from seed, the seedlings springing up all about the parent plants and having the appearance of grass. Do not destroy this "grass" and its promise of future blue glory. *S. bifolia taurica* wears a lighter and, if possible, a lovelier blue, and it flowers a little earlier than the type. The white form of *S. sibirica* is most attractive but to my thinking the pink is not worth planting. *S. atrocaerulea* is very splendid, with a taller and fuller flower spike. *S. amoena* blooms later than do the foregoing kinds, but not so late as the two lovely wood hyacinths, *S. campanulata* [*Hyacinthoides hispanica*] and *S. festalis* (*nutans*). The first is the Spanish wood hyacinth with stalwart stems rising erectly to the height of a foot, strung with bells—blue, lavender, white, or various tones of pink. Some fine forms are blue king, blue queen, skyblue, rosalind, rose queen, peach blossom, and white lady.

S. festalis (*nutans*) [*Hyacinthoides non-scripta*], the English wood hyacinth, is a far more graceful and beloved flower, though it makes less show. The stalk curves lightly like a shepherd's crook or a wand all hung with bells, and whether the common blue form be grown or some of its "improvements," it is an investment to make sure of. None is lovelier than the common sort, but there is a blush queen that is dainty, and a fine white form listed as *S. f. alba major.* Leonidas is said to be an improvement on the type. In English woodlands, the blue forms of these scillas make shadowy pools of dim blue colour, and they will do the same in ours if kept free of rank weeds and underbrush.

S. italica [*Hyacinthoides italien*] also flowers very late—toward the end of May. This is a very old garden friend, having been grown since the early days of the Seventeenth Century. It grows from nine to twelve inches high, and, says Mr. Jacob, when all the flowers are fully developed, they form a fat sugar-loaf-shaped spike.

If your garden is a shady one, plant largely of the scilla family, for they will thrive and be most graciously at home. They will tolerate a sunny situation, but a shaded one is more to their mind.

Very close to scilla is puschkinia, called the striped squill. This is a little bulbous plant growing only three or four inches tall, with flaring bells of very faint blue with a line of deeper colour down the centre of each petal. It is a pretty and dainty little plant, but too pallid to make much of an impression. Its early flowering is the chief of its virtues. *Puschkinia scilloides* and *P. libanotica* [a variety of *P. scilloides*], often offered separately, are, or seem to be, one and the same thing.

Of fritillarias there are a number charmingly fit for use in the rock garden, though they are not often seen there. Indeed, these quaint and interesting bulbous plants are rather generally neglected nowadays; perhaps because of the noise made in the world by the gorgeous

and ever-increasing cottage and darwin tulips, quieter things are being overlooked. The fritillaries, it is true, save for the great crown imperial, are not showy, but several kinds are too charming to be missed. Once, a long time ago, the crown imperial, *Fritillaria imperialis,* made a great deal of noise in the world, and deservedly. It is the first flower mentioned in Parkinson's *Paradisi In Soli,* 1629, and he classes it among lilies.

> Because the Lilly is the more stately flower, among manie; and amongst the wonderfull varitie of Lillies knowne to us in these daies, much more than in former times, . . . the Crowne Imperiall for his stately beautifulness, deservith the first place in this our Garden of Delight, to be here entreated of before all other Lillies.

Perhaps the crown imperial is too large for the rock garden, but I have seen it used effectively on heights in Mrs. Chapman's beautiful rock garden, at "Silvania," where its rich colours shone finely against the background of pale spring green. It is a most exciting plant, thrusting a great nose out of the ground at the first hint of mildness in the atmosphere, and then, if reassured as to weather conditions, shooting upward with the speed of a moon at the pantomime; positively, it can almost be seen to grow. Try a few of these old-fashioned flowers in your rock garden. They are the same now as when Parkinson figured them in his book, having been little tampered with during the centuries between then and now. They like a rich soil and sunshine, and the great stalk should never be cut off, but allowed to mature and die away naturally. They should be planted as early as it is possible to procure them.

The white guinea hen flower or checker lily is lovely and most distinctive with its slender stems and large drooping white bells faintly checkered with green. It likes a dampish spot in partial shade. The type *Fritillaria meleagris* is less beautiful, but a quaint and old-fashioned flower that is good to include among the flowers of the rock garden. Mr. Purdy offers several Western fritillaries that are worth growing. Among them, *F. recurva* is a striking scarlet-flowered sort that is well established in the garden of a neighbour in rich dark soil and shade; and *F. pudica* that grows in my own garden. This is a slender little plant only a few inches tall, carrying a single bright yellow bell. It is from the arid regions of the great basin, says Mr. Purdy, and likes sandy or loose soils in sun.

A very old-fashioned plant not often seen is the star of Bethlehem, *Ornithogalum umbellatum*. Once it was prized in every garden but now it is neglected, and in many neighbourhoods opens its white and green stars along the dusty roadsides and at the edges of field or wood like any weed. Of course, it is too hearty and vigorous for the rock garden proper, but on banks near by, among ferns and honesty and violets, I am glad of its unfailing constellations. Its fault is that its blossoms close at noon, which habit has earned it one of its English names, Betty-go-to-bed-at-noon. If pet names are an indication of popularity, then the star of Bethlehem was undoubtedly once a beloved plant, for there is a long string of them given in *A Dictionary of English Plant Names* (Britten and Holland), among which are 'Nap-at-Noon,' 'Peep-o-Day,' 'Sleepy Dick,' 'Twelve O'Clock,' and many others.

So many of the plants of the rock garden have no pet names, but only long, unpronounceable Latin names, that it is pleasant to find among them a few that have so long been on terms of intimacy with gardening folk that they have been given friendly appellations.

CHAPTER IX

Western Troutlilies

ALL WHO FREQUENT the country in spring are familiar with the yellow troutlilies, dog's-tooth violets, or adder's tongues, as they are variously called, that carpet large tracts of dampish woodland or foregather multitudinously in low copses from Nova Scotia to Ontario, south to Arkansas and Florida. Their curiously mottled leaves closely covering the ground are conspicuous some time before the yellow lilylike flowers appear nodding on their slender stems. This is *Erythronium americanum,* and it has as its seasonal companions spring beauties, violets, anemones, and some flowering shrubs.

Because of the great plentifulness of this troutlily, it is one of the plants that we may with a clear conscience gather freely and also transplant to our gardens without endangering its continued existence in the wild. But, unfortunately, there are two reasons why we do not readily take advantage of this freedom to take and make them our own. In the first place, the long white bulbs of blossoming size are usually buried seven inches below ground, which makes getting at them no small task, and, moreover, in so doing we must uproot hundreds of small ones that may be many years in arriving at a size where they can produce a blossom. The presence of these myriads of nonflowering bulbs provides the second reason why *E. americanum* is not an especially desirable plant for naturalizing.

While its increase is very rapid and we soon have wide stretches of the curious tonguelike leaves, only here and there appears a yellow nodding flower, and that is not reward enough for the trouble of digging and transplanting them. If the leaves remained to carpet the ground throughout the summer, they would be in themselves useful, but they disappear as spring merges into summer and are seen no more until another spring calls them forth.

There is a white troutlily in the east, *E. albidum,* but it is rare. The leaves of this species are not mottled.

But we are not here so much concerned with our rather grudging eastern troutlilies as with their amazing relatives that disport themselves in great multitudes in the cool woods and upon the high slopes of the mountains of the west. These western troutlilies are so little known in eastern gardens that few persons that come to visit my garden have ever seen or even heard of them. And this is a sad pity, for they are among the most individual and delightful of spring-flowering bulbous plants. Not only are there yellow-flowered species, but others are pale pink, deep pink, mauve, cream, white, or bright orange, and many are distinguished by circles of contrasting hues. Moreover, these sprightly beauties take kindly to conditions they find on this side of the country, appearing perfectly hardy and increasing happily if given comfortable quarters.

Considering the fact that the bulbs are comparatively inexpensive, there is every reason, while bulb ordering is in mind, that all who are interested in making the acquaintance of new and charming plants, or in increasing their knowledge of our native flowers, should give the western erythroniums a generous trial.

All the species of erythronium belong to North America save *E. dens-canis,* found in various parts of Europe. This is reddish-purple in colour and is said to be less attractive than the American species. In addition to the two eastern species mentioned above, there are two found in the Rocky Mountains, while in the cool woods and on the high mountains from northern California into Canada, there are nine or ten distinct species with numerous well-defined varieties. All these westerners may with entire safety be brought to our eastern gardens, and will give the greatest satisfaction and delight whether naturalized by the thousand or planted by the half dozen in suitable locations in the rock garden.

A light soil, moist and rich in mould, is their preference, and a cool, shaded position. Those who possess shaded hillsides will do well to naturalize the erythroniums in large numbers. Free drainage is important to them, and wherever the soil is too heavy and clogging, the addition of peat moss, sand, and leaf mould will convert it to the proper consistency. Where the situation is very hot and dry, a mulch of leaves will keep the bulbs in good condition after flowering.

Erythroniums may also be naturalized in grass with success, and as the foliage ripens before the grass needs be cut, such treatment is usually attended by satisfactory results.

The propagation of *E. dens-canis* and of the eastern American species, as well as of a western species, *E. hartwegii,* is by offsets, the rest increase only by seeds, so that it will be found that they increase slowly. In planting, the long white bulb or corm should be set two inches below the surface of the ground, the hole being dug about four inches deep. If the various species of erythronium be planted, a long succession of bloom may be enjoyed.

Earliest to bloom is *E. grandiflorum*. Its carriage is erect and sprightly, and it sometimes reaches a height of nearly two feet. The leaves are a fine rich green, unmottled, and the slender erect stems carry with especial jauntiness from one to three or four handsome bright yellow blossoms that measure nearly two inches across. This species is at home in cool Northern woods and because of the fact that the bright green leaves often thrust through a bank of melting snow in early spring it is locally known as the snow lily. My little plantations of snow lilies are about five years old and show a satisfactory increase.

Also in the woods of the Northwest but higher in the mountains grows the avalanche lily, *E. montanum*, said to be a form of *E. grandiflorum*. It has the same upstanding grace but the flowers are white stained with yellow at the base of the petals while the buds are pinkish. This form is said to be less easy in cultivation than its yellow relative of the lower hills, but where it grows naturally it is as prolific as are buttercups in our summer meadows.

E. hartwegii is one of the best and most sturdy of the species. It is common on the slopes of Mt. Rainier and also in the Sierra Nevadas in California. Its leaves are rather thick and handsomely mottled and the blossoms are orange coloured at the base and creamy for the rest. This species is said to endure a greater degree of heat and drought without apparent suffering than any other. My own clumps have rather a cool place under a spreading spicebush. It is one of the earliest to bloom. *E. hartwegii* is recommended for forcing, being treated as are other bulbs for that purpose.

One of the prettiest and daintiest species is *E. hendersonii* reported from the mountains of south Oregon. The blossoms are a soft pinkish-lilac and are carried with a good deal of "style." The petals are sharply recurved, and the colour toward the centre of the blossoms is nearly black. This quite bewitching troutlily makes patches of lovely delicate colour amid the young green of woodsy places, and is altogether one of the most satisfactory. Among the treasures of the coast ranges of California is *E. californicum* which is considered one of the best for naturalization in the East. Its leaves are richly mottled, and the flowers, borne several on a stem, the colour of rich cream. An exquisite form of *californicum* is white beauty, whose almost pure white blossoms are richly banded with mahogany.

And no collection of these flowers would be complete without a generous number of the type known as *E. revolutum*, and its numerous very beautiful varieties. Characteristic of this type are the tall stout stems and large flowers in various exquisite tints, and the leaves mottled in white. Carl Purdy says that, while these plants thrive in good garden loam, they will do well in heavy soils quite wet in winter. I have not put them to this seemingly drastic test, but grow them in wood soil and loam in a partially shaded place, quite well drained. The type itself, *E. revolutum*, has large flowers that open white but speedily flush with pale purple. Pink beauty is a delicate pale pink in colour. It is said to be found in Humboldt County, California, and I believe there is a white form. *E. johnsonii* [*E. revolutum* var. *johnsonii*] is probably the most lovely of all the race. Its flowers are a pure pink and waxen in texture.

The season covered by the blossoming of the troutlilies in my garden is from mid-April to about mid-May. *E. grandiflorum* leads the display, and it is magnificently brought to a close by the beautiful revolutum forms. Let me say again that, if you do not already know these flowers, do not let the snow fall upon your garden before you have tucked a few of them away in some of the shaded corners of your rock garden or, better still, planted a thousand or more in some woodsy place.

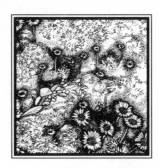

CHAPTER X

Windflowers of the World

WE ARE APT to associate the charming name of windflower chiefly with the fragile blossoms of the damp spring woods—flowers brought into the world on the wings of the spring breezes. But, as a matter of fact, there are windflowers, or anemones, as they are botanically designated, belonging to all the open seasons. Some spring up in the wake of the receding snows on the high mountains, or, like our hepatica, are found early on south-facing slopes or in sheltered hollows of the woods; others belong to the full summer, while the Japanese anemone of the borders defies the frosts of autumn with extreme hardihood, and a lovely show of bloom.

Anemone is a numerous race offering much beauty of a fragile, airy type, and plants suitable for many situations. They are, for the most part, meadow or woodland plants inhabiting the temperate regions of the earth. Very few are true rock plants, though nearly all show to advantage in such a setting as the rock garden offers. The soil suited to a majority of them is a light, rich, warm loam, and though a few like the sunshine full upon them, the greater number are happiest in partial shade.

All who fare to the woods in April without doubt know the American wood anemone, *A. quinquefolia*. Where it grows at all, it is usually quite wildly abundant, the delicate white blossoms flecking the brown floor of the forest like flakes of new-fallen snow, and creating a most charming scene. But when we attempt to reproduce this scene under cultivation we are apt to meet with difficulties. This modest little plant, so lavish in its chosen haunts, is not easy to please under ordinary conditions. Its natural home is in damp, open woods where the soil is decidedly acid. This condition, it must be emphasized, is the quite passionate preference of the wood anemone. The rue anemone (*Syndesmon thalictroides*), usually to be found in its company, is, on the contrary, quite indifferent to diet and will cheerfully exchange the acid shades for any woodsy situation, dry or moist, and with very good grace, even put up with a sunny bank.

But if we would grow the wood anemone, let us give it the proper conditions. It is one of the choice wild flowers that are growing scarce through the thoughtless ravaging of the woods and the inexorable march of the development scheme. If taken from the wild, the plants should be dug with great care—a generous sod lifted—and the whole transplanted to a situation previously prepared for it. The rue anemone is often confused with the wood anemone, but the former may easily be distinguished by its cluster of pink-tinted blossoms, while the other is solitary on its slender stem. Both are but a few inches in height, little low, fragile things that need to be seen in generous numbers to show the full quality of their beauty.

Before the appearance of either of the foregoing, we find the hepatica sending up furry buds amid its winter-worn leaves in sheltered places in the woods. It is, I believe, our earliest wild flower, and as such greatly beloved. Not so long ago, its name was *Anemone hepatica,* but now hepatica is counted a distinct genus, and we have in this country two species, *H. triloba* and *H. acutiloba,* not greatly differing save in the shape of the leaves; nor as to habitat, though I believe *H. acutiloba* is the more common type in

the Northwest. Hepaticas are altogether delightful for naturalizing on banks of damp woodsy soil, or for edging fern beds or borders of wild flowers. And they are quite choice enough for the most exclusive rock garden where their early blooms are appreciated. Various colour forms are found—white, pale purple, pinkish, blue, and of these the blue ones are the most lovely and desirable. Hepaticas are also, sadly enough, becoming scarce, and it is urged that, wherever roads and building operations are invading woodland regions, the anemones and hepaticas and other small and helpless things be rescued and given sanctuary amid congenial surroundings.

Taller and later-flowering native windflowers are *A. canadensis* and *A. virginiana.* The first, called the meadow anemone, is an undeniably handsome plant with a fine upstanding carriage and rather large cream-white blossoms opening from pearly buds. It is an inhabitant of low, moist situations in many parts of the country, and in such places it is an aggressive spreader. Planted in rich soil in the garden, it literally sets out to take the place, but confined to less advantageous positions, to outlying districts of the rock garden, or given the run of a bit of waste land, it is a really desirable plant. Against the summer anemone, *A. virginiana,* the word "weedy" might perhaps be whispered, but for situations not wanted for choicer things even this sort has its merits.

North American anemones, on the whole, while most dainty and lovely, are quite modest and unassuming in appearance. We have none to match some of the glorious species that inhabit various parts of the Old World. Our West Country, however, boasts at least two species that come very close to being glorious. These are *A. patens nuttaliana* and *A. occidentalis*. The first is called the American pasque flower from its likeness to *A. pulsatilla*, the European pasque flower. It is the state flower of North Dakota, where it is popularly known as "crocus." This is a plant of the prairies and low hills of the Northwest where it comes into bloom very early. The large cuplike flowers are pale purple in colour, and the whole plant is covered with silken hairs. It grows in soft sand in full sunshine, and such conditions should be provided for it in the rock garden. Here it thrives on a little raised sunny plain in almost pure sand.

A. occidentalis, the chalice cup, is a most beautiful plant of the mountains of the Northwest, with large silver blossoms that open so early, I am told, as sometimes to force their way through a snowdrift. The blossoms are nearly two inches across and not fragile in appearance as are most anemones, and are mounted on stout serviceable stems a foot or more in height, covered with silken hairs. It is probably the finest of our anemones. In the rock garden, the best place for it would be on a little gravelly slope in full sunshine.

In marked contrast to the splendid chalice cup is another mountain windflower, smallest and most fragile of its kind. This is *A. parviflora,* a dainty little plant with a hairy, reddish stem some four to eight inches tall, topped by a white blossom stained lilac on the outer sepals and filled with golden stamens. It is common throughout the Rockies and mountains of the Northwest in moist ground and rich woods, and it is also to be found in parts of Asia. Larger in all its parts is *A. drummondii,* called the alpine anemone because it is found only in meadows of the highest mountains, "close to perpetual snow." In appearance, this charming species is something like a white buttercup, the outer sepals pale blue. In the garden, these plants would require a situation where the soil is deep and rich, and high enough to insure perfect drainage.

A dozen plants of *A. deltoides* have recently reached me from Oregon. There is a charming drawing of this species in Miss Armstrong's *Western Wild Flowers,* showing a large, solitary blossom carried on a slender stem that is encircled by three palmate leaves. Miss Armstrong says this white flower with its many golden stamens is conspicuous in the dark mountain woods. This gives us an authentic clue to its requirements in the garden. Undoubtedly, these dark mountain forests are acid as to soil, and so we feel sure that this little windflower will respond if planted in the acid soil bed and preferably under evergreen or oak trees.

These are but a few of the windflowers to be had out of our West Country. Those who would embark on the adventure of collecting anemones should seek the cañon anemone, *A. sphemophylla; A. globosa* [*A. multifida*], common in the low valleys of the Rockies; *A. multifida,* a plant of dry meadows, and many more. When we must largely forego the allurements of the sparkling foreign-born of the family, our own assume a special desirability, and in any case they are well worth the slight trouble that must be taken to accommodate them.

And as to those same foreign-born wonders, we need not give them up so easily. We may not for the present import the plants, but the pasque flower is fairly plentiful in nurseries still, and the many forms of *A. japonica* of the autumn borders are to be had without stint. And for the rest, if we are in earnest, we may raise them from seed. Anemones are not the easiest plants in the world to raise from seed, but it may be done. First, it must be understood that the seed must, absolutely *must,* be fresh. This you will understand is essential, because in anemone and in a number of other species, usually found difficult to propagate from seed, "the living germ has but little surrounding nourishment to keep it alive," and unless confided to the earth a short time after maturity, vitality is lost and the seed becomes worthless. On the other hand, seed sown as soon as ripe commonly germinates without delay. Buy from a dealer who is willing to assure you that his seed is newly gathered, and buy in the late summer or autumn, and sow at once. A compost of finely crushed potsherds (clay flowerpots), sand, and peat is recommended as suitable, and flat boxes or pans may be used and placed in a coldframe or covered heavily with leaves in winter.

Among the many beautiful exotic anemones the pasque flower, *A. pulsatilla,* stands out as one of the most striking. Its splendid purple cups opening in early April are a source of perennial delight, and the finely cut, silken leaves and waving, plumy seed vessels are scarcely less ornamental. The plant is easy to grow, loving a dry, rather stiff soil, not too rich, and a position where it receives the sun for half the day at least; and whether in the rock garden, along the edge of a border, or in clumps on a dry hillside is no matter.

And of those undoubted loves that are at present denied us, I must say a word. There is *A. blanda,* the blue winter windflower, that Mr. Farrer tells us decks all the islands and coasts of the eastern Mediterranean in a sheet of colour with the first breath of returning spring. A patch of it, blue and starry, on an April day makes the heart leap. There are pink and white forms, but they cannot compare with the blue. This windflower grows from a little black cylindrical root and if one or two should fall into your hands, cherish them. They will enjoy a good loamy soil and the twiggy protection of little bushes against the blustering winds. There is *A. apennina,* hardly less enchanting, with larger blossoms and more blue petals, that will do with almost any situation, but loves a corner which early catches the spring sunshine. There is our lady of the snows, *A. vernalis* [*Pulsatilla vernalis*], an opalescent pasque flower and the dwarfest of that group, that likes a moist, peaty soil and some shadow, but is even then an uncertainty in gardens. There is the European wood anemone, *A. nemorosa,* and its many fine forms, chief of which are *A. robinsoniana,* with large pale blue blossoms—one of the beauties of the race—and the quaint little double form,

A. nemorosa flore-pleno [*A. nemorosa alba*], most floriferous and amiable. Also there is the yellow wood anemone, *A. ranunculoides,* no more difficult to grow, and well worth a place among the others. These European wood anemones bloom in April. They all appreciate a shaded situation and a soil wherein leaf mould plays a large part.

CHAPTER XI

Variety Among the Violets

IT IS USUAL to think of violets as belonging to that season when the flowery tide of spring is rushing over the earth and violets in infinite variety bloom as if the whole burden of beautifying the world rested upon them alone. And yet there are few weeks in the year, except when the ground is covered with snow or frozen solid, when we may not find a violet of some sort blossoming, not, of course, with its wild spring prodigality, but in a gently unexpected way that is very pleasant and cheering.

All through the heat of summer, certain of them, if kept from seeding, will flower quite freely, and even at this present late season, when the air is alight with the yellow leaves of the tulip trees fluttering down from their high perches, and frosts steal nightly upon the garden, robbing it stealthily of its treasure, it is amazing how many different kinds of violets, or violas, to speak botanically, are to be found lifting their small faces to the untrustworthy sun as confidingly as in April.

The little ceremony of finding the first violet of the year has come down to most of us from childhood as a happy memory. I do not remember, however, in those far-off days, ever having noted the date of the last one. But I do this now, and the discovery of a violet, perhaps, when snow has begun to sift down from the leaden sky seems quite as much a matter of wonder and interest as the shy venturer at the other end of the year.

I have never found one of these flowers in January, but it seems not an impossible triumph, for once in mid-February I turned back the snow from a corner of the rock garden and found a witch-faced pansy peering at me inscrutably, and friends have told me that they have found Johnny-jump-ups in their gardens in every month of the year.

This year-round companionship that we may expect from violets is one of the good reasons for giving space to as many of them as possible. A quite small garden may hold many kinds of them without fear of crowding out other desirable plants; for most violets are easy to please and do not object, where space is a consideration, to being tucked about in nooks and corners where they need be noticed only when in bloom. Indeed, this seems to be the most fitting way to grow these modest flowers. They are not for bold plantings in conspicuous places, but for secluded regions where we must seek them out and may enjoy their quiet beauty in peace. True, a number of them self-sow with a freedom that leads us to suspect a determination to command notice at all seasons and in all places, so that they acquire the bad reputation of weeds, but the worst of these offenders may be excluded from the garden wholly, or confined to some locality where their prodigality will not be a nuisance.

Viola is the family name, and it includes a multitude of small and lovely delights: pansies—such gorgeous beings—and the pert Johnny-jump-ups said to be the ancestors of the pansies; the lovely bedding violas, so much used abroad, and more than two hundred species that inhabit the woods, the meadows, the plains, the mountain slopes and heights of this country and most of the temperate world.

It is too bad indeed that with such beauty and variety to choose from we should be satisfied with knowing only such violets as grow in near-by woods and meadows. Leaving out the commonest sorts and a sad number of

veritable charmers, here are a dozen species with a few varieties that will add much to the pleasure and beauty of any garden.

First, then, taking them alphabetically, there is *Viola arenaria rosea* [*V. rupestris*], a dainty European species with bright pink—well, faintly magenta—blossoms borne in the greatest profusion. It is a sprightly being, and its hue is unusual for one of its family, making patches of soft colour in the rock garden at a season when there are few pink flowers. Its habit is tidy and tufted, and though it self-sows rather freely, it is seldom in the way. It also crosses promiscuously with neighbour violets, and it is not unusual to find funny little piebald babies about the garden that have no merit save their funniness. After the generosity of its spring blossoming, *V. arenaria* [*V. rupestris*] keeps a few flowers going until after hard frosts. It is easily raised from seed.

The twin-flowered violet, *V. biflora* [*V. pedata 'biflora'*], is wee and dainty, with rounded leaves and two bright yellow blossoms to a stem. The mission of this small creature is not a brilliant one, but, given the run of a flight of shaded steps, it will quietly take possession of the cracks and crevices, and in their season the little gilded blossoms make a charming show.

V. blanda, our native sweet-scented white violet, found in low moist places in many parts of the East, is almost the earliest of its kind to bloom. One often comes upon it most unexpectedly, when March experiences a melting mood, arrested first, perhaps, by its delicate but searching fragrance. It is one of the most useful and lovable of our native species. It spreads quickly, making wide mats in shaded places, and if *Scilla sibirica* be planted thickly beneath these mats, a charming spring picture results, when the innumerable white violets and the brilliant blue bells spring into life at the same time. *V. blanda* likes shade, and is one of the best companions along a woodland path.

From Bosnia comes a choice little violet that bears the name of its native land, *V. bosniaca.* With me and with most persons from whom I have reports of its habits, it is a biennial, self-sowing in a restrained sort of way. But occasionally I hear of it as behaving in the manner of a perennial, and those for whom it is thus permanent are fortunate indeed, for the small Bosnian is quite a unique beauty, and one must have it even at the price of raising it yearly from seed. The blossoms are large and of a most delightful pink colour—no magenta this time—and they are continued throughout the summer. This treasure is for the rock garden in full sun or half shade in a soil compounded of sand and leaf mould. It comes readily from seed, and no lover of violets should miss the opportunity of knowing it.

Our little Canada violet, *V. canadensis,* is fairly well known. It is one of those generous sorts seldom found out of bloom, and so to be cherished. It seems positively to delight in the autumn frosts, and one is quite sure of finding it flowering freely among the brown and scarlet leaves in late November. The plants are branching and bushy, growing to ten inches, the blossoms white tinged with lavender and delicately scented. It is for a woodsy place where it will seed itself about freely though not so as to become a nuisance. There is something especially gay and friendly about this species, and where it is known it is always beloved. Out in the West grows its very near relative, *V. rugulosa,* a more stalwart individual altogether, though having many of the characteristics of the Canada violet. It has the same busy branching growth and the larger blossoms are white tinged with lavender. It also is seldom out of bloom. With me it grows contentedly in a low place in full sunshine, as well as in the shade. It is to be had of most Western dealers, and is well worth a place in any garden.

Many gardens are adorned with the horned pansy, *V. cornuta,* and its many beautiful varieties. This is an alpine pansy of spreading growth, small leaves and the habit of wild floriferousness. If seeding is prevented by conscientious snipping off of all dead flowers, the plants will present a most beauteous appearance for the greater part of the season, beginning in the early spring. Some of its finest varieties are *V. c. rosea, V. c. alba,* the garden form *george wermig,* the flowers of which are of a magnificent rich purple hue, and *papilio,* large, sprightly and showing a lovely combination of bright lavender and white. These are the showiest members of the family, barring the florists' pansies, and are delightful for edging garden beds and borders or for adorning the rock garden.

V. elatior is a distinct European species, growing a foot or more tall, erect and bushy. The blossoms that come in early May are large and of a lovely pale blue colour. Though not a native, it loses no time in establishing itself as such by sowing its seed most freely in all directions. This habit makes it rather too rampageous for a choice location, but it is not fastidious and may be relegated to any out-of-the-way situation whether in sun or shade. I have never found this species blossoming save in the spring at its appointed time.

From far Macedonia comes a most beautiful and useful species, *V. gracilis*. This has something of the habit of the horned pansies, but is altogether neater and more compact. It spreads into close, broad mats and bears an extraordinary number of purple velvet blossoms poised on slender stems over a long season. It seems occasionally to bloom itself to death, but this may often be prevented by cutting the plants back sharply after flowering and working a reviving mixture of sand and leaf soil in among the growths. For the top of a wall or the rock garden, no more charming plant could be found. It thrives well in a well-drained soil in any open situation. Various forms of *V. gracilis* are offered—'Purple Robe,' 'Lord Nelson,' and numerous others—but they are all definitely larger and stouter than the type and have lost what Mr. Farrer calls the freakish, elfin loveliness of *V. gracilis,* no less than its intensity of dark and velvety violence.

No garden should be without a bed or border or at very least a patch of the sweet violet, *V. odorata,* for it would be a thousand pities to miss the pleasure of their warm, rich fragrance—like that of hothouse violets—that freights the brisk March breezes, does the sun shine warmly for a few days in that month of many moods. Buy a dozen plants of *V. odorata,*

or better still a hundred, and set them out in a sheltered place in good soil where the sun rests for at least part of the day and know the pleasure of delicious nosegays from your own garden while winter still lingers. Every year or two the plants should be divided and reset if they are to continue flowering with freedom, and because of this necessity our store of them rapidly increases, and soon we have enough to share with friends and neighbours. One may have them white, mauve, lavender, and purple, and a bed of them looks like a charming bit of old chintz.

The big common purple violet, *V. papilionacea* [*V. sororaria*], common in low ground everywhere, is much too strenuous a spreader to bring into the garden if one hopes to grow much of anything else, but its white form is most lovely to encourage along the edges of a fern border or in any moist, shaded place. There is also a blue and white form, known as the confederate violet, with large flowers carried on long stems, that is most ornamental. The confederate violet, like its blue relative, is a violent self-sower, and because of this habit has gained the name, by which it is known in some localities, of Sherman's raiders, but it is strikingly beautiful, especially where it may be grown in large patches. M. Correvon was so delighted with it when he visited my garden that he took back several large clumps of it to his wonderful gardens in Switzerland.

The bird's-foot violet, *V. pedata,* is well known but not always so well understood. It is a plant of sandy wastes and pine barrens where it grows profusely in sun or shade. But where it is plentiful one may be assured that the soil is acid, and too many of its admirers, unaware of this fact, bring it in from the wild or secure it from nurseries, and try to satisfy it with a diet of ordinary soil or one containing lime. In these cases, the plants linger on for a few months and then disappear. Give it the soil of its choice—one of rotted oak leaves, pine or hemlock needles, and sand, and there will be no trouble in keeping the bird's-foot violet. It is one of the beauties of the race, especially in its bicolour form, and to be considered and cherished in every way. The white form is rare and lovely but not comparable to *V. p. bicolor*.

It has been very difficult to choose a dozen violets for distinction, and so I am minded to add a few more for the sake of those who find violets alluring and desire to make the acquaintance of a greater number. Of native species I would suggest the following: *V. pedatifida, V. striata, V. glabella, V. rotundifolia, V. primulaefolia, V. lanceolata, V. nuttalli, V. ocellata.* Of foreign species, *V. alpina, V. lutea, V. calcarata, V. cenisia, V. altaica,* and *V. pinnata.*

CHAPTER XII

Irises That Fit the Rock Garden

Irises are so many, so amazingly various, so almost universally desirable that one without acres to devote to them is in a quandary how to choose among them. But one who threads his way among the splendid crowd in search of adornments for his rock garden only finds the embarrassment materially lessened.

The irises we choose for the rock garden, if we are to uphold the best traditions of this Floral Kingdom of Lilliput, should, of course, be dwarf of stature. No beauty of the spacious borders, long-stemmed and with huge blossoms, should have a place there, nor should any tall member of the beardless section—*I. aurea* [*I. crocea*], *I. ochroleuca* [*I. orientalis*] and the rest—be they ever so regal, arise to disparage some tiny, lovely thing. These, like the great-flowered cottage and darwin tulips, the big trumpet daffodils, are for the glorification of the borders, while the little gay wild tulips, the tiniest among the daffodils, the smallest members of the iris tribe, are cherished in sequestered nooks, along little safe ledges, on the high windy tableland of the rock garden. There they are safe from pushing neighbours, there they may have special soil and special aspects made to order for them, there they may show the full quality of their fragile beauty without coming into competition with the bulk and gorgeousness of the border beauties.

Perhaps the height of irises used in the rock garden should not exceed one foot, though in the case of some species, very slender as to foliage and with flowers airy as butterflies, a few taller species may be allowed. A few we shall find that do not accomplish a greater eminence in the world than three or four inches. These are delightful indeed.

Probably the first we shall come upon in our search for minia-

ture types and varieties will be found in catalogues under the head of dwarf bearded irises. These are little sisters of the border beauties known as tall bearded irises. They range in height from four or five inches to about twelve inches, and they bloom very early—during April and early May. They are compact, quite wildly floriferous, making splendid spreads of colour over the hillsides of the rock garden, almost as many hued as their tall prototypes and, like them, of exceeding amiability.

For the most part, these irises are forms of hybrids of several widely distributed European species. Hybridizers have of late been so busy with them that their name approaches legion, and there are unhappily many poor ones both in form and colour, as well as many that so nearly duplicate each other that confusion spreads from catalogues to gardens and the result of expenditure is too often disappointment. At the present time the American Iris Society is doing a noble work in trying out these dwarfs and sifting from among the fine and distinct kinds the duplicates and those of inferior colour and habit. Soon we shall have lists purged of all save the distinct and the lovely, and our choosing will be a matter of certainty.

In the meantime, here are a number that may be relied upon to give complete satisfaction. There is no doubt that the fat little elves that derive from I. pumila are the most enchanting. The first of these to flower—about April eighth with me—is I. atroviolacea. It is the smallest, not exceeding four inches over all. Its blossoms are a good purple and look very well near a patch of the lovely blush-pink *Arabis albida rosea*. Very dwarf also and early flowering are the two "gray-sky-blue" forms, I. caerulea and I. azurea, both rather scarce, but worth taking a deal of trouble to find, for few plants of any kind provide us with such lovely breadths of colour in the spring. I. gracilis is small, silver-gray with claret markings and fragrant; I. macrocarpa is purple and there is a white form of I. pumila that must be delightful, but I have not yet found it.

Following close upon the heels of these small charmers come others of slightly greater height. They flower in late April and the early days of May, and are from eight to twelve or fourteen inches tall. A good selection is the following: 'Socrates,' a fine claret-hued variety of nice habit and form; cyanea, deep blue-purple; 'Black Midget,' very dark purple with interesting almost black buds; 'Orange Queen,' deep yellow, with a large blossom; 'Glee,' a lovely soft tone of yellow, with a longer period of blossoming than any dwarf known to me. Lutea and excelsa are very good yellows, the first paler than the second, and both quite dwarf; I. statellae, creamy white, delightfully free and very sweet; the 'Bride,' a lovely gray-white about ten inches tall that should be in every collection.

These dwarf bearded irises love a sunny situation in well-drained soil. They do well in the ordinary soil of the rock garden if plenty of humus is added and they are given an occasional dressing of bone meal.

Very different in appearance from the foregoing varieties are four little species from foreign parts that grace the rock garden exceedingly. They are slender, with narrow leaves and slight stems carrying lovely butterfly blossoms. They are *I. arenaria, I. gracilipes, I. ruthenica,* and *I. minuta.* These are not so readily procured as are the dwarf bearded sorts. One may have a long quest through foreign seed lists and through domestic iris catalogues before the four are assembled, but it is a proud day when it comes, and worth all the waiting and the trouble.

I. arenaria, the sand iris, is a minute Hungarian species with a wiry creeping rhizome. It requires to be planted a half inch deep in sandy soil with a layer of good soil just beneath where the feeding roots may find sustenance. It is a sun lover and spreads about rapidly, making nice patches that in early April are entirely covered with large bright yellow blossoms as vivacious and as ephemeral as a flight of yellow butterflies. Seed of this species is sometimes offered in foreign catalogues, and this, if fresh, germinates quickly, and the little plants are ready to flower the second year from the sowing. Once in a while plants are offered in an American catalogue, but not often, strange to say, for it is a most precious small treasure, and not really difficult to grow.

While *I. arenaria* spreads about and holds its yellow blossoms low to the earth, *I. gracilipes* arises slenderly to a height of about eight inches. It is, perhaps, the most lovely of the dwarf irises. In time, it makes a nice clump of narrow green leaves lightly ribbed, from among which arise in mid-May in great profusion delicate stems bearing aloft the most exquisite fragile blossoms, pale lavender-blue in colour and thin, almost, as tissue. This valuable species hails from wooded slopes in Japan where it grows in loose vegetable soil. Such a position suits it in the rock garden—a little slope shaded for a part of the day and a well-drained soil rich in leaf mould. An occasional top-dressing of this nourishing food is a consideration well repaid.

I. ruthenica is a dainty and delightful species whose range in nature extends from Hungary to East China and Korea. Its height is about eight inches, its blossoms blue-lavender, the falls spreading and attractively veined with white. It has the added grace of delightful fragrance. The leaves are very narrow. This plant requires full sunshine and a soil of humus or leaf mould well mixed with stone chips and a little sand to insure drainage.

I. minuta is a quaint little soul whose natural haunts are not known—that is, it is not known in a wild state. It was brought from gardens around Tokyo and Yokohama to Western gardens, but is still very rarely met with. It is probably not sufficiently striking to take the eye of iris lovers accustomed to the gorgeousness of the larger forms. But for the rock gardener whose eye is keen for small bits of beauty it is a treasure. Its sprightly blossoms are yellow. With me it thrives in a soil of leaf mould and sandy grit with a top-dressing of stone chips, and in a sunny situation, though a large rock at the back protects it from the afternoon sun.

Besides these four undoubted rock garden treasures there are a number of taller species

—taller, but slender and with blossoms lightly made and lightly carried. Of these are *I. chryso-graphes*, from China, a lovely velvety red-purple; *I. forresti*, with charming yellow blossoms, that appear in late May or early June, and *I. bulleyana*, that blooms at the same time, but bears soft blue blossoms. It is a somewhat larger and stronger-growing plant. The three are from western China and like a low position in the rock garden where moisture gathers.

In my own rock garden I also grow *I. tectorum alba*, for, though its blossoms are larger than those of other irises admitted, its supreme beauty seems to demand a special setting, and it is not tall, nor pervasive. It likes, too, the sunshine, the protection, and the thoroughly drained soil there to be found. The type, a delightful mottled blue in colour, is a fine plant, but the white form is to my thinking the most beautiful of all the great family. *I. tectorum* belongs to the same section—the evansia or crested section—as do *I. gracilipes* mentioned above, and *I. cristata*, one of the most delightful of our native species.

Native irises

When we come to think of native irises, it is with a distinct thrill, for here is a field that has been little explored but which promises infinite returns. The Western coast states are especially rich in beautiful species and these are almost unknown in the East save among a few adventurous spirits who are ever reaching out to the far places of the earth in the hope of finding something new under the sun. Not a great deal is known as yet concerning how to make these irises of the Far West completely happy in our Eastern gardens, but gardening folk have only just begun to realize how much beauty and interest is to be found among them, and therefore to desire them. It is believed that they have a strong dislike for lime and that they should be grown in a deep vegetable soil where the sun reaches them for but part of the day. Mr. B. Y. Morrison, whose monograph, Garden Irises[1] should be in the hands of everyone interested in the subject, has this to say of the Pacific coast species:

> These are dwarf plants for the most part with charming little flowers of very delicate colouring. They are somewhat difficult to manage in gardens and are not successful in any climate where winter cold destroys the evergreen foliage. Plants should be secured just as the new growths are starting, as the very scanty root growth is all made at that time. Transplanting should be done as little as possible, because the root system is always meagre and the rhizomes are so slender that they perish before new roots can be formed. One of the easiest species to manage in the East has been *Iris douglasiana*, which has flowers of cream colour and lavender, often veined on the falls with the darker colours. *Iris purdyi* and *Iris bracteata* are similar save in the stem characters. *Iris tenax* from the northern part of the Pacific slope is hardier and more easily grown, but the easiest of all is *Iris longipetala*, which grows in close clumps

---

[1] *U.S. Department of Agriculture, Farmer's Bulletin 1406.*

with stiff grayish green foliage, slender stalks bearing charming flowers of characteristic shape and delicate pale lilac colouring. This is related to *Iris missouriensis* of the Rocky Mountain regions and *Iris montana,* a kindred form; and all are of easy growth in the Eastern States as compared with those of the wooded slopes of the coast countries.

I. tenax has been for several years quite conclusively established in my garden and it is a delightful kind with dainty flowers varying from claret through mauve to almost pure white. *I. longipetala* and *I. missouriensis* have proved perfectly amenable. And a small species, *I. gormani* [*I. tenax*], sent me from the mountains of Oregon has bloomed enchantingly for two seasons in a bed of leaf mould situated where it is shaded for rather more than half of the day. It appears delicate, however, and I do not feel at all sure of it yet.

Fresh seed of the Western species of iris is not difficult to obtain and it is probably by this means that we shall have the greatest success in growing and establishing them.

Even the wild irises of the East and South receive scant recognition considering their beauty and usefulness, and the fact that they are not at all difficult to grow. Probably *I. cristata,* that is native of the Southern states and extends westward to the Great Lakes and the Ozark Mountains, is the only one that receives anything like the attention it deserves. This little creeping species is as easy to grow as any plant in the garden, though it is said to prefer partial shade and a moist soil. However

this may be, it makes lovely spreads of lilac colour—pale or deep—on the sunny slopes of the rock garden, doubtless finding the moisture it requires beneath the stones. It spreads rapidly, and the plants may be divided soon after flowering and the stock thus easily increased. The white form is rare, but quite exquisitely beautiful. With me it has not proved as strong a grower as the type, but quite hardy.

I. lacustris, found on the shores of the Great Lakes, somewhat resembles *I. cristata,* but is slenderer in all its parts and is not so vigorous a grower. *I. verna* is a species of great charm when well grown. And to have it well grown means acid soil. In this medium it behaves in a most satisfactory manner either in full sun or in partial shade, waxing fine and luxuriant, and giving its bright lavender blossoms, gold-banded at the haft, in great profusion. But in a normally sweet soil it immediately becomes an invalid and finally passes away.

I. verna is found on dry hillsides from southern Pennsylvania to Georgia and Texas, and I have seen it spreading about over the sand hills of North Carolina in great patches fully exposed to the sun. It is a slender species not more than eight inches tall.

I. versicolor is too "propagatious" for the rock garden, but *I. prismatica,* though sometimes nearly two feet tall, is so light and altogether lovely that it may be given a place in some low and rather damp situation. It is well placed beside a little pool where the soil is acid. Both these are found in low-lying meadows along the Atlantic coast. *I. foliosa* [*I. brevi-*

caulis] and *I. fulva*, both growing naturally in dampish places in the South, are so distinct as to merit a place in the rock garden in spite of the fact that they are above the height of plants usually admitted. The former has bright blue blossoms, large and very striking, borne down among the leaves; the latter is a beautiful terracotta in colour. It should be grown in rich black soil, where it may be kept moist in times of drought, or in a naturally damp situation.

I. foliosa sometimes makes itself a nuisance by its too generous seeding, the little plants coming up in all directions and, as they grow quickly, soon making trouble in situations where they are not wanted. *I. tripetala* [*I. tridentata*] is less attractive than many, but, as it is a small thing, place may be found for a plant or two. *I. hookeri* and *I. setosa canadensis* are also candidates for a corner in the rock garden of an iris lover.

CHAPTER XIII

Poppies of Sorts

CHARM IS THE poppy's birthright, and this indefinable quality is its chief stock in trade. Sheer charm it is that wins for these whims of the wind their host of ardent admirers. Without fragrance, sometimes, indeed, confessing a quite "evil odour," as the old books say, the blossoms fleeting as the day and almost useless for cutting, wearing often a colour that is an impertinent challenge to every other flower; the plants lacking all the qualities supposed to animate a reliable garden plant, the poppy yet tosses a careless head above many a plodding green soul, secure in the knowledge that few can remain insensible to the witchery of its flashing hues, its fragile, fugitive, provocative beauty.

There is not space here to consider the enchantments of annual poppies, whose name is legion and all of whom are lovely. We must begin at once with the perennial and biennial sorts, for there are a good many of these that poppy lovers, present or prospective, will want to have a word about. First let us say that all poppies come readily and profusely from seed, germinating in from one to three weeks after sowing; that they are all difficult to transplant, deeply resenting disturbance once they have got well settled, so that it is always wiser to raise them from seed and move them while they are very small, or to sow the seed directly where the plants are to grow, rather than to buy them ready grown. Delightful results follow the sowing of alpine or Iceland poppies in nooks and corners of the rock garden, or in the chinks of a sunny dry wall.

All poppies, it may be said, are ardent sun lovers, and persons with very shaded gardens had best leave them out of the counting, though I have known that gay Spanish vagabond, *Papaver rupifragum*, to take to a half-shaded bank with apparent satisfaction when its room was more desired than its company in the choicer regions of the rock garden. And the oriental poppy will give very fair results where it receives the sunshine for only part of the day. They all do best in a well-drained soil, but for the mountain species this is an absolute necessity, and these must have free wind and free sunshine as well.

In many gardens, a red flower is regarded as a crime, and the fiercely scarlet oriental poppy would no more be admitted than a convict in his ignominious stripes. For these sensitive ones, the florists have conjured up pale pink sorts, soft rose tones, shrimp-pink, and even a white one. All these are very lovely, but a gardener who cannot suffer a bit of red or scarlet in his garden must turn his back upon some of the most alluring members of the poppy clan.

Besides the well-known oriental poppy, there are one or two other kinds that belong essentially to the garden borders. There is *P. bracteatum*, a Siberian species, thought by some to be finer than the oriental poppy in habit. Its colour is a most rich and vibrant red—not scarlet—and each petal is stained at the base with dusky colour. Then there is *P. pilosum*, a hairy-stemmed plant from Mediterranean shores, tall, lax, with flowers of a strange blood-orange hue that open out flat. It is a reliable perennial, good for borders but better for rough banks and waste places, where its incorrigible seed-sowing will not become a nuisance or a menace to choicer plants. *P. heldreichii*, often listed, is a form of the above, smaller and more compact of habit and with smaller flowers.

P. rupifragum is also a steadfast perennial.

This is a most engaging species, Spanish by birth, and said to decorate lavishly the rugged slopes of the Pyrenees with its rags of gallant colour. The blossoms of this species are sadly fugitive, falling on a hot day, sometimes before noon, though if cut very early in the morning they will last twenty-four hours or more indoors.

This Spanish poppy forms a stout rosette of narrow, long, lobed, much indented leaves, hairy and bright green; it sends up to a height of eighteen inches a continuous succession of bare wiry stems surmounted by a single silken blossom of a lively apricot colour. If seeding is sedulously prevented, these blossoms will continue to materialize all summer, indeed, until frost. In poor, dry soil it is as happy as in a richer mixture, and in fact keeps its form far better when not too well fed. It is adapted to border or rock garden, but in the latter location its too free self-sowing must be looked out for.

A narrow border planted with the Spanish poppy and the 'Heavenly Blue' flax, *Linum perenne*, will bring delight to the eye for many weeks of the late spring and summer.

The Iceland poppy, *P. nudicaule*, while it will grow in borders, is far happier in the rock garden or on the wall top where the drainage is free and assured. We constantly hear the plaint that the Iceland poppy is not hardy. But as a matter of fact it is reported as one of the most northern flowering plants known—"so extremely northern," wrote Canon Ellacombe, "that I was told by one of the officers of the North Pole Expedition, that if there was land, there he would expect to find the Iceland Poppy." But while this undoubtedly hardy plant is indifferent to any number of degrees of frost, it is not proof against even a little standing moisture. Free drainage it must have. Wherefore it is only safe in a light sandy soil and in a somewhat raised position. Seed of Iceland poppies sown in a frame in February or March and the seedlings set out when large enough to handle will begin to bloom by mid-July and continue until frost. Once established happily, they will be always in the garden, for while the individual plants are short-lived, they seed freely and spring up of themselves in generous numbers. Tufts of these plants with their tall, slender stems and large silk-crepe blossoms associate well with mats of spreading sunroses, helianthemum, in the rock garden or at the wall top. They both bloom profusely when the great tide of early spring blossoms has gone over, leaving us a little bereft and bare.

A fine strain of Iceland poppies is called 'Pearls of Dawn.' The blossoms are delicately crinkled and display a wide range of lovely soft tones from cream through pink and saffron to orange. The munstead strain, too, gives an infinite number of hues, both tender and brilliant. A pure white variety of beauty is white queen, and in tangerine we have the most vibrant, hot orange-red colour known to the garden, and plants unusually sturdy that bear their blossoms aloft on tall strong stems. There are one or two double-flowered varieties also.

The Tibet poppy, recently introduced, somewhat resembles the Icelander in appearance, but is smaller and altogether more compact, with stems not so tall and a delightful succession of blossoms of pure golden yellow, often having a few extra petals which give them the air of being semi-double. Well placed, this species seems to be a fairly reliable perennial, but it is wholly unable to endure standing moisture at any season, often going off during a spell of wet and muggy weather in summer, and seldom surviving a wet, open winter unless planted in an elevated position in soil that is very well drained. The Tibet poppy is an important acquisition to the rock gardener. It is quite distinct from other poppies, and its dwarf habit and brilliant blossoms make it an ideal plant for use among the stones and boulders. Like others of its tribe, it matures a good deal of seed and self-sows, though not pervasively. It blooms later than either the Iceland or the alpine poppy, beginning to unfold its first golden blossoms in this garden at the very end of May.

P. alpinum is a true alpine; that is, it is found growing high upon the mountains above the limit of timber trees. But it is also found in subalpine regions and will even condescend to lowland gardens if not insulted by a fat clogging soil and a low miasmic situation.

In its natural haunts the alpine poppy is found principally on chalky formations or in granite débris of the high Alps. Do not seek to detain it in any ordinary border. Give it the highest, sunniest, windiest situation at your command, in soil that is light and sandy and made sharply pervious to moisture by the intermixture of many small stone chips. It is wiser to raise the alpine poppy from seed than to buy the plants, and as in the case of the Iceland poppy, seed sown early in the year will produce flowering plants by midsummer. Tiny seedlings or the seed itself may be tucked into the crannies of a dry retaining wall, and it is doubtful if any more entrancing picture could be devised than an old gray wall, its every joint and crevice bursting with the gray tufts and airy glancing blossoms of this loveliest of poppies.

The alpine poppy is the fairy of the race—a little low tuft of most delicate silver lace leaves and large (for the size of the plant), infinitely fragile blossoms continuously borne throughout the summer, if too much seed be not allowed to mature. It is perfectly hardy in the face of winter cold, but it is not a long-lived plant and is best treated as a biennial. It self-sows, however, where it is made to feel at home, so there is little trouble in keeping it about the rock garden. A mixed packet of seed from a reliable house will produce enchanting results—lovely blossoms in every delicate tint save blue and lavender, and some with delicately fringed petals.

The enthusiast may be interested in growing some of the distinct alpine species. M. Henri Correvon has pointed out that where the alpine poppy grows on limestone the blossoms are white, and where on the granite they are yellow or orange. *P. burseri* is a most exquisite white-flowered type, and *P. kerneri* bears airy yellow cups somewhat larger than the foregoing; *P. rhaeticum* (*aurantiacum*), of the Dolomites,

is resplendent with tufts of blue-gray foliage and large citron-coloured blossoms. *P. pyrenaicum* is dwarfer than the other forms and is usually found at higher altitudes. The flowers are white.

It is most interesting to grow all these various forms of the alpine poppy, but it is impossible to keep them in their integrity. "The bees work upon them, and they cross with extraordinary facility even when the various species are planted far apart," says M. Correvon. This is true of all poppies. I found last year that a number of seedlings of the Tibet poppy had taken on the orange-red tinge of their neighbour, the tangerine Iceland poppy.

And then there is a small group of biennial or monocarpic poppies that all who are infected with the mania for these delightful flowers will want to grow. These, while less stable and more fugitive even than the others of the race, have a fascination as great as any and an individuality peculiarly their own. "Their predilection for death," says Mr. Farrer, "can be easily counter-balanced by always raising the seed they leave behind them, so as incessantly to have a stock coming on." But, like the others of the race, they self-sow, albeit sparingly, so that if we fail to gather and sow the seed we need not fear to lose them quite. These biennial poppies are perhaps too lax and unsubstantial for the borders, too tall and flopping for the small rock garden, but space must be found for them somewhere, for they are altogether too lovely to be foregone. The rock garden offers the best situation for them, for they relish the light, well-drained soil, and against the stones the intricate beauty of their striking foliage is seen to great advantage.

The rosette of blue-silver leaves is as lovely as any flower, but this species has the added gift of a fountain of pale vermilion blossoms sent up toward the end of May and continuing nearly all the summer and autumn. The buds are round, the blossoms open out flat and are sadly fleeting, but no plant known to me presents a more attractive colour scheme. There is also *P. tauricolum* from the Levant with brick-red blossoms, whose seed I am unable now to discover in any catalogue; *P. floribundum,* with scarlet blossoms and an amazing rosette of fine-cut glaucous leaves, which eludes me also; and *P. triniifolium,* whose wondrous silver rosette is its whole fortune, for its purplish blossoms are no sooner borne than gone.

Collecting poppies is one of the gayest sports of rock gardening and always productive of delightful results. None of these blithe flowers is difficult to grow, and their response to sunshine and free drainage is always immediate.

CHAPTER XIV

Pinks of Perfection

Every garden, whatever its character or the scope of its interests, has room for pinks of some type or variety. Most gardens have room and reason for a great many, the more the better, and it is not claiming too much for these flowers to say that the more of them a garden holds the more friendly and fragrant and altogether delightful will that garden be. Where shade predominates or the exposure is mainly toward the north, only a few of this sun-loving race may be enjoyed, but these few are well worth while and hold their own among the best. The owner of a sunny garden, on the other hand, may literally revel in pinks, and if he number a rock garden among his blessings, may grow, not only all the hardy border pinks and carnations, but the many enchanting species that require the special conditions of soil, aspect, and drainage that can be assured them only in a rock garden or in the chinks of a dry wall.

The dianthus is essentially of the Old World. We have no representative of the race on this side of the water, though the little Deptford pink, *Dianthus armeria,* an annual, runs wild in many localities and is included in some of our books on native wildflowers; and the spicy little Scotch or grass pinks have escaped from gardens and gone a-roving on Cape Cod and in several neighbourhoods where gardens have long flourished. The mountains of southern Europe and the shores of the Mediterranean are festooned and sprigged with innumerable pinks, thrusting out of rocky crevices, carpeting the moraines, growing freely in the grassy meadows; and in this choice, geographically, of a dwelling place, is exemplified their love of warmth, of light, of drought, of free drainage, and, in most cases, of lime. This does not mean that these pinks are not winter hardy. On the contrary, to most of them cold is no deterrent to health and happiness, but they nearly all object to a moisture-clogged soil, and for the most part they are grateful for the light and heat of the sun full upon them.

All pinks are raised from seed with such ease and promptitude—germination taking place commonly within a week of sowing—that they should be among the first subjects to claim the attention of the beginning gardener. They intermarry, too, with extraordinary facility, so that one having a varied collection to begin with soon finds himself the happy possessor of innumerable intermediate forms, all delightful.

There are so many kinds of pinks available that it is a difficult task to choose a few among them for remark. The following notes can give but a fraction of an idea of all the delight that is to be got out of a wide acquaintance with the race.

Various forms of *D. plumarius,* the Scotch or grass pink (called also the Vermont pink in this country), are happily well known and much grown in American gardens, though not nearly so much as it would be felicitous to have them. No plants are more serviceable or pleasing as border edgings, and none so subtly fill the garden with an atmosphere of friendly simplicity. The type grows wild in middle and eastern Europe, luxuriant in narrow blue-green foliage and masses of pale, spicy, fringy blossoms borne in late May and June. From this type many fine garden hybrids have been developed.

Of the three white sorts, 'Mrs. Sinkins,' 'Her Majesty,' and 'White Reserve,' though all are lovely, I think the last named is less apt to burst its calyx, and it is, moreover, a fairly constant bloomer through the season. 'Essex Witch' and 'Lord Lyons' are pink; 'Louisa M. Alcott,' deep pink; 'Souvenir de Sale,' delicate pink; 'Lady Betty,' pale pink with a deeper centre and a firm calyx; 'Homer,' dark red; and 'Little Dorrit' is white with a fleck of red at the heart—a hardy and long-blooming variety.

Hardy garden carnations there are, too, nice for use near the front of the borders and providing many long-stemmed scented blossoms for cutting. These are best treated as biennials and raised yearly from seed, the little plants being put in their permanent places when large enough to fend for themselves. Among them, delightful colour variations are found—chocolate, yellow, pink, rose, scarlet, white, picotee, striped, and many more.

The 'Maiden Pink,' *D. deltoides,* is for border or rock garden. It is a hearty, happy, ramping species, quickly forming wide flat mats of small dark leaves, and fairly bristling in late May with five-inch stems carrying small bright rose or white spotted flowers that are not fragrant. Drought has no terrors for it, and neglect seems but to hearten it. In the rock garden its generous spread must often be discouraged lest it submerge some fragile and choicer neighbour. Very close to *D. deltoides*— indeed, seeming to be but slightly glorified forms of it—are *D. graniticus* and *D. caucasicus* [*D. chinensis*]. *D. prichardii* also resembles it, but is a smaller and neater plant, fitter for the choice assemblage of the rock garden than the others.

Quite the queen of the easy pinks, either for rock garden or wall-top, is the Cheddar pink, *D. caesius* (*D. glaucus*) [*D. grationopolitanus*], compact of habit, blue-green of foliage, riotous of rosy blooms, deliciously fragrant. It is a native of the Cheddar Cliffs of England and of the mountains of Central Europe. It wants full sunshine and loves to hang from a crevice of wall or ledge. It is the stand-by of every rock gardener and a perennial joy. Close to it is *D. suavis*, a larger and less compact plant but as friendly and sweet. Also allied to the Cheddar pink is *D. furcatus* which makes small cushions of dark blunt leaves and throws out countless stems carrying small starry blossoms, pink and white. It is a charming sort. But the most engaging of this group is *D. c. arvernensis* [*D. monspessulanus*], that makes a very small blue-green cushion above which wave the characteristic sweet pink blossoms on stems less than three inches long. The spread of this little treasure seldom exceeds three or four inches. This minute species has the look of the aloof and difficult, but, as a matter of fact, it is an easy doer, probably the least difficult of the smaller, choicer kinds, asking only sunshine and a nourishing, gritty soil impeccably drained.

The sand pink, *D. arenarius*, is another charmer upon which to pin one's faith with entire confidence. Its mats of narrow dark green foliage spread rather widely, and the character of the pure white, deliciously fragrant blossoms is well shown. It is one of the few pinks that will endure partial shade, and it has the endearing habit of blooming off and on all through the summer. *D. squarrosus* from sunny places in Southern Russia is close to it, but in the latter plant the leaves are stiffer and rather greener, and the blossoms are pink. It is as easy to grow as the sand pink but somewhat more prejudiced in favour of a sunny location. A rock gardener would do well to start his collection of pinks with *D. arenarius* and *D. caesius* [*D. grationopolitanus*]. Few are lovelier and none is more readily grown.

D. superbus, a tall fringy beauty reported as growing wild in woods and damp meadows of central and southern Europe, and in western Asia and Japan, from the plains up to 6,000 feet, will also thrive in partial shade, and it flowers from June until September. Rather taller than the kinds we have mentioned, *D. superbus* has green grassy leaves and charming ragged flowers of a soft lavender colour, quite ineffably sweet. It is best treated as a biennial, for the plants are short-lived, and it likes a rather rich, woodsy soil. A sister plant is *D. monspessulanus* which, however, requires drier and sunnier conditions. This has the same fringy, fragrant blossoms, but they are pink, or, more rarely, pure white. Both these species are delightful in high places among the larger stones.

D. gallicus is a rather untidy fellow and takes up considerable space, but two points in particular recommend it. First, its quite superlative fragrance, even for a pink; and the fact that it continues to bloom after most of its kind have lapsed into mounds of soft green or gray foliage. Give it an out-of-the-way corner and let it spread about freely, and it will give much pleasure to eye and nose.

And now here are a few for the very keen and careful. This does not at all mean that any excess of coddling or consideration is required. Few pinks are very demanding, and fewer still capricious. But some of the choice mountain species must have their home surroundings fairly closely approximated if they are to tarry in our lowland gardens. *D. alpinus,* indeed, one of the most coveted species, has so far proved rather unresponsive in this country. Garden doctors on both sides of the water disagree as to its necessities. Mr. Farrer describes it as "sheeting the high moors of the Styrian limestones with miles of bright foliage," but so far, I am bound to confess, *D. alpinus* has refused to sheet more than a few inches of my limestones, and this after a deal of consideration and every sort of incentive offered it. A mixture of brown peat and loam with plenty of lime and absolute drainage, but with plenty of water also during the growing season, and frequent top-dressings worked in under the short growth, is said to be the sum of its desires. Thus considered, we are told, sun or light shade are all one to it. One point is a comfort: *D. alpinus* comes readily from seed, so we may continue to experiment until we find ideal conditions.

Closely allied to *D. alpinus* and even a more striking and desirable beauty, is *D. callizonus,* from the Alps of Transylvania. Its large blossoms are bright pink with a band of rich embroidery on each petal. Its treatment should be the same.

D. neglectus [*D. pavonis*] is an easier plant and one of the most precious of its race. Its mats of narrow leaves are close and firm, and its lovely bright pink blossoms, buff on the reverse, are borne in the greatest profusion. A perfectly drained, deep soil, sandy and rather poor, and with little or no lime, in a sunny situation makes it happy. Its habit of exhausting its health through blossoming may be offset by immediate top-dressing with sandy loam and cutting the faded blossoms before seed has formed. If you raise your plants from seed, tuck the seedlings away on the sunny, stony slopes of the rock garden while they are still quite small, for *D. neglectus,* I find, dislikes disturbance once it is established.

D. freynii and *D. microlepis* are two dainty and wholly alluring small species from high mountains whose charms are somewhat similar. *D. freynii* makes a minute, tight cushion of bluish, narrow leaves ornamented with little stemless pinks, white or rose, the whole affair no more than two inches high. It is for a secure crevice with a deep root run of calcareous soil behind. The small close mat of *D. microlepis* is somewhat greener, the small leaves a trifle broader. The blossoms are pink or white, starry, and set close to the foliage. It requires a thoroughly drained soil of loam, sand, leaf soil, and plenty of grit and a position in full sun. In the spring, a little light soil worked in about the tufts is helpful.

D. sylvestris (*D. inodorus*) is a beauty which,

contrary to the implication of its name, does not pine for sylvan glades, but revels in the hottest, dryest, sunniest situations at our command. It makes a tuft of narrow, sharp dark leaves from which spray out many very slender stems bearing clear pink, smooth-edged, fragrant blossoms. It is a charming species which should be in every rock garden and given a high place where its graceful bending stems may show to advantage. Among seedlings of *D. sylvestris* there will be found a decided choice as to clarity of colour and size of blossom. Only the best should be kept. A choice and lovely form of *D. sylvestris* is *D. frigidus* [*D. s.* var. *frigidus*], smaller and more compact throughout and deserving the utmost care and comfort we can give it. The soil and situation suggested for *D. microlepis* will be satisfactory.

And here are two more choice little beings that no lover of pinks should miss. *D. brevicaulis,* from the high Alps of Taurus, is a squat little elf with a tight tuft of very narrow leaves, and mauve toothed blossoms, faintly yellow on the reverse of the petals, held close to the tuft. *D. integer* is a variable species with flowers pink or white arising on stems four to six inches tall from a neat dark cushion. The petals of this pink are usually smooth, but occasionally lightly scalloped. A situation on a little stony slope facing south or east should make it comfortable. It must be remembered that all these little pinks must be protected from the encroachments of larger plants. They cannot survive being pressed upon or overrun. They will grow cheerfully among small things

like themselves, but no ramping globe trotter should be allowed near them.

And most pinks are rather hearty eaters, however diminutive and dainty they may appear. While they demand free drainage, they also relish a nourishing soil, even old rotted manure in the mixture—but it must be very well decomposed—does not cause them to turn their charming heads away. I have been amazed at the fine growth made during the last year by some tiny seedlings of *D. freynii* and *D. gelidus* [*D. glacialis*] that are planted on a little slope of a recently made addition to the rock garden, the soil for which has a good deal of very old manure incorporated in it. And they have bloomed well. Too much enrichment, however, would cause them to grow fat and lazy and little interested in putting forth flowers. *D. sylvestris* is certainly best in a poorer soil, as is *D. arenarius*.

D. glacialis has a reputation for being a difficult subject, and it has proved so with me until now. Authorities seemed not to agree upon the requirements of this attractive little species, but two small plants are now flourishing in my garden in peaty soil and sand and with the shelter of a big stone on the south to shade them from the hottest sun. On the other hand, *D. gelidus* [*D. glacialis*], said to be a form of *glacialis,* is flourishing in full sunshine in the sweet fat soil described above. One can only experiment endlessly and keep humble. Both *glacialis* and *gelidus* are delightful small species, the one with bright green leaves and flowers very like those of *alpinus,* though smaller; the other makes a closer mat, and the pink blossoms are spotted with white in the throat.

I have always been a dianthus enthusiast and it seems to me not too much to say that no race of flowers brings such delicious returns to the rock gardener for so little trouble and expenditure. They are easily raised from seed, and most of them are spicily sweet as well as beautiful.

CHAPTER XV

The Versatile Phlox Family

IT IS WITH quite pardonable pride that we lay claim to the illustrious phlox clan as our very own. There are known in the world some thirty-five or more species of phlox, and all of them, save one Westerner that extends its wanderings into Siberia, make their home exclusively in North America. They are to be found scattered over most of the United States, though the greater number of them inhabit the hills and prairies of the West and Middle West; and the Eastern species, while abounding in New York, Pennsylvania, and many localities south and west, seem to shun the New England States. Woods, thickets, dry hillsides, wide prairies, alpine heights, and even arctic regions know them, one species or another, and all are perennial save one; and this one, *Phlox drummondi*, a native of Texas and thereabouts, is one of our most important summer annuals.

It is a facile race, bestowing upon the summer garden in the various forms of *P. paniculata* and *P. suffruticosa* [*P. corolina*], the tall border beauties, more than half its magnificence; furnishing many lovely untamed sorts for wood and wild garden; giving us the moss pink to veil our rough banks or gaily edge the borders, not to mention a vast number of authentic gems for the rock garden. Few if any plant genera bring to the garden such radiant colour, such rich fragrance, such almost universal amiability.

Of course much has been done for various of the phloxes by man. Real improvement has been wrought, which is not always the case when the hybridist sets his hand to change the character of a wild flower. Sometimes attributes are lost more precious than any gained. But it has not been so with the phloxes. Poise and finish have been bestowed upon them, and in the case of the tall border

varieties, colours so splendid that the name phlox, a Greek word meaning "flame," seems far from inappropriate.

One does not readily trace relationship between the sumptuous and stately summer phloxes and the rather shabby and sad-coloured wayfarer through thin woods and along roadsides of Pennsylvania south and westward. But this humble itinerant is none other than *P. paniculata* which, married in some cases to another vagabond, the 'Wild Sweet William' (*P. maculata*), is the fairly immediate progenitor of all our tall border varieties. There are scores of descendants now with fine names and clothed as was never Solomon or any other potentate. Forgotten is the weak magenta colour worn by the parents, the small ragged flower-head, and in their place are every conceivable tint and tone save the pure blues, and great wedge-shaped flower heads in some cases almost a foot in length. The soil for these highly cultured subjects should be a deep, rich loam, neither stiff with clay nor too sandy, and they should never want for water during dry weather. To allow them to grow into large clumps is a mistake. Three or four stems give the best results in the size and quality of the blooms.

Every two or three years the clumps should be lifted and separated, the quick young side shoots replanted in sweet, newly dug soil, and the exhausted centre thrown away. If these phloxes are allowed to seed, it will be found that the majority of the progeny have "gone native." If these are allowed to survive, they will quickly run out the highly developed vari-eties. Many a puzzled gardener finds her neglected bed of 'Elizabeth Campbell' or some other fine variety suddenly overrun with the "old purple" sort and wonders why.

The annual *P. drummondi*, too, has made phenomenal strides toward perfection since Drummond in 1835 gathered the seeds from the sandy wastes of Texas and sent them to England. It is now to be had, as they say in the advertisements, in all the wanted colours (save blue) and is without doubt one of the six most popular annuals for summer decoration.

Our moss pink, *P. subulata*, has also come in for a share of the florist's attention. In Nature, this little plant in its dim magenta gown scrambles over rocky exposed banks and wanders through fields in parts of New York and all the states southward to Florida, faring as far west as Kentucky and Michigan. Some very lovely forms of it are now to be had. Vivid is the most extolled. Its blossoms are a clear bright pink, innocent of the magenta tone which is conspicuous in so many of the family. The habit of vivid is close and compact, and it is extremely slow in growth, so that it may be used among choice rock plants and alpines where the free spreading of some of the other kinds would be a menace. It blooms with characteristic prodigality.

P. subulata 'Nelsonii' also hugs the ground, appearing like a rich moss when out of bloom and quite obliterated by a froth of white blossoms for several weeks in spring. It is not so rampant, and is far neater in habit than the white form of the common *P. subulata*.

More lovely than any, however, it seems to

me, is the variety known as *Phlox subulata* 'G. F. Wilson.' This is loose and springing in growth, forming wide mats of dusty green that in April quite disappear beneath the wealth of sweet round blossoms whose colour should ever be described in the inspired words of Mr. Farrer as moonlit blue. This sort is too vehement for small rock gardens but is superb where there is room for its generous spread; for banks, etc. The variety *P. s. lilacina* is often sent out in its name but should not be accepted, as in comparison with the true variety it appears a weak thing with little character.

There are numerous other named varieties of *P. subulata,* but the foregoing are the best available in this country, and all are far superior to the common magenta type so generally planted. This, while well enough with only gray stones to oppose it, is roused to vindictiveness by the presence of almost any flower colour. What we owe to the beauty and amiability of the moss pinks can scarce be told. Seldom do they refuse a situation, however exposed and uninviting, always making shift to spread their dusty-green mats and to materialize the masses of fragrant blossoms. They bloom from mid-April well into May, and frequently vouchsafe a second lesser blossoming in the autumn.

A wide general use may also be made of the wild blue phlox, *P. divaricata* (*P. canadensis*), a slender, headlong, crowding plant with round lavender-blue blossoms, sweetly scented and joyously profuse in the early days of May and onward into June. Once established, this plant increases at a riotous rate, springing up in all sorts of nooks and corners to the beautification of all its surroundings. Where it is made to account strictly for its behaviour, seeding is not allowed and the clumps are taken up and divided every two or three years. This is a fitting subject for the wild garden, the borders, or outlying districts of the rock garden where its exuberance can do no harm. It makes a lovely setting for the wild British tulip—*Tulipa sylvestris,* with its gay butter-yellow blossoms, and if the foamflower, *Tiarella cordifolia,* be stationed near them, a beautiful picture is the result. It also mingles most felicitously with golden alyssum and other gay blossoms of the season. A lovely white form came to me from friends in North Dakota where both forms apparently grow freely. *P. divaricata* has a wide range in the United States and Canada, preferring light woods where the soil is deep and rich, and in such places it often stains wide areas with its tender colour.

The mountain phlox, *P. ovata* (*P. corolina*), is an effective plant for rock gardens or narrow borders where it will not be pressed upon by stalwart neighbours. It grows a foot or more tall and bears in May on erect stems round pink blossoms of a very good tone. The mountain phlox thrives best where the soil is somewhat acid. Its home in the wild is in upland regions from Pennsylvania south to Alabama.

Pink, too, and very gay and fluffy in appearance, is *P. amoena,* a dwarf, creeping, and very willing species common in dry lands through Virginia, Kentucky, and southward. It rushes willingly to the aid of the rock gardener who seeks a gay display in a dry place, and is good also in little colonies along the border edge. Its height is about five inches.

The foregoing species are happily quite well known and grow in many gardens. But there are numerous others sure to bring pleasure to any who will go to the small pains of providing conditions in which they may thrive. *P. stolonifera* (*P. reptans*), the creeping phlox, that surges over the ground in a tangle of slender, half-procumbent stems, carrying loose cymes of bright crimson or pure lavender blossoms, is an attractive subject for planting a little slope in partial shade in the rock garden. Its natural range is through Pennsylvania to Georgia, mostly in upland regions.

The *Standard Cyclopedia of Horticulture* refers to *P. bifida* as rarely cultivated. This is quite true, though it is one of the most lovely of its kind and not difficult. It is one of the many fine native plants that are unaccountably neglected. That it is worth cultivating, no one who looks at its portrait will gainsay. *P. bifida* is found on prairies from Michigan to Montana and Tennessee. It was sent to me, a small slip, in a biscuit box a few years ago and set out in the rock garden in a little bed of peat and sand, where its companions are bird's-foot violets and bluets (Quaker ladies). There it has prospered, and in its season is one of the most engaging plants in the garden. The blossoms are a soft blue-white, the whole plant "dusty" with little hairs, the foliage dark green, narrow, and stiff. It flowers in April. It would benefit the gardening world if nurserymen in its home districts would propagate and

distribute this altogether delightful plant.

P. argillacea was discovered, I believe, by Dr. Clute. Its natural habitat is in barren, gravelly tracts of Illinois and parts of the Middle West. It grows to a height of a foot or more, the stems more erect than those of *P. divaricata*, and bears small heads of silvery-lilac flowers, faintly sweet, in May and June. It is pleasant for a half wild situation and increases satisfactorily, though not with the abandon of some of the others.

And still farther west, nestled in the mountains, staining the vast plains, washing the dry hillsides with lovely colour, are many beautiful and desirable species, the greater number of which are not yet in cultivation, though a few have found their way to the gardens of specialists and enthusiasts. *P. kelseyi* is a little prostrate species, having narrow stiffish leaves along its flung branches and rather large white blossoms solitary at the ends. This is one of the choice mountain forms that in our Eastern gardens must be treated with care & solicitude.

P. douglasii is another small and perfectly delightful species of the Western mountains that is at last established here after a long hunt for it. It came, as do so many of my most cherished treasures, through the generosity of a gardening friend. Margaret Armstrong, in her *Western Wild Flowers*, writes of it thus:

A charming little plant, with woody stems a few inches tall and partly creeping along the ground, densely crowded with numerous needle-like leaves, sometimes over a foot across and suggesting some sort of prickly moss. These prickly cushions are sprinkled all over with pretty lilac flowers and the effect is most attractive.

My cushions are still very small, as they have been resident with me only a year, but they nevertheless gave me a glimpse of their dainty beauty by blooming quite profusely before they had been many weeks in the garden.

P. multiflora is a delightful cushioned form found in the Rockies that is not at all difficult to suit. It bears pink or white flowers in great profusion. Of *P. caespitosa* and *P. stansburyi* our British gardening friends speak enthusiastically, but so far as I know they are not in cultivation here. They are both small things that would be warmly welcomed in rock gardens were they placed within our reach.

CHAPTER XVI

Choosing Among the Campanulas

CAMPANULA is a vast and versatile race, widely distributed in the Northern Hemisphere, containing a great number of popular garden and rock-garden plants, as well as many charming kinds that have as yet found only a small public, and others that still waste their charms in wild and little travelled regions of the earth. They are for the most part perennial and biennial in character with a few annuals that are of less account. The colours range from white through tones of lavender to cool lavender-blue and rich purple. There are a few yellow-flowered species, but these are difficult to satisfy and not of great importance from the gardener's viewpoint. Among the Canterbury bells, we have a fine pink variety, but these are not for the rock garden.

When the gay profusion of spring bulbs is past and the resplendent flush of June on the wane, we look about for perennial plants that will carry the blossomy tradition into the later season. It is then we turn with gratitude to the soft-toned bells and stars of the campanulas that are making themselves felt in various parts of the garden. These plants belong almost entirely to the summer, and their clean, cool hues are especially appreciated at that florid season.

A large number of the campanulas are far too tall and strong-growing to be allowed a place in the ordinary rock garden, but there are a few of the taller sorts so ungarden-wise in appearance that, if the rock garden is extensive, or where a wild garden or little wood adjoins, they may be grown most effectively. I would mention among these tall campanulas the peach-leaved bellflower, *C.*

persicifolia, an important border plant, but one which is delightful grown high and at the back of a shaded region of the rock garden where it will not interfere with smaller plants. The white-flowered form is especially beautiful with a woodland background.

C. alliariifolia is a pretty spreading plant about two feet tall, with grayish leaves and many white bells, that is charming in a half wild setting, and the rampion of old-time gardens, *C. rapunculoides,* is a good companion for it. The stems of rampion are erect and at midsummer are hung with deeply scalloped lavender bells. Both of these plants are determined spreaders and, of course, should not be allowed in the rock garden itself, but only in the "undressed" environs, if such there be.

Here, too, is the place for a cheerful self-sowing native, *C. americana,* found from Canada to Iowa, south to Florida and Arkansas, growing in low ground usually in shade. Its slender stems, from two to four feet tall, are set with lovely lavender stars. It is an annual, and persons of exacting taste would certainly accuse it of weediness; but it has a certain wild grace, and where it gathers in little colonies the effect is lovely.

Weedy, too, I dare say, is *C. patula,* that Mr. Farrer pictures as sometimes filling the alpine meadows with a tossing sea of hot lilac-lavender. It is certainly not what might be termed an "elegant" plant, nor one to be selected for borders, but I love to encourage it in odd corners and enjoy thoroughly its slender wands of pinky-lavender shallow bells. It is a fairly tall plant, reaching a height of from two to three feet, and it is a biennial, self-sowing with sufficient freedom to insure its permanence. The dull name of spreading bellflower has been assigned to *C. patula* by some authorities, but certain old books call it by the far prettier and more expressive one of fair-in-sight; and fair to the sight it most certainly is.

And now to speak of some of the small bellflowers that exactly fit the rock garden. These are many and unfailingly delightful. The high festival of the rock garden has almost come to an end by the middle of June, but a generous and comprehensive planting of the dwarf campanulas will keep it bright with bloom and full of interest for many weeks longer.

Most of these plants are made happy in a light, sandy loam with plenty of limestone chips, and in our climate the majority are glad to be protected from the sun for a part of the day. They do not like to grow beneath trees, but may be placed on the east side of a stone or on a little slope facing north or east, and will be quite satisfied.

A few species are said to abhor lime. Of these are *C. pulloides, C. allionii* [*C. alpestris*], and *C. pulla.* I have had no experience with the last two, but *C. pulloides* is growing and thriving here in a soil that certainly has some lime in it. For these so-called lime haters, a soil of peat and sand is recommended with an admixture of granite or sandstone chips. All the little bellflowers are worthy of the choicest situations and should be protected against the encroachments of stronger-growing plants. All may be increased by division or raised from seed, but the seeds are very small, and those of many perennial species slow to germinate. It is best to sow them in pots or pans of finely sifted loam and sand placed in a greenhouse or coldframe.

First to bloom here is *C. muralis* [*C. portenschlagiana*], a most exquisite but sturdy species from the mountains of southern Europe, whose height does not exceed four inches but whose luxuriant mat of foliage often widens out to the circumference of a dinner plate. In early June, the large lovely purple flowers quite obscure the greenery, and it flowers again in the autumn. At the same time blooms *Dianthus neglectus*, that gay and floriferous small pink, and the two together make a most bonny picture. The foliage of *C. muralis* [*C. portenschlagiana*] is evergreen. Various forms of this species differing but little, one from the other, are *minor, major,* and *bavarica;* any of these, or the type, are the best of the dwarf campanulas for the beginning rock gardener.

First in beauty, however, to my thinking, of all the dwarf bellflowers is *C. garganica*, nor is it difficult to grow. Compact of habit, not more than three inches high, with little toothed heart-shaped leaves, this little plant is literally covered with flat lavender-blue stars in early June and for several weeks onward. There is a pure white form that is also most lovely, and numerous variations, some with hairy leaves, or flowers bluer or less blue, and all growing with the same heartiness in the rock garden or in a chink of an old wall. *C. garganica* and its various forms belong to the rocks of Italy and to the heights along the Adriatic.

A very dwarf and most appealing small species is *C. pusilla* [*C. cochleariifolia*], that runs about the little terraces of the rock garden by means of its rapidly increasing stolons and trickles down between the crevices, spreading out over the lower levels for all the world like a little waterfall. The gay little bells, white, pale or deep blue, are borne in July in wild profusion, quite obliterating the small, shining leaves. A loamy, gritty soil seems to be what this wee bellflower desires, and it grows in partial shade or full sun with equal cheerfulness. Its profuse blossoming sometimes impairs its vitality, and it is well to give it a top-dressing of leaf mould and sand twice a year. This is a charming plant for the chinks of an old wall, for the crevices between stone steps, and for the edges of stone paths. It mingles delightfully with other small plants, seeming to do them no hurt.

C. stansfieldii, a bushy little plant with larger dark blue bells, is a real beauty, but does not roam about, in my garden at least, so satisfactorily as does the small *pusilla* [*C. cochleariifolia*]. The foliage is pale green and dies down wholly in the winter. It appears to like a cool situation in partial shade and a soil containing a good deal of lime.

C. pulloides is an amiable and lovely species that should early find a place in every rock garden, for it is not among the difficult beauties, yet is a beauty of quite certain standing. Its rich violet-blue bells are borne in profusion in July and August, and it creeps about in a friendly manner in any loamy, stony soil, increasing into goodly patches in a short time.

C. pulloides is said to be a chance hybrid of garden origin. Its parents are not exactly known, but it has been suggested that the Carpathian harebell with its sturdy constitution is one, and *C. pulla*, capricious but quite dazzlingly beautiful, the other.

C. raddeana is an easy dear where it may have a stone between it and the long afternoon sun; and a soil that is well drained and lightened with grit and leaf mould. Its habit is tufted, and it bears clusters of deep purple bells on six-inch stiffish stems above the pretty heart-shaped leaves. It is of fairly recent introduction and should receive a warm welcome, for it has no crotchets and makes a really lovely display of rich-hued bells. These are a half dozen little bellflowers that should find a place in every rock garden whether large or small. Not one of them is difficult to grow, and each contributes beauty of an uncommon kind.

The harebell, or Scotch bluebell, *C. rotundifolia* which we share with most of the countries of the world in one form or another, while taller and requiring more room than the little species just enumerated, is no less indispensable. Most persons are familiar with its showers of delicate stems and fragile bells, white or gray-blue. This is a plant for partial shade and a soil of leaf mould and grit among larger stones. It begins to bloom in early July and continues often, though with lessening profusion, until late in the fall.

A beautiful harebell is *C. hostii* [*C. rotundifolia*]. This is a dwarfer and more close-set plant altogether, and its "bells" are larger and more open. It is, I think, a more generally desirable plant for use in the rock garden than the common harebell. Its habit is less ethereal and airy, and it makes a richer and more solid mass of colour. There is also a most beautiful white form of it.

C. scheuchzeri [*C. linifolia*] is an alpine form of *C. rotundifolia*. It is a taller and more robust plant with larger and bluer blossoms. It is at home in high pastures and stony, grassy places, rarely descending, it is said, below about seven thousand feet. In the garden, however, it flourishes and it will stand more sun than our harebell if its feet be set in a loose vegetable soil with plenty of grit.

Everyone who embarks upon the enterprise of collecting campanulas will sooner or later want to grow the noble and beautiful bell of the Alps, *C. barbata*. This plant, while not advertised as difficult or classed as a biennial, has certainly a most precarious hold on life in most gardens. It is best to treat it frankly as a biennial and raise a few plants every year from seed. Then, should our luck be unusually good and a few plants linger past the usual age limit, we shall have so much the more beauty for our pains, and shall not run the risk of being without it altogether. *C. barbata* is one of the most distinguished beauties of its race. It grows commonly about a foot tall and bears large deeply scalloped bells of a most exquisite pure porcelain blue. Its natural home is in alpine and subalpine pastures and meadows. In the rock garden, it must grow where the drainage is most thorough and absolute. The rest is on the lap of the gods.

C. speciosa [*C. glomerata* var. *speciosa*] is a much

heralded species which is new to my garden. So far, its wide, flat rosettes of rather harsh, grayish foliage look in the most magnificent health. It is a biennial, and when the stout stem arises to the height of a foot and hangs out large deep purple bells almost as large as those of a Canterbury bell, the show will soon be over. It is a native of the Pyrenees and said to be a most conspicuously handsome species, well worth the trouble of annual sowing.

Another quite glorious biennial is *C. mirabilis,* from the Caucasus. It sends up a veritable fountain of lovely large pale blue bells on a branching stem about a foot tall. It would be well to make a practice of sowing a few seeds every year of these three lovely species—*C. barbata, C. speciosa* [*C. glomerata* var. *speciosa*], and *C. mirabilis,* and if there be a woodsy or waste corner to be decorated, *C. patula* and *C. americana* should be added.

Last to be mentioned is the Carpathian harebell, *C. carpatica,* probably the best known of any of the dwarfer kinds. It is a most useful plant for edging the garden borders, and is also a fine thing in the rock garden when it can be given a situation well away from smaller plants, which its hearty manner of spreading would soon overcome. There are numerous so-called improvements on the original type. Some exhibiting larger flowers, or flatter, but none being more exuberant and floriferous. All are easily raised from seed, or the plants may be endlessly pulled to pieces and so multiplied; nothing is easier than to have a fine stock of this beautiful plant, nor is there any difficulty about making it happy. Any fair soil suits it, and it thrives equally well in sun or partial shade. *C. turbinata* [*C. carpatica* var. *turbinata*] is so like it that it seems possible that it may be only a variation of the type. The true *turbinata* is said to have hairier foliage in a closer tuft and larger flowers borne only a few inches above the leaves.

CHAPTER XVII

The Steadfast Sedum

WHEN WE embark upon the adventure of building and planting a rock garden, we are advised by various interested spectators to grow largely of sedums, or stonecrops, as they are commonly called. No stonecrop, we are given to understand, would have the heart to blast our budding enthusiasms by refusing to live; any soil will suit them, any situation, and they increase at a rate unknown to any other rock plant. Pin our faith to sedums and avoid despair. Thus we are admonished!

But after several summers and winters have passed over our experiment and we, by honest toil and not wholly heeding the advice of those early admonishers, find ourselves clinging to the fringes of the rock gardening elect, we hear a different story: that sedums are the refuge of the lazy rock gardener, or his confession of weakness; that a rock garden largely clothed with these genial plants doubtless belongs to one too indifferent to grow choicer things, or too unskilled; that sedums are utterly commonplace and too "easy" to hold the interest of the experienced.

Doubtless some of all this is true, but, as a matter of fact, the genus sedum is far too vast to be generalized about. Some, it is true, are so easy to grow that merely laying them upon the surface of the ground and turning a careless shoulder is sufficient to insure them in our midst forever, but, on the other hand, I have come to issue with certain species and come off badly beaten. The hilarious encroachments of some we must curb with no uncertain hand, but others (a minority, it is true) we must coax and tend with care. Nor is beauty a word often used in connection with this primarily useful race, yet a few have both beauty and distinction of blossom, and the foliage of nearly all is fine and luxuriant. Just what we should do without sedums in the rock garden I am not prepared to say. They fill a hundred uses, come to our rescue times without number.

According to Lloyd Praeger, a sedum authority, these plants are found pretty much all over the world: in Africa close to the Equator, in Iceland, Greenland, Nova Zembla, Arctic Siberia, and Alaska, pushing close to the icy fastnesses; nearly all over Europe, in the United States and Canada; in Central and South America and Mexico, the Atlantic Islands, the Caucasus, Siberia and Central Asia, the Himalayan regions, China, Japan—an enormous family merging into other families, not always clearly defined, and among which great confusion reigns. The nomenclature generally is in a tangle. Some species bear many names, others go about under names that do not belong to them, again names appear in books and catalogues which belong to no known species. And among many of the species there is a close resemblance. It is, indeed, a wise man who knows his sedums.

Sedums are succulent plants with leaves flat to cylindrical, smooth and shining generally, and for the most part evergreen. As a rule, the foliage is more valuable than the flowers, forming richly luxuriant mats, often finely coloured. The blossoms belong to the summer and are yellow, white, or a rather dull rose. There is a single pure pink kind, one high scarlet, one blue. As to height, there are stalwarts almost two feet in height down the scale to the veriest little groundlings. Concerning propagation, little need be said. Any bit firmly

pressed into the earth will straightway root and bud, and the tale is told of certain species that if a leaf be inserted in the earth it will soon be a thriving plant. Most of the species are perennial, but there are a few biennial and annual sorts.

When it comes to choosing among this great family, one is sunk in indecision, so many to select from and so many apt to be on the side of the commonplace. Of the tall sorts, few, it seems to me, are worth growing save *S. spectabile* [*Hylotelephium spectabile*], a quite noble sort with powder-blue leaves and "chalk-pink" blossoms in the late summer. This, the so-called showy sedum, is too tall for a small rock garden but shows up well in one of fair extent. Its late blossoming season makes it valuable in the rock garden.

S. altissimum [*S. sediforme*] is fairly tall, sometimes reaching a height of ten inches. It makes an erect bushy mass, grayish in colour and topped by pale straw-coloured blossoms quite different from the greenish yellow tone affected by so many of the race. This is a fine plant for a hot, exposed position. It abounds about the whole Mediterranean basin.

Frequently, we cast about for a plant that will cover a flat rock with beautiful and luxuriant foliage, or throw a kindly veil over unsightly portions of the rock garden, or swing a curtain of rejuvenating greenery from the crevices of some old and broken wall. Many sedums will accomplish these amenities. Perhaps the best of these is *S. spurium* which produces masses of stems that root as they go and a close-woven mat of rich, shining leaves beautiful at all seasons. The low-toned, rose-coloured flowers come at the end of the shoots in the late summer and are decorative. There is a brighter coloured form and one with whitish blossoms.

Very close to *spurium* is *S. stoloniferum* (*ibericum*) that is valuable for the same uses. It is possible to use this plant in damper situations than will be accepted by many of the clan. *S. ewersi* [*Hylotelephium ewersi*] is a lovely, half bushy, half scrambling kind, whose gray-blue leaves would win it a place in any collection of fine plants without its rounded heads of wine-coloured blossoms that finish the stems in late summer. It is herbaceous in character, quite losing its leaves in winter. *S. kamtschaticum* is a low-growing, trailing and creeping species with shining dark leaves and rich coloured orange-yellow flowers that will grow in sun or shade and in the poorest soil. It makes a good border edging as well as being suitable for the rock garden.

While praising the quite delightful Chinese species, *S. sarmentosum*, one must also sound a warning against it. Its way of running flat along a dry wall face, rooting in the crevices as it goes, and soon covering the whole with its pale green shining foliage, is very effective. It will also cover bare, unsightly stretches of ground in the same quick way, the lax, slender branches often running eighteen inches in a season and not rising more than an inch from the earth. In late June, the expanse is covered with cymes of yellow starry blossoms making a show that is quite lovely. But because of its very virtues it must on no account be al-lowed in the neighbourhood of the choice and cherished. Every detached piece will root and grow apace and before we are aware of the approach of trouble, we find this wily plant in possession of sacred ground and all it contains. Enjoy it by all means, but put it in a safe place and watch it even there.

A trio of rather uninteresting kinds that are prominent in catalogues but are not really pretty enough for use as anything but fillers in unconsidered places, are *S. rupestre* [*S. reflexum*], *S. sexangulare*, and *S. reflexum*. They are fairly low-growing, bear a profusion of yellow flowers, rather acid in tone, in summer, and are ambitious spreaders. It is rather too bad to give much space to these commonplace varieties when there are so many better things to be had.

There is the little *S. acre*, once called kit-o'-the-wall. It is very close-growing, making a neat, bright evergreen mat and bearing a shower of yellow flowers in June. Kit-o'-the-wall is found quite on its own in many rural neighbourhoods, creeping in and out of the crevices of old walls or binding the roadsides with its neat and shining green.

Very dwarf and pretty, too, is *S. lydium*, dainty in appearance and not too expansive of habit. Its blossoms are white. *S. album* also is a delightful kind, though it is a ramper and requires watching. This species masquerades in the catalogues under many names and appears to have many forms, all pretty much alike when you get them. In dry locations, its fat leaves turn bright red, and in June its blossoms are a froth of white—very gay and decorative. A beauty, this, to furbish up old walls or difficult corners, but a thief in the night where one's choicest dears are concerned. An ingratiating thief also is *S. anglicum,* "low and matted, with fat leaves like bluish globules on three-inch stems, that bear a branched head of rather large white stars." These globules seem to become detached easily and carried by the wind or some evil instinct of their own, roll about until they manage to lodge in the midst of some choice and fragile plant, where they immediately root and grow lustily, with the inevitable tragic result.

And now we are among the real jewels of the clan, the little lovely kinds that are held dear for their own sakes and not for utilitarian reasons. Two Caucasian biennials are perhaps at the head of this list. They are *S. pilosum* and *S. sempervivoides.* The former, perhaps the brightest jewel in the sedum crown, forms a little downy rosette much like a soft sempervivum during the first year from seed, and entrances us the second year by maturing in May a rounded head of exquisite and gentle pure pink blossoms, far lovelier than those displayed by many a more pretentious plant. *S. sempervivoides* forms a rather flat and fleshy rosette of dull green and in summer sends aloft a bronzy stem topped by a loose spray of dazzling scarlet blossoms. Both these beauties require warmth and light and a soil that is light and stony.

S. dasyphyllum is among the loveliest, making a little pile or mat of fat globules that stand for leaves, soft gray in colour, and studded toward the end of June with small lovely white or flushed blossoms that look like exquisite bits of enamelwork. *S. brevifolium* is close to it but has sub-globular mealy leaves and white flowers. Both these plants, while appearing very choice and aloof, are easily satisfied in warm sunny situations of the rock garden, but they must be assured a dry bed in winter.

S. caeruleum is an emerald-green annual that bears blue blossoms and prefers a dampish situation. *S. glaucum (hispanicum)* [*S. reflexum 'Minus'*] is annual or biennial, dwarf, charming, a vagrant, sowing its seeds hither and yon. The plant is perhaps three inches tall, and bears one-sided sprays of white flowers with distinct black anthers.

The foregoing species are all foreign born, but we must take space to mention some of the native kinds that we are beginning very slowly to get acquainted with. Three Eastern species deserve more than casual attention. *S. ternatum,* found in Virginia and thereabouts, and in New York rarely, is the first of all the stonecrops to bloom in my garden, usually being at its best toward the end of May. It is most effective when covered with its sprays of creamy stars. Sun or half shade suits it.

Closely following it is *S. nevii,* with lovely rosetted gray foliage and white flowers early in June. It belongs to the Southern states—Virginia, Missouri, Alabama. But quite the prettiest is *S. pulchellum,* like a wee spruce tree, bright green, that hoists over its head in early June the most fetching three-cornered pink umbrellas. It is an annual, but self-sows freely, so once you have it there is little fear of losing it. It is said to inhabit cool limestone ledges and dampish places in Virginia, but I have not found it set in this preference.

Mexican sedums, of which there are many, are too tender for our climate, but the West and the Northwest are well supplied with them. These Western sedums are not so easy to grow as those of which we have been speaking, and persons who have been experimenting with them have decided that what they require is a slightly acid soil. Where trouble with them is experienced in the limy soil of the rock garden, it is well to give them a trial in acid soil. Many of them enjoy partial shade. *S. oregonum* has proved very amenable, as has *S. gormani* (acid soil and sun). Other sorts that are most interesting are *S. divergens, S. douglasi* [*S. stenopetalum 'Douglasii'*], *S. obtusatum, S. purdyi* [*S. spathulifolium purdyi*], and *S. spathulifolium.*

Sempervivums

Sempervivums, or houseleeks, belong to the same order as do the sedums, and they are even easier to grow and more indestructible than the latter, that is, when attention is paid to their few requirements. These are, hot sun and a poor, well-drained soil; they will flourish, indeed, in little or no soil on the tops of rocks or rammed into narrow crevices of walls, increasing their fleshy rosettes until wide mats of them spread out over the rock surface. It can hardly be said that these plants are beautiful when compared to many of the small inhabitants of the rock garden, but they are exceedingly interesting, and at seasons when there is

little colour in the garden, their rosettes, sometimes bright green, or green tipped with brown or purplish red, or wholly red, or like the cobweb houseleek, covered with white hairs like a cobweb, claim our attention and gratitude. They blossom in summer.

The genus includes about a hundred species, but many of them are not hardy out of doors in our climate. Nurseries commonly offer eight or ten kinds, all of which will prove amusing and useful. The cobweb houseleek, *Sempervivum arachnoideum,* makes mounds of tight green rosettes with innumerable fine threads woven from point to point exactly like a cobweb; hence its common name. The hotter its situation, it is said, the whiter its threads and the more numerous. Its curious spikes of red flowers are quite effective. There are numerous forms of it, some with larger rosettes.

Other species with small rosettes are *S. braunii,* with open, pointed rosettes, bright green, sometimes tipped with brown, the whole very neat and tight in effect, and spikes of yellow flowers. *S. funckii* is a free grower, adding to its pale green rosettes at an amazing rate and sending up spikes of purplish flowers in summer. *S. globiferum* has bright green small rosettes tipped with brown.

Some of the larger kinds are very handsome. The best is *S. triste,* with red rosettes and spikes of red flowers. *S. rubicundum* is also effective, with orange-red leaves tipped with green. *S. schotti* also shows red tints and is distinct. *S. calcareum* has handsome glaucous blue rosettes two or three inches across, tipped with purple.

A very nice species. *S. pittonii* has tongue-shaped leaves covered with short hairs & a purple spot at the tip. It is an uncommon species.

S. tectorum is the common houseleek, often found half covering old walls in country neighbourhoods with its large showy rosettes. It has numerous forms. A section of the rock garden given over wholly to sempervivums is a most interesting feature. I have seen several such congregations, and when the houseleeks are thus grown their individuality and quaint charm are best displayed. Such a section of the garden should, of course, be arranged in full sun.

CHAPTER XVIII

Colour in the Rock Garden

ALTHOUGH THESE notes have to do with colour in the rock garden, they are not by any means to be understood as advocating a colour scheme. A rock garden is supposedly the best report we can give of a rugged natural scene, and what more incongruous than a pattern of tints and tones, each the happy complement of the other, nicely fitted among jutting crags and winding valleys?

Someone has said that a rock garden should appear neat but natural; and we might add that, while we may go to great pains to make its colour associations lovely, they should appear quite careless and unpremeditated.

In no other phase of gardening may such exquisite colour associations be invoked with so little thought and planning and nowhere else do we ever have such amazing colours and textures to do with. Nothing is easier than to make charming pictures in the rock garden. Indeed, more often than not they make themselves, seeming to delight in surprising us with gay entanglements where roots have run together bringing about the most felicitous alliances, or where seeds have crossed a wide stretch of country to spring up and take their part in a scene that is the gayer for their coming.

Sometimes the picture will be no larger than your hand, again it will cover a hillside, again, at certain seasons, all the garden will blaze and shimmer with breadths of azure, of rose, of gold, of gray, and, here and there, bits and patches of high scarlet that give life and meaning and a touch of the unexpected to the enchanting scene.

We may plant closely in the rock garden and underplant with

hundreds of little bulbs so that more than one display takes place on each bit of ground. But in doing this we must guard against planting the rampageous spreaders against the little choice things that could not save themselves; or covering such small bulbs as the wild crocuses or muscaris with a blanket the thickness of *Arabis albida* [*Arabis caucasica*]. The warm lavender blossoms of *Crocus sieberi* come delightfully through the loose gray weave of *Androsace primuloides*, which later will wave a hundred pink umbrellas to hide the fading crocus grass. The white grape hyacinth, *Muscari botryoides alba*, whose flower head is like a cone of small seed pearls, is charming among mats of mauve and purple-flowered aubrietia.

All this is no gardener's dream, but a gay reality for all who follow the few rules. We do not, however, go about its attainment, especially if we are beginning gardeners, in quite the usual way. It is curious, but a fact, that to bring lovely colour into the rock garden we must first forget all about it and give our close attention to more practical matters.

It is clear, of course, that to achieve riotous colour the plants must bloom their ardent best, and that to do this they must be in perfect health. The health of the plants, then, is our first consideration. When we realize that the plants we gather together in the rock garden hail from all climates, altitudes, aspects, it is at once plain that our chief preoccupation must be to reproduce for them as nearly as possible the conditions that surround them in their homelands—the right soil, the right aspect, the right amount of moisture, lime or no

lime, sweet or acid, and whether a windy height or a sheltered nook is the sum of their desires; in short, we must *know* our plants. Find out about them from books, by asking questions, by writing to nurseries, botanical gardens, or to anyone who supposedly might know their ways and their necessities. When orders are sent in the spring or early autumn for rock plants, keep a copy and search out the needs of every plant before it arrives in order that it may have the right sort of situation and conditions ready for it upon its arrival. Thus only can we obviate ill health and speedy demise, thus only can we bring about that gay and gracious colour that should be found in every rock garden.

Consider also the plants in relation to the carefully modelled topography of the little landscape. Plant high on the heights to accentuate the difference in level, give to each declivity its graceful trailer, to each flat stone its mosslike creeper: give to each plant a position where it not only feels but looks at home. Nothing so adds to the reality of the little scene as this.

And now, having dutifully planted our rock garden with these practical matters in mind, and having begun to look it over with a sharp eye for discordant notes, we find surprisingly few. Of course, some magenta splendour may have run foul of a patch of scarlet poppies, or the crude yellow of *Alyssum saxatile* [*Aurinia saxatilis*] be elbowing a group of choice pink Spanish scillas, but on the whole there will be little to offend the most supersensitive eye. And for this reason we have two factors of the utmost importance working for us in the interests of peace and harmony.

In the first place, there are the stones, both great and small, soft-toned, neutral, thrusting a shoulder between angry contestants, separating or reconciling enemies, forming an inimitable background for flashing hues. Let no one underrate the value of the stones. Many of them are very beautiful in themselves and take their place in the general scheme with as much significance as the plants or shrubs. The Japanese pay great sums for beautiful stones to adorn their gardens, and there are unalterable rules for their employment. There is a chapter entitled "Garden Stones" in Mrs. Basil Taylor's *Japanese Gardens*, which should be of great interest and assistance to all who propose to make stones the basis of a garden.

And then there is the markedly beautiful foliage contributed by many of the plants. Some rock plants, it is true, when they have done their gorgeous bit, lapse into obscurity, and might be mistaken for meek little weeds. But a great number, if they had no blossoms at all to give us, would still be of the highest value because of the broad mats and mounds, trails, and little bushes of soft-toned lasting foliage they provide—gray, silver, hoary, bronze, blue-green, which, like the stones, act as mediators in this region of many and brilliant hues.

Some of the most useful of the gray and hoary-leaved mediators are the following:

Antennarias in variety
Anthemis montana
Arabis albida
 [*Arabis caucasica*]
Arabis albida flore
 pleno [*A. c. 'flore pleno'*]
Artemisia frigida
Artemisia canadensis
 [*A. campestris borealis*]
Artemisia
 pedemontana
Aubrietias, many
 varieties
Cerastium
 tomentosum
Dianthus caesius
 [*D. gratianopolitanus*]
Dianthus suavis
Euphorbia myrsinites
Festuca glauca (a little tufted grass)

Gypsophila repens
Helianthemum
 rhodantha
 carneum, and
 others
Lavender (dwarf)
Nepmussini
Papaver caucasicum
 [*P. fugax*]
Santolina
 chamaecyparissus
Santolina incana
 (lavender cotton)
 [*S. chamaecyparissus*]
Sedum sieboldii
 [*Hylotelephium sieboldii*]
Stachys lanata
 [*S. byzantina*]
Veronica incana

All these, it must be kept in mind, are free-growing ramping things which, while they may be arranged to add immensely to the beauty of the garden, especially at off seasons, so to speak, are all to be watched carefully and kept out of the neighbourhood of small plants which they would quickly vanquish. But these small things also have their little gray pacifists, and a free planting of them is just as important. Here are some of the prettiest.

Achillea serbica
Alyssum saxatile
 [*Aurinia saxatilis*]

Alyssum saxatile
 citrinum [*Aurinia saxatilis 'Citrinum'*]

Achillea argentea
 [*A. umbellata*]
Achillea huteri

Achillea kellereri
Achillea umbellata

The Tibet poppy behind a bush of white-flowered helianthemum with its hoary foliage.

The brilliant rose-pink blossoms of *Dianthus neglectus* [*D. pavonis*] are lovely with a mat of purple-flowered *Campanula muralis* [*C. portenschlagiana*] near by.

Veronica prostrata, with its masses of bright blue flower-spikes, may be allowed to mingle with the white-flowered Maiden pink, *Dianthus deltoides*. Both strong growers.

Allium moly, the Spanish onion, and star of Bethlehem are two summer bulbous plants that appear well together in a partially shaded place.

Gypsophila repens, the creeping chalk plant, with its many white flowers and gray foliage, makes a delightful mat for the wiry, purple-flowered *Calamintha alpina* to tumble over.

No better setting can be found for our wild bluebell, *Campanula rotundifolia*, than a shaded corner among small ferns.

Calluna vulgaris and *Aster liniariifolius* make a delightful association for the late summer.

Silene schafta, *Oenothera caespitosa*, and *Ceratostigma plumbaginoides* are three graces of the late summer and autumn, bright pink, pure white, gentian blue. They blossom for a long time.

Geranium wallichianum, mauve flowers and reddening leaves climbing over a small evergreen.

Sedum sieboldii [*Hylotelephium sieboldii*] with the charming autumn *Crocus speciosus*.

Chrysanthemum arcticum near a bush of gray-leaved lavender.

Helleborus niger amid the brown leaves.

CHAPTER XIX

Shrubs That Fit the Rock Garden

SINCE WE ARE creating our rock garden as closely as possible in the likeness of a rugged natural scene, the omission of trees and shrubs would be a serious blunder. Indeed, their importance in helping us toward reality in our fashioning is hardly to be over-estimated. With their aid we are enabled to create a convincing picture of what might otherwise appear, in spite of our best efforts, a rather meaningless pile of stones. Evergreens in particular, as Mr. Farrer has pointed out, "when properly placed, have the most astounding power of giving place and composition. They can make any rock look high or low, natural or artificial, near or far." Furthermore, when the blossoms and leaves of the deciduous shrubs have departed, the evergreens, both broad-leaved and narrow-leaved, remain to give life and strength and coherence to the little landscape.

Few rules may be laid down for the placing of shrubs and trees in the rock garden, for each miniature scene will require to be treated according to its individual necessities and possibilities, and no two of these little scenes will be the same. Each builder must strive to see for himself where the planting of an erect or spreading tree, or a group of little bushes will best serve to confirm his effort to bring about the illusion of height, of vastness, of wildness, or to draw the various parts of the construction together, making of it a harmonious and expressive whole.

But a good deal may be said concerning the choice of trees and shrubs to be used. And, first and most important, it must be urged that they be not only of a size to fit the scale of their surroundings when planted, but of a type to *remain* in scale with them. To plant young specimens of large-growing trees or shrubs is to find that in a surprisingly short time they have outgrown their surroundings; and not only this, but have destroyed entirely the illusion they were intended to foster, dwarfing the hills, drawing in the little plains, reducing the jutting cliffs to mere upright stones of puny eminence, instead of endowing these features with majesty and strength.

A ten-inch specimen of *Picea excelsa* [*P. abies*], the Norway spruce, when set out against a boulder in a small rock garden, appears wholly relevant and at home. But five years' time finds it a giant among pygmies, and with the passing of another five or ten years it would stand confessed, if it had not been before removed, a stripling forest tree upon a pile of earth and stones which its growth has rendered utterly insignificant and meaningless.

But happily there are a great number of naturally dwarf trees and shrubs, as well as numerous kinds whose growth is so slow that they may safely be used in the rock garden without danger of outgrowing their quarters for many years. And among them none are so useful and so wholly fascinating as the little conifers. The pygmy spruces are especially picturesque and in keeping with rugged scenery. Some have the dwarfed and contorted aspect of trees long exposed to the fury of the elements on real alpine heights. *P. e. Gregoriana* [*P. abies 'Gregoriana'*], and *P. e. Maxwelli* [*P. a. 'Maxwelli'*] are two that create this illusion. They are low, broad, irregular in outline, and give the

effect of having reached a great age. *P. e. pygmaea* [*P. a. pygmaea*] has the habit of its great relative, the Norway spruce, but grows only a few feet high. No little tree is more effective in a miniature landscape than *Picea alba albertiana conica*. Its form is very slender and pointed, with branches close set and twiggy and densely covered with bright green leaves. Very realistic effects may be contrived by planting a number of these little pointed trees on a rugged slope, or using a single specimen at the foot of a cliff. This spruce is said to prefer partial shade and a not too dry situation.

Of the junipers, *J. sabina tamariscifolia*, hoary and almost prostrate, is one of the best. It is beautiful at all seasons. Small specimens of the Swedish juniper, *J. communis suecica*, may fill a situation where a spirelike tree is required. Its growth is exceedingly slow, and its dense habit and gray-green foliage very attractive. *Juniperus communis depressa* is also a fine subject where there is room for its generous spread.

Retinispora obtusa nana [*Chamaecyparis obtusa*] is a delightful bushy evergreen for the rock garden, and some will like its "golden" form, though I think it is bad practice to use these golden or variegated forms in what purports to be a natural scene. Of the pines, *Pinus montana Mughus* [*P. mugo*] is the best. Its habit is low and spreading, and though it finally covers considerable ground, its development is deliberate. *Taxus cuspidata brevifolia* may be used in the rock garden, but it must be remembered that while this fine hardy form of the Japanese yew is very low-growing, it spreads out very widely and so requires plenty of space. *T. canadensis,* our native yew, grows well in shade, however dense, and enjoys a dampish soil.

The arborvitæ tribe contributes a most engaging small subject in *Thuja occidentalis little gem*, a mound of soft foliage growing broader than tall. *T. o. pygmaea* is an erect little bush with gray-green foliage, and *T. o. spaethi*, with foliage dark in summer and bronze in winter, is highly desirable.

These are but a very few of the small conifers available. It is a good plan, productive of much pleasure and information, to visit a nursery where a fine collection of these miniature trees is to be seen. Choice may then be made of the types best suited to the situations where it is desired to use them.

The dwarf cotoneasters are a host in themselves in clothing the rock garden with beauty. Many of them are evergreen, and all have small attractive blossoms followed by brilliant fruit literally encrusting the branches. *C. horizontalis* is the most widely used, but the spraylike branches of this fine species reach out so broadly in a short time that it is not suited to small rock gardens. *C. humifusa* [*C. dammeri*] is a creeping form that roots as it goes, but its spread is easily kept in check. It is low and close-growing and makes a fine subject for hanging over a cliff or for covering rough places. *C. adpressus* is very dwarf, and its leaves turn so grand a scarlet in the autumn that it is invaluable. *C. himalaica* makes splendid little bushes, and others of the genus useful in the rock garden are *C. thymifolia* and *C. microphyllus glacialis*.

Among low-growing barberries, none is finer than *B. verruculosa*, that has beautiful shining evergreen leaves tinged with scarlet in winter, and a distinct habit of growth. *B. thunbergii minor*, a dwarf compact form of the well-known hedge barberry, is valuable for its brilliant autumn colouring. *B. stenophylla* has fine arching sprays and lustrous foliage. It is too large for very small rock gardens.

I would urge all who have not made acquaintance with the little brooms to seek and make their own a few at least of the many species and varieties. If they are not to be had ready grown in this country one need not be discouraged, for they are easily raised from seed, and the charm of their gay blossoms and distinct forms fills one with the desire to know as many as possible. *Cytisus ardoinii* is a most engaging little bushling with half-trailing branches little more than six inches above the ground. In spring these are alight with yellow blossoms. *Genista prostrata* flings its branches about in a delightful manner and in late April covers them with golden bloom. *G. dalmatica* [*G. sylvestris*], a little alpine gorse, is one of the best, a fuzzy spreading bush but a few inches high, good to plant where it may curl over a jutting cliff. *G. sagittalis* is a creeping shrub about six inches tall with curiously winged stems and bright yellow blossoms conspicuous in the June garden. Other good forms are *G. pilosa*, for dry, gravelly places, and *G. hispanica*, reaching a height of eighteen inches and flowering all summer. The brooms all love sunshine and thrive best in well-drained sandy loam.

For early flowering in the rock garden, *Erica*

carnea and its white form are indispensable. The March sunshine often causes the little bells to open, and when they are planted in thickets on a gentle slope and interplanted with some of the early scillas, there could be no prettier picture. The soil best suited to them is composed of peat and sand, and they enjoy full sunshine. The same soil and aspect are right for the numerous forms of the common heather, *Calluna vulgaris*, which makes such delightful breadths of ruddy colour among the stones in the late summer and autumn.

Valuable all the year are bushes of dwarf lavender. It is hardier than the taller growing kinds and if cut over soon after flowering remains sturdy and compact. It gives a wealth of scented spikes in summer that last for a long time. Lavender cotton (santolina) is another gray shrub that enjoys, as does the true lavender, a sunny position in well-drained, sandy soil.

Daphne cneorum is probably more often seen in rock gardens than any other shrub. Its low, branching growth and delightful, almost continuous blossoming make it justly popular. Its relative, the exquisite *D. blagayana* with clusters of creamy, fragrant flowers, is scarce and difficult. Peat and loam, cool and well-drained, and partial shade are its necessities, if you are so lucky as to secure it. *Abelia chinensis* and *Viburnum carlesii* are fine shrubs for large rock gardens, the former flowering all summer and fall, and the viburnum early in the spring. Numerous azaleas are suitable for our use, among them the splendid *A. hinodigiri* [a form

of *Rhododendron obtusum*] whose garment of brilliant cerise in April is the most conspicuous thing in the garden. Two very dwarf spiraeas, *S. crispifolia* and *S. decumbens*, may adorn the smallest rock gardens; and two little ivies, *Hedera conglomerata* [*H. helix* var. *conglomerata*] and *H. minima* [also var. of *H. helix*], are exceedingly quaint and interesting. They do not climb, but hug a vertical cliff with interesting effect, or may be allowed to sprawl over a flat stone.

All the foregoing are foreign born. America, however, is rich in dwarf shrubs—just how rich we have as yet but a small idea. The heath tribe alone offers immense variety and beauty. These require acid soil and in most cases shade or partial shade. *Vaccinium vitis-idaea* is a most enchanting small Arctic huckleberry, found also on the high mountains of New England. It grows only a few inches high, its tiny leaves are evergreen and lustrous, and it bears in spring pink bells followed by dark berries. *Gaylussacia brachycera* (*Vaccinium buxifolium*), the box huckleberry, is another diminutive gem. Its home is in pine barrens of Pennsylvania, New Jersey, and Delaware. Both may be accommodated in the smallest rock gardens.

Leiophyllum buxifolium, the sand myrtle, grows also in sandy barrens. It reaches a height of two feet, is evergreen, and in spring is covered with a mass of creamy blossoms. A prostrate form, *L. b. prostratum*, comes from the mountains of North Carolina and is very desirable. *Chamaedaphne calyculata*, cassandra, is taller than the sand myrtle but not so tall as to preclude its use in rock gardens. Its blossoms come early and last a long time. *Andromeda polifolia,* the marsh rosemary, is a native of cold bogs in Northern places. It requires a deep, peaty soil. *Kalmia angustifolia,* sheep laurel, is gay in summer with bright pink blossoms; and *K. glauca,* the swamp laurel, earlier to bloom, is a charming thing. Both require a deep, moist, peaty soil.

Now within our reach through the patience and enterprise of a Colorado nurseryman is *K. microphylla,* a diminutive laurel that grows in the Rocky Mountains. It is only two or three inches tall, its leaves small and shining, and its bright pink blossoms almost continuously borne. It is a difficult subject to make happy, for its alpine bog is not easily reproduced. But it appears to be established in a low part of my rock garden in leaf mould and brown peat, and also in Mr. Durand's garden in very acid soil. I am still praying over it, but not so often as at first.

Other heaths that should be sought out are *Ledum groenlandicum,* the lovely Labrador tea; *Cassiope mertensiana* of the Northwestern moun-

tains; and the false red heather, *Phyllodoce empetriformis,* that is abundant in the alpine meadows of the same region, and is now offered, I think, by the trade.

Three quite lovely little willows from our West country should have a place in every rock garden where there is room for them. *Salix bracycarpa,* found on Rollins Pass quite near the timber line, has yellow twigs and gray leaves. *S. glaucops* is rather similar but is a more rapidly growing shrub. The best, perhaps, is *S. repens argentea* [*S. arenaria*], a creeper with silver leaves.

From the West also come several dwarf shrubs that there is not space here to mention. The resources of the West have as yet hardly been guessed at, but the keen searcher may confidently expect to bring forth many treasures. Nor has mention been made of all the shrubs offered by the East and the Southeast for the furnishing of the rock garden, but enough has been said to show clearly that the sylva of the rock garden may be as interesting and varied as its flora.

CHAPTER XX

The Late Rock Garden

Aᴼᴛᴇʀ ᴛʜᴇ spring freshet of radiant bloom has passed over the rock garden, our little cosmopolis is apt to lapse into a period of sober quiet unless we have given a good deal of thought to planting for summer bloom. In any case, April, May, and June are the gala months in a rock garden—its festival of all nations with the representatives of each striving to outdo the others in gaiety and beauty of mien and array; but, though the scene may be less brilliant, there is no reason for a lack of interest and colour throughout the summer and autumn.

Many persons are near their gardens during the summer and early autumn only, and in this case it is well to give over the whole area to plants that come to their blossoming during this period, and in any rock garden generous space should be allowed them. Though they are fewer in number than the spring-flowering plants and perhaps lack something of the glancing freshness and sparkle that characterize the early comers, there is beauty among the summer and autumn rock plants, and when the long, hot days are upon us we are grateful to them for their sturdy indifference to the soaring mercury.

True, many spring-flowering plants give a scattering bloom all through the summer and autumn. Others having reposed through the heated season, experience a rejuvenescence, with the coming of cool nights and refreshing dews, and vouchsafe a second blossoming. Both these classes may be considered when planting a summer garden. Among the first are notably the poppies. Established plants of *Papaver nudicaule*, the Iceland poppy, beginning to bloom toward the end of April, will continue, if seed pods are not allowed to form, straight through the summer and autumn and more than likely wave a scarlet rag of defiance at you as you draw on the winter blanket. A noble Icelander named tangerine is especially satisfactory in this respect, sending up an amazing succession of crinkled orange-scarlet blooms for at least six months. It is sure to please all who love to crown their heights with a bit of flashing colour.

P. rupifragum, the biennial *P. caucasicum* [*P. fugax*], the various forms of the alpine poppy, and the Tibet poppy, will, if not allowed to form too much seed, bloom on until the frosts and sometimes longer.

Potentilla alba, while one of the earliest plants to open an eye upon the awakening world, is among the last to quiet down if, indeed, this pretty cousin of the strawberries ever really sleeps.

Corydalis lutea, the little yellow fumatory, blooms from May first until hard frost has put an end to its charming effervescence.

Summer days abate little the enthusiasm of the various forms of *Viola cornuta* if they are given an occasional clipping over, and of course one must not forget the jaunty Johnny-jump-ups who both toil and spin right round the year, even beneath the snows.

Among the plants that bloom again after having rested during the heat of the day are many kinds of violets. The bird's-foot violet, *Viola pedata,* the white Canada violet, *V. canadensis,* and a quaint little pink treasure the sand violet, *V. arenaria rosea* [*V. rupestris*], appear especially refreshed and lively after the siesta and blossom profusely. Others with this pleasant habit are *Phlox subulata,* most of the geraniums

and erodiums, numerous campanulas, but notably *C. muralis* [*C. portenschlagiana*]; houstonia, aubrietias, *Dryas octopetala,* all sorts of primroses, nepeta, *Trollius laxus,* thrifts, and pinks and a host more. Some of these are always to be counted upon to brighten the autumn garden. Occasionally, some spring-flowering plant that has never before so favoured us will burst into bloom among the reddening leaves of October. Then, indeed, we feel that we have received a gift. Last year, toward the end of the month I found a long-spurred yellow columbine in full flower, and near it a parkman's crab, its crooked branches sprinkled over with rosy blooms!

Among the summer families, that of oenothera stands out. Not difficult to please—indeed, sometimes too ready in their response to our request to beautify the summer garden—they flower over a long period, revelling in the heat and sunshine, unmindful of drought. The blossoms are large, lovely, papery things, white, yellow, or pale pink. Among the best is *Oe. caespitosa,* that has flat widely ramifying rosettes from which arise huge pale blossoms on very short stems over a long period. *Oe. brachycarpa* has hoary foliage and wide yellow blossoms. These two hug the ground but spread over it with considerable rapidity. *Oe. tetraptera* arises to a height of a foot. It is a beautiful Western species, opening an endless succession of snowy blossoms punctually at sundown. Whatever it may be in its home environment it is here a biennial scattering its hardy seeds widely. *Oe. speciosa* is taller still and should be given a place only in large rock gardens where there is room for its rapid increase. A small and unassuming biennial with yellow blossoms is *Oe. pumila.* It self-sows about the garden, but is too small ever to be a menace. This American family is a large one and the above are but a few of the many species to be had.

While most of the spring-flowering campanulas bloom occasionally during the rest of the season, a number of this choice family are at their best when the cool blue or white of their bell-like blossoms is most welcome and refreshing. Of these is the well-known and profuse-flowering *Campanula carpatica,* the Carpathian harebell. It has several improved forms with larger or more open blossoms, and all are lovely. Near it is *C. turbinata* [*C. carpatica* var. *turbinata*], the true form seldom seen, with grayer and hairier leaves and gray-blue blossoms, and a more compact habit than the last.

Our native harebell, *C. rotundifolia,* blooms all through the summer and autumn and is a most lovely and fragile thing to be cherished in cool corners where ramping neighbours may not overcome it. The white form is less attractive than the blue but is nice for a contrast. *C. stansfieldii*—which Mr. Farrer calls a gift from Heaven—is a small delightful plant flowering early in July, as does another small charmer, *C. pulloides,* that bears large dark blue bells in profusion. These are for a favoured position in gritty soil where the morning sun will reach them. *C. punctata,* from the Alps of Japan, is also an attractive species, having long creamy waxen bells well spotted inside with red.

Geranium wallichianum, a fine prostrate spe-

cies of this large family, begins to bloom at the end of June and continues until frost, not even asking to have the seed pods removed. It is a most graceful and gracious plant when allowed to scramble at will over rocks in half-shaded situations. The blossoms are wide salvers of a fine lilac colour, paling toward the centre. It is easily raised from seed and quite hardy.

Silene schafta is brightly indefatigable in furnishing the summer garden with its mats of deep pink blossoms. A sunny situation suits it, and it is easily raised from seed. *Funkia minor* blooms in August with the greater, but less lovely, members of its family, a quaint little prototype of *F. subcordata,* carrying its virginal white "lilies" on stems only six or eight inches tall. It is seldom seen. *Linum capitatum* is a beautiful yellow-flowered flax that blooms much later than the better-known *L. flavum.*

More yellow is furnished the late garden by the numerous fine hypericums, some of which bloom off and on until fall, by the golden aster, *Chrysogonum virginianum* and by a quaint little plant called *Inula ensifolia,* that has many big and lusty relatives but which is itself only a few inches tall.

Dianthus gallicus is not the choicest of its race, but it is not to be despised these shortening days, and besides, it broadcasts a fragrance that would at any season give it eminence. The cluster-headed pinks, *D. cruentus, D. carthusianorum, D. giganteus,* I frankly dislike as being utterly unpinklike, but they are colour for the summer rock garden.

Scabiosa pterocephala [*Pterocephala perennis*] is a

quaint, rather pallid, but engaging little plant whose gray mat is studded over in August with rather large pale lavender "pincushions." It is squeamish about damp, and must have a comfortable place among stones, where water will not settle about it. *Tunica saxifraga* and *Asperula cynanchica* are two small frivolous-appearing creatures that grow and sow in sunny places without ministrations from us. The one has very fine foliage and masses of small pale pink blossoms, the other is a tangle of threadlike stems and tiny white flowers. Though frail in appearance they can both become a nuisance among plants whose hold upon life is less of the strangle kind.

Many beautiful gentians bloom during the summer and autumn. "In their native homes," says Sir James Cotter, "they grow in vast patches and provide a spectacle of wonderful beauty to those who have the opportunity to see them there."

Some of us have seen the fringed gentian growing in such profusion—a sight surely never to be forgotten—but it is not so easy to reproduce even in a small way in the rock garden this superb gesture of Nature's. For gentians are difficult plants to deal with—capricious and demanding, and I am sometimes quite sure they do not themselves know what they want.

Two summer-flowering species are *G. freyniana* [var. of *G. septemfida*] and *G. septemfida*—the one having large beautiful blue flowers in July and said to like a soil of sandy loam and peat in shade; the other, no less beautiful "requires full sun and a mixture of moist, sandy

peat and loam." Both these are sojourning in my garden for the moment along with the entrancing *G. farreri*, whose long pale trumpets should surely be carried aloft by angels instead of attached to little green earthly tufts. How long they will remain, I cannot say. They have bloomed for two seasons in succession, but they do not set my heart at rest by waxing fat and lush.

G. przewalskii, they say, is easy, but its name is certainly against it, and I do not feel drawn toward it. One easy doer is here, however, in the person of an American species, *G. linearis*, a slender erect plant no more than a foot high, with a cluster of blue tubes at the top of each shoot. It came to me from the Northwest, was put into a bed of leaf mould and loam, and forgotten. In the spring, before it appeared, its bed was dug up and other things put in, but it nevertheless appeared—a little depleted as to numbers, it is true—and bloomed. It is said to like bogs, but, at any rate, it has the good manners not to press its preferences when away from home.

And as the weeks roll on toward autumn, we continue to look for flowers in the rock garden and need not be disappointed. Little slopes covered with the common heather or ling, *Calluna vulgaris*, are pleasant to look upon. There are both pale and rosy-purple kinds, and some whose foliage is touched with "gold or silver." These little bushes are not especially particular as to soil or situation, but if they can choose, they like sand and peat and sunshine and all the winds that blow. In their neighbourhood plant the little native *Aster liniariifolius,* rather heather-like itself in appearance, with big lavender-blue asters that blend happily with the flowers of the ling. This is a nice late summer and autumn picture.

And then we have that beautiful plant, so handicapped by its terrible name that it is seldom spoken of in pleasant garden conversation, *Ceratostigma plumbaginoides* (*Plumbago larpentae*), that more certainly than any other glorifies the autumn garden. It dearly loves to send its roots down among buried stones, and when once established, will every year provide a splendid display of bright blue flowers above its crimson-tinted foliage.

Saxifraga fortunei is rare in this country but dearly prized where possessed for its rosette of thick bronzy leaves and its banner of white fringy blossoms held aloft in October. Still later blooms *Chrysanthemum arcticum,* a fat-leaved little plant with many white daisies and a pungent scent. It will grow anywhere and self-sows. Though modest, it seems a lovely thing in November's shorn garden.

A word must be said, too, of the autumn crocuses. Only in spring do we find such fragile beauty as in these slender vases or rounded goblets that open out at the touch of the warm noonday sun. There is room in most gardens for a great many of them stowed here and there in nooks and crannies. They occupy little space, and the more you tuck away the greater will be your surprise and delight when they appear in little battalions, so soft coloured, so seemingly fragile, yet so brave in the face of frosts. Some lovely kinds are *C. salzmanii* [*C. serotinus* ssp. *salzmanii*], *C. sativus* (a rather shy

bloomer with me), *C. zonatus* [*C. kotschyanus*], *C. asturicus, C. cancellatus, C. speciosus.* If none other, plant *speciosus* and *zonatus* [*C. kotschyanus*].

A few more plants for summer and autumn blossoming are the following: *Sedum sieboldii* [*Hylotelephium sieboldii*] and numerous other sedums, *Vittadenia triloba,* dwarf lavender, *Bellis caerulescens, Campanula patula, C. americana, Coreopsis rosea, Allium cyaneum, A. stellatum, A. cernuum, Campanula tommasiniana.*

A brief word must now be said concerning work in the summer garden, for upon our faithfulness during this season largely depends not only its present comeliness, but also the beauty of the following spring. All plants should be kept growing strongly, and this spells water in dry weather. Not stingy sprinklings, but in times of drought, thorough soakings so the ground is wet for several inches down. This should be done at least once a week, or better, every five days. After a scorching day, when the small inhabitants of the rock garden appear weary and spent, a spraying with the fine nozzle of the hose is a beneficent attention well repaid by the smiling faces that greet us on the morrow. In dry weather, this may be done every day at sundown.

Spring is essentially neat and restrained; summer is lax and careless. It is important that the summer garden be kept tidy. Many plants that have blossomed earlier will now appear straggling and unattractive. To these we give a sharp shearing with a long pair of scissors, snipping off the spent flower stems and a fair portion of foliage. This treatment works wonders. At first they look a little forlorn, but soon regain the mounded neatness that characterizes them in spring, and they are in good condition to stand the winter with its various hardships. Among the plants that will require this treatment are arabis, alyssum, aubrietia, *Arenaria montana*, aethionema, iberis, *Saponaria ocymoides*, the strong-growing pinks, *Phlox divaricata*, nepeta, *Veronica rupestris* and *V. prostrata*, many violas, and others. Withered flowers should be snipped from all plants unless it is desired to secure seed.

CHAPTER XXI

Sowing the Rock Garden

FOR THE ENTHUSIAST with a little time at his disposal and a trifle each of perseverance and ardour in his make-up, by far the best way of assembling a comprehensive collection of rock plants is to raise them from seed. Besides being probably the most interesting of gardening experiences, there are great practical advantages to be derived from following this method. In the first place, the difference in the expense of growing our plants from seed and buying them ready-grown is enormous. For the price of a few dozen rare or unusual plants, or, for that matter, of quite common ones, we may have, if we are sufficiently keen and painstaking, literally hundreds of our own raising—enough for our own use and plenty to share with fellow enthusiasts, or to use in that gay barter and trade which has ever been so pleasant and so profitable a feature of the pursuit of gardening.

Moreover, in propagating plants from seed, we are following Nature's methods, and the home-grown seedling is apt to be, if properly brought up, a sturdier youngster than the nursery-grown plant, and is ready to take up life in the wide world of the rock garden with considerably more zest and vigour. The plant that has undergone a railroad journey, even when well packed and transported with the minimum of delay, has suffered a loss of vitality, and consequently takes time to steady itself in its new surroundings and to become acclimatized. But our own seedlings may be lifted with a ball of earth and set out in their permanent places in the twinkling of an eye, the dear innocents not so much as suspecting that they have left the shelter of the nursery forever and are embarked on independent careers.

It is of the greatest advantage, moreover, that they may be

transplanted at a time when weather conditions are most favourable to their uninter-
rupted growth, as during a period of cloudy
weather or on a day when rain is pending. The
home-grown seedling has usually the good
fortune also to be moved while still small
enough to adapt itself readily to any quarters,
however narrow. Many a full-sized plant is
mangled and torn beyond recovery in the attempt to insert it in some narrow crevice of
the rock work, or in the tight joints of paved
path or dry wall, that could in seedlinghood
have been easily slipped in and happily established.

But perhaps the greatest boon derived by
the rock gardener through the use of seeds is
that his roving, acquisitive spirit is set free—
free to follow his desire hither and yon, far and
near, and to make his own almost any loveliness that has touched his fancy. Today, in this
country, only a few nurseries as yet specialize
in rock plants, and thus far the general nurseries are able to offer only the most ordinary
varieties. Gradually, we are learning how and
where to seek the rare and beautiful plants of
our own country, but because of the quarantine enactment against the importation of
plants, we should have small knowledge of the
treasures of other countries were it not for
seeds. Seeds enable us to laugh in the face of
these limitations and prohibitions. They are
the open-sesame to a world of illimitable delights.

Nature sows her seeds as soon as ripe and,
while it is not necessary in all cases that we follow her example, in certain others it is highly

expedient, even necessary that we do so. Seeds
of a great variety of plants may be carried over
the winter and sown in spring with perfectly
satisfactory results, but there are others which,
if subjected to this delay, will not germinate
for a year or more; and when those seeds are
concerned whose vegetative power is short-
lived germination will be extremely irregular
and uncertain, if it takes place at all. Seeds of
the following species should be sown as soon
as ripe or certainly by early winter: primula,
helleborus, delphinium (very short-lived),
anemone (very short-lived), trollius, ranunculus, ceratostigma, hepatica, omphalodes,
paeonia, phlox, soldanella, adonis, aconitum,
pulmonaria, geum, acaena, androsace, cyclamen, dodecatheon, dryas, onosma, saxifrage,
and ramondia.

For myself I prefer late autumn or early
winter sowing for all species save those that
germinate very readily, and even in their case
no harm is done if it is more convenient to
make one task of the seed sowing. At this late
season, indeed, Nature seems to lift the burden of responsibility from our shoulders and,
once we have properly set the stage, there
seems little for us to do save await results with
cheerful confidence. Freezing has a very compelling effect upon hard shells, and it is well
known that melting snow has a penetrative
power that the most rock-ribbed or dilatory
find hard to resist. Autumn is not usually regarded as the season for rummaging in seed
catalogues, but as a matter of fact there is no
better. Seed purchased from a reliable house at
this season is sure to be fresh, and this, of

course, with the species whose vitality is short-lived, is of paramount importance, and with all seeds an advantage.

For our enterprise, a coldframe is a prime necessity. For, though the seed of numerous hardy species may, with some chance of success, be sown directly in the open ground, the hazards are too many to make the taking worth while for even the commonest kinds. The frame enables us to safeguard the seeds from all manner of perils; from beating rains that would wash them out of the soil, from prowling animals and hungry birds, from extremes of heat and cold, damp and drought. And when the tiny seedlings appear, the frame becomes a nursery where these new babies may receive the care and protection necessary to take them safely past the dangers that beset the paths of infant plants.

Almost any sort of frame that may be at hand will do, but if a new one is to be built, I would most earnestly urge that whatever its length, its depth from front to back be no greater than may easily be reached across. This facilitates enormously all dealings with it, enabling us to reach all parts without undue stretching or straining.

My own frames are contrived in twelve sections, each section being but 2½ feet deep by 3 feet wide; a most comfortable size. They extend along a picket fence and the sash are hinged to the back of the frame and when not required may be raised and fastened to the fence by means of a hook in the sash and an eye in the fence. Thus all lifting of the heavy lights is obviated and safe storage provided close at hand. Many persons make use of a patented wire and celluloid material in the sash instead of glass, and this has the advantage of lightness and of being unbreakable.

The situation for the frames should be chosen with some care. On no account should they face due south; such an exposure would put the young seedlings cruelly at the mercy of the sun in summer, from which it would be extremely difficult to protect them. On the other hand, they should not have to face the bitter winds of winter. An eastern aspect with some protection on the north in the form of a wall, a fence or shrubbery is the most satisfactory.

The majority of gardeners sow their seeds in boxes or pans of prepared soil, which are then placed in frames. But, after many years of experiment, I find sowing directly in the soil in the frame is productive of more satisfactory results in the long run; and it is a much less laborious method for the person whose concerns are many besides that of gardening. My contention is substantiated by A. J. Macself, whose book, *Plants from Seed*, should be in the library of all who are interested in this special phase of gardening.

If asked to give reasons for this point of view [says Mr. Macself], I should claim that the soil of a well-made bed is subject to less variation of temperature than the small body of soil in a pan or box, and that considerably more watering is required for the small receptacles than for a fairly deep and properly drained bed. That, to my mind, is of great importance, not on the score of labour-saving, but because artificial watering, however carefully done, is a task to be reduced to the minimum in the interests of the seedlings. . . . My records for years prove convincingly that failures in the pans are out of all proportion to those in frame beds.

In preparing a seed bed in a frame, it is important to insure ready drainage by placing at the bottom a thick layer of broken stone; upon this foundation may be laid several inches of sphagnum moss to keep the earth from percolating through the stones; then a few inches of unscreened earth, and on top of all half a foot of a prepared mixture. Scientists are telling us a great deal about the use of specific composts to insure the germination and subsequent healthy growth of hitherto recalcitrant species. But to grow successfully a great number of beautiful and desirable rock plants and alpines no more is necessary than a light, gritty, and porous mixture, sweet and wholesome, and made fine by being put through a fairly coarse sieve.

A compost composed of one part clean sharp sand, one part leaf mould, and one part sweet loam, with the addition of a little powdered limestone and some fine charcoal is very satisfactory. In this mixture may be grown most of the species of the following genera:

Achillea,	Aquilegia,	Aubrietia,
Aethionema,	Arabis,	Bellis,
Allium,	Arenaria,	Bellium,
Alyssum,	Armeria,	Campanula,
Anchusa,	Asperula,	Corydalis,
Anthemis,	Aster,	Delphinium,
Dianthus,	Iris,	Primula,
Draba,	Leontopodium,	Saponaria,
Erigeron,	Linaria,	Scabiosa,
Erodium,	Linum,	Sedum,
Erysimum,	Lychnis,	Silene,
Genista,	Mertensia,	Thymus,
Geranium,	Myosotis,	Tunica,
Gypsophila,	Papaver,	Veronica,
Helianthemum,	Penstemon,	Viola,
Hypericum,	Polemonium,	Wahlenbergia,
Iberis,	Potentilla.	

That the compost should be sweet and wholesome is of the greatest importance, and it should be remembered that leaf mould taken directly from a pit or compost heap is pretty certain to be sour. Before using it should be spread out for several days to sun and air. The charcoal and lime, however, do much toward converting it to sweetness.

For androsaces, saxifragas, sempervivums, and the rarer species of dianthus, draba, and silene, Mr. Macself recommends a compost composed of one half sweet fibrous loam, and the other half made up of porous lime rubble, burnt earth or brick, sand and charcoal crushed "so that it will pass through a riddle with nine holes to the square inch."

For such peat-loving plants as ramondia, haberlia, soldanella, shortia, ferns, dodecatheon, arnica, and others, the mixture used should be composed of peat, fibrous loam, charcoal, and pulverized brick rubble.

If only one frame is to be used, partitions of boards may separate the different composts; otherwise it is advisable to give to each a separate frame. Seeds that are slow to germinate should always be given a frame or a pan to themselves in order that they may not be disturbed by the early rising of the more expeditious.

Several hours before sowing, the soil in the frame should be made quite level and given a thorough soaking with the fine spray of the hose. A fine, windless day in late November or early December may be chosen for the pleasant task. Seed sown earlier may be encouraged to germinate in a week or so, in which case the tiny seedlings would have gained no hold upon the soil before cold weather arrives and would be thrown out and destroyed by the freezing and thawing that our climate is subject to.

No paraphernalia are required save a box of soil made a trifle sandier than that used in the frames, a bundle of wooden labels, and a lath, or narrow strip of wood, cut to fit the depth of the frame. By pressing this strip of wood lightly into the soil at intervals of three inches, straight, smooth-surfaced rows are made upon which the seed is thinly scattered and immediately covered with the sandy soil to a depth of about twice their own size. Very fine seed will require only the merest sprinkling of soil.

The importance of thin sowing cannot be too emphatically stressed, for if, when the seedlings appear, they are overcrowded, they shut off the health-giving light and air from each other, and rot sets in, often causing the loss of an entire planting. Some seeds are so small that it is almost impossible to avoid sowing them too thickly. In this case, a little silver sand may be mixed with the seed in the packet before sowing. Each row should be clearly labelled with the name of the plant and the date of sowing.

When planting is completed, the sash is lowered, but not closed tightly. A brick laid flat on the edge of the frame serves to keep it open far enough to insure the free circulation of air necessary to prevent the growth of moss or fungus; and occasionally, on a fine day, it is well to lift the sash and allow a good airing. Mats that come for the purpose or pieces of burlap are placed over the sash and remain in place until germination starts in the spring.

If the earth has been saturated before sowing, no further watering will be necessary. But, after the first of January whenever there is a thick fall of snow, the frames should be opened wide to receive it. "Snow broth," as has been said, is a most potent force in stirring little green souls to life and energy, and on no account should this rite be omitted. If it so happens that one is not at hand during the winter to tend the frames, the sash may be left off altogether and salt hay be filled in over the sleeping seeds to protect them from beating rains which would wash them out of the soil. It is not wise to make use of leaves for this purpose, as in so doing we are introducing whatever disease germs may be on the leaves, to say nothing of the eggs of rapacious insects and worms which, in the fullness of time, will arise and destroy the tiny, tender seedlings; nothing could be more to their taste. I realized this danger only after several bitter experiences.

Light screens made of lath fastened two inches apart to horizontal pieces may also be used to deflect the force of the rains.

And then it will come about some fine day during March probably shortly after the frames have received a lap full of soft thick snow, that the dark earth will be discovered all pricked over with delicate green embroidery, where before was no sign of life at all. And let me assure you that there are few more gratifying occasions in life than when one perches upon the edge of a frame, the perfidious March sunshine nuzzling about one's coat collar, and sharp breezes nipping one's recklessly exposed ankles, and gazes upon those rows of tiny green things, realizing that from high Chinese bogs, from Pyrenean slopes, from sunny Southern isles, from alpine pastures, we have called them to dwell together and make gay and full of vivid interest the hills and valleys of our rock garden.

But, of course, success is not wholly ours until these babies have been safely piloted through the dangers of infancy to sturdy seedlinghood. As soon as germination takes place, the mats must be removed from the frames in order that the seedlings shall receive plenty of light. On fine mild days, the sash may be lifted during the best part of the day, for light and air are as essential to the healthy development of these young plants as to any other young things. Next to light and air, the proper degree of moisture is the chief matter to be looked after.

On no account must the earth be allowed to dry out. One lapse of this kind would prob-ably result in the loss of all the little plants. Nor must the soil be oversaturated. This results in the dread trouble known as damping off, a fungous disease that causes the stems to rot at the soil line, laying the seedlings low in heart-breaking numbers. This is a tragic business for which I know no certain remedy, once it starts, save to transplant the unaffected seedlings to fresh and airy quarters as expeditiously as possible. "Powdered charcoal dusted over the surface is a useful preventive of the disease, but when it has actually made its appearance the best thing is to dust flowers of sulphur over the whole surface." [Macself.]

In watering seedlings, a long-nosed English can should be used and the finest possible rose spray. Never, by any chance, the rose of an ordinary garden can.

If, in spite of our care, the seedlings appear crowded, thinning should be done drastically, and done before trouble has had time to start. A tiny pair of tweezers, such as is used in extracting splinters, is a handy implement for this delicate operation. Later, the remaining seedlings, as they develop and require more room, may be removed to beds of prepared soil near the frames or pricked out in other frames. Seedlings may be transplanted directly from the frames to their permanent places in the rock garden, if they may there be given the same degree of care. Strawberry boxes and peach cartons are invaluable for protecting newly planted seedlings from the strength of the sun; these may be removed at sundown and replaced in the morning. On no account should inverted flower pots be used for this purpose, as, by excluding air, they engender a damp heat that frequently causes the young plant to faint and die.

As the spring advances and the sun's rays become more powerful, the light screens before mentioned may be used to protect the young plants from too great heat during their life in the frames as well as when they are moved to the beds outside.

"Raise seedlings of everything," said that great British gardener, F. W. Burbidge, "and hybrids, if you can." And this is sound advice.

For the beginning rock gardener wishing to make a start by raising a certain number of his plants from seed I should recommend the following:

Achillea serbica
   [*A. sibirica*]
Aethionema persicum
Alyssum saxatile
   citrinum [*Aurinia saxatilis 'citrinum'*]
Anchusa
   myosotidiflora
   [*Brunnera macrophylla*]
Anthemis montana
Aquilegia flabellata
   nana
Arabis alpina
Arabis aubrietioides
Arenaria montana
Armeria maritima
Asperula cyananchica
Aubrietia (any)

Campanula carpatica
Cheiranthus allionii
   [*Erysimum allionii*]
Dianthus arenarius
Dianthus deltoides
Dianthus caesius
Draba aizoides
Erysimum pulchellum
Gypsophila repens
Iberis sempervirens
Linaria alpina
Linum alpinum
Lychnis alpina
Papaver nudicaule
Primula vulgaris
Primula elatior
Primula japonica
Saponaria ocymoides
Silene schafta

Tunica saxifraga
Veronica incana

Viola cornuta, many
   varieties
Viola gracilis

Seed of biennial plants, save where they sow themselves with sufficient freedom, should be sown yearly, and also that of certain perennials which in our climate must be classed as short-lived. Important among these are the following:

Androsace
   coronopifolia
   [*A. lactifolia*]
Aquilegia, many kinds
Bellis rotundifolia
   caerulescens
   [*B. caerulescens*]
Bellium bellidioides
Calandrinia umbellata
   (rather tender)
Campanula americana
Campanula barbata
Campanula mirabilis
Campanula speciosa
   [*C. glamerata* var. speciosa*]
Campanula thyrsoides
Cheiranthus allionii
   [*Erysimum allionii*]
Cheiranthus alpinus
Dianthus
   monspessulanus
Dianthus superbus
Erinus alpinus
Linaria alpina
Linaria cymballaria

Lychnis alpina (the
   white form is the
   prettiest)
Mentzelia decapitata
Myosotis (many
   kinds)
Oenothera pumila
Oenothera
   taraxacifolia
Papaver alpinum
Papaver caucasicum
   [*P. fugax*]
Papaver nudicaule
Penstemon alpinus
Penstemon caeruleus
Primula cockburniana
   and its hybrids
Saxifraga cymbalaria
Saxifraga longifolia
Sedum pilosum
Sedum sempervivoides
Viola bosniaca
Viola cornuta (many
   kinds)
Viola Bowles' Black

CHAPTER XXII

Opportunity In a Shaded Rock Garden

To MANY MINDS, the idea of a shaded rock garden seems to present insurmountable difficulties. Continually one hears the plaint, "We have nothing but shade, so there is no use in trying to have a rock garden." And many, thereupon, do not try, or, if they do, too often confine their efforts to the sun-loving alpines which quite reasonably, under such conditions, sicken and die, leaving discouragement or passive resignation in their wake; and the shaded area is then, more than likely, planted to stolid rhododendrons or abandoned to rank weeds that know too well how to take advantage of its rich possibilities.

Now this seems quite too bad, for rich possibilities for a very lovely and special kind of rock garden do lie in shade. Of course, the ideal rock garden boasts many aspects, but ideal conditions are not always at our command, and, "Far from the shaded rock garden being a matter to bemoan," says an English writer, "it is an opportunity to be grasped."

It is unfortunate that a skeptical attitude of mind toward shade in the garden has been unintentionally fostered by the compilers of catalogues and the writers of garden books generally, particularly when dealing with rock and alpine plants. Continually the sun-loving alpine is extolled and presented while the plant that loves shadow is given scant publicity, if any, at all. As a matter of fact, there are a vast number of beautiful and desirable plants that will flourish in shaded places, many of which absolutely demand such situations if they are to live in health and display the full quality of their beauty.

For this reason, the work of making a successful rock garden in shade must begin in the *mind* of the builder. That storehouse of visions must be cleared of certain cherished pictures before a groundwork of success may be laid; pictures of sun-baked slopes studded with brilliant small pinks, heights misty with waving alpine poppies, cliffs veiled with the fragrant-leaved plants that drape the hot cliffs above the Mediterranean; all these and many more he must thrust out, and in their places put others of quite different character but in no wise inferior in beauty. Let him see, instead, green glades presided over by that mysterious beauty, the pink lady's slipper, little umbrageous dells radiant with primroses, mossy, meandering paths that lead past forests of waving ferns, or grassy slopes starred with constellations of Quaker ladies; little pools of English bluebells, slopes flecked all over with snowdrops among brown leaves, groups of the rarely lovely shortia enthroned beneath a dark hemlock, many kinds of orchids, trilliums, and so on.

A sense of mystery and of expectation may be contrived in a shadowed garden if it be of some extent, and none need fear a lack of variety or of beauty among the plants. But these must be, as I have before said, genuine shade lovers and not pathetic homesick creatures that will pine and sicken for the light of the sun full upon them; though it is true that shade is often the equivalent of root moisture which makes it possible sometimes for us to content a moisture-loving plant of the sun in a half-shaded situation.

There are, however, two kinds of shade to be considered: there is that cool and grateful shade cast by a large rock, or a wall, or a north aspect, or distant trees, where the soil is nearly always pleasantly moist but seldom acid, and a free circulation of air is assured; and then there is the shade cast by directly overhanging branches. It must be confessed that the first type is available for growing a greater variety of plants, for in such a situation will thrive many alpines that haunt the northern slopes of mountains and that, while revelling in the tempered light, are also dependent upon a free circulation of air and would perish where was the least suggestion of dankness.

Nevertheless, we in this country need not fear overhanging branches in the same degree as do British gardeners; the dread "drip" which for them is a matter for continual wailings and warnings is not so terrible a bogie to us. England's skies drip a good deal more than do ours, and mists and fogs roll in from all sides, so that a situation beneath trees is sure to be intolerably dank and humid. But in our dryer and more sunny climate trees often provide a gentle half light for which many a plant that in England must be grown in a fully exposed position is plainly grateful.

Did we, however, exclude from our tree-shaded garden all the plants that, while enjoying shadow, must yet have an abundance of light and air, we should still have the whole realm of beautiful woodland plants, both mountain and lowland, to draw upon; and of the richness of this source few can have any doubt who have made even a slight study of our native wild flowers; and we should have, as well, a great number of bulbous plants that find in a half light no detriment to their health and hardiness, many indeed, thriving and spreading more luxuriantly than they do in full sunshine.

In planning a rock garden in shade, it must be remembered that it is as important to arrange varying aspects and conditions as it is in the sunny garden. Bleak northern slopes and the more genial southern exposures will have their candidates; heights and hollows call for different types of inhabitants; beds of loam and leaf mould, dry stony places, dampish spots and bogs may be provided, and soils from sweet or limy to various degrees of acidity to meet the needs of a wide variety of possible tenants. And, of course, there must be varying degrees of shade; some plants are happy in the gloom beneath evergreen trees, but others among the shade-lovers enjoy the light of the sun for a few hours a day. It is well to endeavour to provide for the needs of all. Where trees stand too thickly, they may be thinned out until there is a clearing in which to build, and low overhanging branches should be cut off in order that air and light may penetrate freely.

The rock garden shaded by trees will undoubtedly have to be watered frequently in dry weather, for trees are thirsty folk and absorb all available moisture; they are hungry, too, and unless their fallen leaves be allowed to lie upon the ground and rot, thus keeping up a supply of nourishing food in the form of leaf mould, artificial feeding will have to be re-sorted to. In the case of plants that like a sweet, wholesome soil, a mixture of loam, leaf mould, and a little sand will do; the acid soil plants—and they are many for the shaded rock garden—will need to be fed with a mixture of rotted oak leaves, bits of rotted wood and bark, and pine or hemlock needles. The plants with a taste for acid soil should be assigned certain regions to themselves, some in fairly dense shade and others out in the light. Old chestnut stumps or rotted logs well placed add much to the picturesque appearance of their quarters, besides helping materially to keep up the acidity in the soil.

Paths may be mere woodland trails with ferns and violets and other low verdure crowding their verges; or stepping stones may be used with such little green creepers as *Arenaria balearica, A. caespitosa* [*Sagina subulata*], and *Mentha requienii* outlining the joints. Steps should be rugged and should appear as much a part of the construction as possible. In their crevices many small things may be grown.

A wide and beautiful use of bulbs constitutes one of the greatest opportunities of the shady garden. Tulips and most of the crocus species will want sunshine for at least half the day, but the great majority of others thrive exceedingly. Daffodils flourish and are most exquisite in the half light; scillas of all sorts will grow and spread in shade even beneath evergreen trees; snowdrops are much better in shade than in sun; the charming checker lily loves a dampish spot in light shade; the spring and summer snowflakes (*Leucojum vernum* and *L. aestivum*) delight in a light soil in partial shade; grape hyacinths, stars of Bethlehem, erythroniums may all be enjoyed to the fullest extent. And for the rest, here is a list of plants suited for the uses outlined in this chapter. They will delight the heart of any rock gardener. Plant them in little colonies of one kind, not as specimens, where there is space so to do.

For ordinary soil (loam, leaf mould, and sand)

Aconitum—*A. uncinatum* (climbing monkshood). Rich soil, shade, moisture. Flowers blue.

Actea—*A. alba* (baneberry). Flowers white, white china berries, 18 ins. Half shade.

Adonis—*A. amurensis* and *A. vernalis*. Light shade, flowers yellow.

Ajuga—*A. genevensis Brockbankii* (bugle). Sends out no runners. Fine spikes of blue flowers.

Allium (onion)—*A. moly.* Yellow flowers, 8 ins. *A. cernuum,* nodding lavender flowers, 12 ins. *A. stellatum,* rose flowers, 18 ins. *A. cyaneum,* sky-blue, 6 ins.

Anchusa—*A. myosotidiflora.* Light shade, sharp drainage, 18 ins., sky-blue flowers. Showy.

Androsace—*A. laggeri* [*A. carnea* var. *laggeri*]. Bright pink, 2 ins. Light shade, open situation. *A. lanuginosa, A. sarmentosa, A. carnea,* half shade, open situation.

Anemone—*A. blanda, A. apennina, A. nemorosa, A. robinsoniana, A. sylvestris,* and others. Light shade.

Aquilegia (columbine)—Many kinds may be grown in light soil in partial shade.

Arenaria—*A. balearica,* tiny green creeper with white flowers. *A. caespitosa,* a little green moss. *A. montana,* trailing plant with large white flowers. Light shade.

Asarum (wild ginger)—Plants with handsome leaves. *A. canadense, A. hartwegii* (leaves mottled with white). Damp soil in deep shade.

Asperula—*A. odorata* (sweet woodruff). Low-growing with white flowers and fragrant foliage. Open woods.

Caltha—*C. palustris* (marsh marigold). Golden flowers in spring. Bog.

Campanula (bellflower)—*C. divaricata, C. rotundifolia, C. Hostii* [var. of *C. rotundifolia*], *C. pulloides,* and numerous others. Light shade.

Cardamine—*C. pratensis* (lady's smock). Biennial with white or pink flowers. Damp places.

Claytonia—*C. virginica* (spring beauty). Pink flowers. Open moist woods.

Corydalis—*C. cheilanthifolia, C. nobilis,* and *C. lutea,* lovely species with fern-like leaves. *C. aurea* and *C. sempervirens* are native biennials that self-sow. Dry places.

Cyclamen—*C. coum* (tender), *C. europaeum* [*C. purpurascens*], *C. atkinsi, C. hederifolium.* A light loose wood-soil and a somewhat raised position.

Cypripedium—*C. parviflorum* [*C. calceolus* var. *parviflorum*] (yellow lady's slipper). Under deciduous trees.

Daphne—*D. cneorum.* Fragrant pink flowers. Half shade.

Dentaria—*D. diphylla, D. laciniata* [*Cardamine lacinata*]. Rich wood soil.

Dianthus—*D. alpinus, D. arenarius.* Open

shade, not under trees.

Dicentra—*D. canadensis* (squirrel corn), fragrant pinkish flowers, rich soil under trees. *D. cucullaria* (Dutchman's breeches), creamy flowers. Same situation. *D. eximia*, a taller plant, half shade.

Digitalis—*D. ambigua* [*D. grandiflora*] (yellow perennial foxglove). Light shade.

Dodecatheon—*D. meadia* (American shooting star). Rose-coloured flowers, cool, moist situation.

Doronicum—Several species, large yellow daisy-like flowers. Open situation.

Epimedium—Delightful plants with fine foliage that thrive under trees. Flowers, pink, rose, white, or yellow.

Eranthis—*E. hyemalis* (winter aconite). Very early spring. Yellow, 3 ins. Thrives under trees.

Erica—*E. carnea*—Light shade, open position.

Erinus—*E. alpinus*. Pretty little plant for open situation among stones. Well-drained soil. Pink or white. 4 ins.

Funkia—*F. minor* [*Hosta minor*]. Small daylily with fragrant white blossoms.

Gentiana—*G. verna*. Partial shade, cool rooting medium. Open.

Geranium—*G. ibericum*, *G. sanguineum*, *G. maculatum*, and others. Open places.

Haberlea—*H. rhodopensis*. Flowers, lavender-blue. Vertical fissures.

Helleborus—*H. niger* (Christmas rose). *H. orientalis* (Lenten rose). Rich soil under trees.

Hepatica—*H. triloba*. Under trees. *H. acutiloba*, same situation. They like sheltered banks.

Hypoxis—*H. hirsuta* (yellow-eyed grass). Open woods, very sandy soil. 6 in.

Incarvillea—*I. grandiflora* [*I. mairei* var. *grandiflora*]. Deep loamy soil with leaf mould, partial, shade. 10 in. Rose-purple flowers.

Ionopsidium—*I. acaule* (violet cress). Little annual that will self-sow freely in shaded places. Violet flowers.

Iris—*I. cristata* (crested iris). Open woods, dampish places. Blue, 5 in.

Iris—*I. gracilipes*. Partial shade, well-drained soil.

Iris—*I. lacustris*. Partial shade, dampish soil.

Iris—*I. prismatica*. Open woods, dampish places. 2 ft.

Jeffersonia—*J. diphylla* (twinleaf). Lovely little plant with white starry blossoms; damp shade, sandy leaf soil.

Lilium—Many species are suited for open places in the shaded rock garden.

Linaria—*L. alpina*. Brilliant little annual. Open places. Seed.

Linaria—*L. cymbalaria* (Kenilworth ivy). Small creeper with white or violet blossoms. Open shade.

Lithospermum—*L. prostratum* [*Lithodora diffusa*]. Brilliant blue flowers, trailing habit. Half shade, open; warm aspect, soil of peat and loam. Dislikes lime.

Lobelia—*L. cardinalis* (cardinal flower). Damp places. 18 in., scarlet flowers.

Lysimachia—*L. nummularia* (moneywort). Long trailing branches close to the ground, yellow flowers. Suited for covering waste places. Lovely but to be watched.

Mazus—*M. pumilio.* Small-leaved creeper with purple flowers. Suited for creeping about in dry places between the joints of stones.[1]

Mentha—*M. requienii.* Tiny creeping plant for damp places. Strongly mint-scented.

Mertensia—*M. virginica* (Virginia bluebells). Beautiful plant for damp position. 18 ins.

Mitella—*M. diphylla* (bishop's cap). Partial shade; spikes of white fringed flowers. 6 to 10 ins.

Myosotis (forget-me-not)—All kinds of forget-me-nots grow in shade.

Nierembergia—*N. rivularis* (cup flower). Open situation in gritty soil.

Omphalodes—*O. verna* (blue-eyed Mary). This and the white form grow well in damp soil and half shade.

Papaver (poppy)—*P. nudicaule* and *P. rupifragum* will grow well in shade not overhung by trees. High position, well-drained soil.

Phlox—*P. amoena, P. divaricata, P. subulata, P. ovata, P. stolonifera.* Light soil.

Podophyllum—*P. peltatum* (mayapple). Rich woods.

Polemonium—*P. reptans* (dwarf Jacob's ladder). Not too dense shade.

Polygonatum—*P. commutatum* (*giganteum*) [*P. biflorum*] (Solomon's seal). Handsome in clumps in dry shade.

Primula—*P. vulgaris, P. elatior, P. veris, P. japonica, P. pulverulenta, P. frondosa, P. luteola,* and many other species. They like lime.

Pulmonaria—*P. angustifolia* (lungwort). Brilliant blue flowers in early spring. Warm exposure. Good soil. There is a pink-flowered form and a white one, also the old Jerusalem cowslip or spotted dog, *P. saccharata.*

Ramondia—*R. pyrenaica* [*R. myconi*]. Beautiful plant forming handsome green rosette with violet flowers with yellow eye borne on stems 4 ins. high. Vertical position between stones, light, damp, peaty soil. North aspect.

Romanzoffia—*R. sitchensis.* Light, gritty soil, in light shade. 4 ins. high. May.

Sanguinaria—*S. canadensis* (bloodroot). Almost any position where the shade is not too dense.

Saxifraga—*S. umbrosa* (London pride) will grow under trees. The mossy species will all grow in partial shade. *S. fortunei,* partial shade, gritty soil. *S. granulata, S. ceratophylla* [*S. trifurcata*], *S. rotundifolia* all like good gritty soil in light open shade.

Sedum (stonecrop)— *S. acre, S. anglicum, S. nevii, S. pulchellum, S. telephioides, S. ternatum,* and others.

Silene—*S. virginica* (fire pink). Brilliant scarlet flowers. Poor soil, light shade.

Soldanella—*S. alpina.* Likes moisture in summer but dry feet in winter. Soil of peat, leaf mould, and a little sand. Partial shade but not beneath trees.

Spigelia—*S. marilandica* (pinkroot). Deep, moist, sandy peat.

Symphyandra—*S. hoffmanii.* Biennial growing 18 ins. tall with drooping white bells. Not too dense shade. Self-sows.

---

[1] *This plant is frequently sent as* Mazus rugosus; *the latter, however, is an annual from India.*

Syndesmon—*S. thalictroides* (rue anemone). Anywhere in shade. 3 ins.

Synthyris—*S. reniformis, S. rotundifolia* [*S. reniformis*]. Lovely spring-flowering plants with blue flowers. Light shade.

Tiarella—*T. cordifolia* (foamflower). Heads of starry white flowers, creeping habit. 6 ins. Divide occasionally. *T. unifoliata* sends out no runners. Taller and very handsome. Good woods soil.

Trientalis—*T. borealis* (star flower). Pretty little plant for cool, mossy situation.

Trillium—*T. grandiflorum, T. erectum, T. sessile, T. rivale* like rich, moist woodland conditions.

Uvularia (bellwort)—*U. grandiflora* and *U. perfoliata*. Yellow and cream respectively. Rich woodland soil.

Vagnera—*V. racemosa* (false Solomon's seal). Tall plant with creamy, plumelike flowers.

Vinca—*V. minor*. Both the blue and the white variety are lovely in waste places under trees.

Viola (violet)—*V. biflora, V. cornuta, V. blanda, V. lanceolata, V. striata, V. primuliaefolia, V. odorata*, and many more.

For acid soil (rotted oak leaves, pine or hemlock needles, bits of rooted wood or bark, white sand)

Andromeda—*A. polifolia* (bog rosemary). A little shrub liking an acid bog in not very dense shade. Lovely.

Anemone—*A. quinquefolia* (native windflower). Not very dense shade.

Azalea—Numerous species and varieties.

Chamaedaphne—*C. calyculata* (leatherleaf). Shrub growing 2 ft. tall with white blossoms along the stems in spring.

Chimaphila—*C. umbellata* (pipsissewa). Dry places under evergreens. Flowers white or pinkish. *C. maculata* (spotted wintergreen), dry woods.

Clintonia (bluebead)—*C. borealis*, very acid soil under evergreens. *C. umbellulata* (speckled clintonia), shade and rich woods soil.

Coptis—*C. trifolia* (goldthread). Pretty little plant for damp acid soil and shade.

Cornus—*C. canadensis* (bunchberry). Delightful little dogwood that thrives in cool damp places under trees.

Cypripedium—*C. acaule* (pink lady's slipper). Very acid soil under pine or hemlock trees. *C. montanum*, fine hardy California species with white flowers, slightly acid soil. *C. hirsutum* [*C. reginae*] (showy lady's slipper), swamps and wet mossy woods.

Dalibarda—*D. repens*. Lovely low-growing creeping plant for fairly deep shade. Flowers white in June.

Delphinium—*D. nudicaule* (scarlet larkspur). Dry places in open situation. Dies down after flowering.

Empetrum—*E. nigrum* (crowberry). Little low native shrub.

Epigaea—*E. repens* (trailing arbutus). Very acid soil in shade or half sun.

Epipactus—*E. pubescens* [*Goodyera pubescens*] (downy rattlesnake plantain). Handsome leaves in a flat rosette.

Gaultheria—*G. procumbens* (wintergreen). Under evergreens in dry woods.

Gaylussacia—*G. brachycera* (box huckleberry). Little shrub from wooded hillsides.

Galax—*G. aphylla.* Beautiful leaves and wands of white flowers. Very acid soil.

Habenaria—*H. ciliaris* (yellow fringed orchis). Wet places in not too dense shade. *H. blephariglottis* (white fringed orchis), boggy places, only light shade.

Helonias—*H. bullata* (swamp pink). For boggy places.

Houstonia—*H. caerulea* (Quaker lady, bluet). Lovely for little slopes in half shade. *H. serpyllifolia,* makes mats of tiny leaves. Very pretty.

Iris—*I. verna.* Brilliant little iris for half shade or sun.

Kalmia (laurel)—*K. angustifolia* (lambkill). Moist places. *K. microphylla* [*K. polifolia* var. *microphylla*], from high bogs of the Rocky Mountains. *K. glauca* (bog kalmia).

Leiophyllum (sand myrtle)—Dainty white-flowered shrubs for dry sandy places. *L. buxifolium* is taller than *L. prostratum* [a var. of *L. buxifolium*].

Lilium—*L. philadelphicum* (wood lily). Dry shade under deciduous trees.

Linnaea—*L. borealis americana* (American twinflower). Exquisite little creeping plant with pink flowers. Moist, mossy places.

Maianthemum—*M. canadense.* Shade of deciduous trees, dry or moist situations.

Mitchella—*M. repens* (partridgeberry). Tiny creeper with pink flowers followed by scarlet berries. Dry or moist woods.

Oxalis—*O. acetosella* (wood sorrel). Deep woods.

Polygala—*P. paucifolia* (gay wings). Charming little plant with pink blossoms for light soil in shade.

Potentilla—*P. tridentata* (evergreen cinquefoil). Exposed rocky or gravelly places. Very acid soil. Only a few inches tall.

Pyrola—*P. elliptica* (shinleaf), dry shade. *P. americana,* dry, sandy places in shade.

Shortia—*S. galacifolia* (oconee bells). Beautiful plant with shining leaves and white fringed blossoms. Very acid soil under evergreens.

Silene—*S. pennsylvanica* (peat pink). Brilliant-flowered little plant for dry rocky places in light shade.

Trillium (wakerobin)—*T. undulatum.* Very acid soil.

Vaccinium—*V. vitis-idaea* (cowberry). Little creeping shrub, 6 to 10 ins. tall. Pink flowers. Dry places.

Viola—*V. pedata* (bird's-foot violet). Sandy acid soil in light shade.

Ferns

Ferns play a most significant part in the spectacle of beauty unfolded week by week in the shaded rock garden. The earliest mildness stirs the eager young crosiers to action in sheltered places, and long before winter's grasp is relaxed they begin to uncoil and restlessly to push aside their brown leaf blanket. All through the summer and autumn their fresh beauty lasts unimpaired, and many remain cheerfully green throughout the dark days of winter. Thoreau wrote, "Nature made ferns for pure leaves, to see what she could do in that line." How successful was the experiment is evidenced by the innumerable forms of loveliness to be found among them.

Ferns are perennial and if happily situated extend the sphere of their green beauty luxuriantly from year to year. The greater number of them are lovers of cool shaded places where the soil is moist and of a moderate degree of acidity. Certain of them, however, demand a strongly acid soil, others are found on calcareous rocks, and a few crave the light of the sun. Nearly all ferns are easily established in the garden if attention be paid to their very modest requirements, and once settled in quarters that are congenial to them will need little attention thereafter. They may be moved with success at almost any season, though perhaps spring is the most satisfactory time, the main point to observe being that the roots shall not be exposed to the air and so become dry.

After planting, the ground about them should be kept continuously moist until they are established. A mulch of leaves or litter is a help in this respect. Ferns are a sure investment in pleasure, making of the shaded garden that is well furnished with them a cool retreat in the heat of summer days. Few plants can be naturalized with finer effect.

In a spacious rock or wild garden all sorts of ferns may find a place, from the little lowly ones to the tallest and most stately kinds. The following list contains with a few exceptions only the smaller species, those that may be included in a rock garden of moderate dimensions. In order to realize to the full their peculiar grace and charm these little ferns should be planted in colonies of five or seven of a kind, or more if space permits; and snowdrops and scillas, winter aconites and Christmas roses should be set among them. All of these are early risers and together create a little festival in the cold springtime at which we shall delight to be present.

Adiantum—*A. pedatum* (maidenhair fern). 12 to 18 ins. Moist situation under deciduous trees other than oaks.

Aspidium—*A. aculeatum braunii* [*Polystichum aculeatum*] (braun's holly fern). 12 to 15 ins. Moist, rich soil among rocks. Fronds yellow-green.

Aspidium—*A. cristatum* [*Dryopteris cristata*] (crested fern). 12 ins. Moist places.

Aspidium—*A. spinulosum* [*Dryopteris spinulosa*] (spinulose wood fern). 12 to 18 ins. Rocky banks in rich soil.

Asplenium—*A. ebenum* [*A. platyneuron*] (ebony spleenwort). 6 to 12 ins., very slender. Dry rocky places and a leaf-mouldy soil. Evergreen.

Asplenium—*A. trichomanes* (maidenhair spleenwort). 3 to 6 ins. A dainty and distinctive little fern forming a tuft of bright evergreen fronds. A shady situation in rocky clefts.

Camptosorus—*C. rhyzophyllus* [*Asplenium rhizophyllum*] (the walking leaf). Prostrate, evergreen. Deep shade in moist, rich loam.

Cheilanthes—*C. vestita* [*C. lanosa*] (hairy lipfern). 6 to 8 ins. Evergreen. The delicate fronds are soft gray-green. Acid soil among rocks.

Cryptogramma—*C. acrostichoides* (rock brake). 6 to 8 ins. A small evergreen fern from the Pacific coast. Forms nice little tufts in rocky places in slightly acid soil.

Cystopteris—*C. bulbifera* (bulbiferous bladder fern). 6 to 12 ins. Deep shade in moist leaf-mouldy soil.

Cystopteris—*C. fragilis* (the fragile bladder fern). 6 to 8 ins. Lovely bright green little fern with delicately cut fronds. Thrives in any shady well-drained soil.

Lygodium—*L. palmatum* (the climbing fern). One of the rarest of ferns. Give a moist hollow in very acid soil.

Osmunda—*O. regalis* (the royal fern). Perhaps the most beautiful of all ferns. Moist shade.

Pellaea—*P. densa* (Oregon cliff brake). 4 to 8 ins. Delightful little fern of the Western mountains. Raised situation in leaf soil and shade.

Pellaea—*P. atropurpurea* (cliff brake). 4 to 12 ins. Thick evergreen leaves, purplish-gray-green in colour. Woodsy soil among rocks.

Phedopteris—*P. polypodioides* (long beech fern). 6 to 8 ins. Spreads quickly in damp shaded places among rocks.

Phedopteris—*P. dryopteris* [*Gymnocarpium dryopteris*] (the oak fern). 6 to 8 ins. Lovely little fern for moist rocky places in shade.

Polypodium—*P. falcatum* (kellogg's polypody). 6 to 12 ins. Small fern from the Northwest growing well in leaf soil. Among rocks. Lime.

Polypodium—*P. vulgare* (common polypody). 4 to 8 ins. Evergreen fern for dry shaded places, often growing on rocks or old stumps or logs.

Woodsia—*W. ilvensis* (rusty woodsia). 4 to 8 ins. Quaint little fern growing in exposed places on cliffs or hilltops. Acid soil.

Woodsia—*W. obtusa* (obtuse woodsia). 6 to 12 ins. Shaded places among stones.

CHAPTER XXIII

Putting the Rock Garden to Bed

WHEN THE ROCK garden has been made quite safe and snug for the winter, one has rather the comfortable, relaxed feeling enjoyed when the children are tucked into bed at night and a quiet interval by the glowing lamp looms ahead. One draws a long breath. Very engaging have the small charges been withal, infinite in the variety of their moods and manifestations, but sometimes willful or exacting, occasionally downright unmanageable, and it is pleasant for a time to regard them in retrospect and to look forward to their gay and spontaneous awakening. Recalcitrance is forgotten, disappointment minimized, and only smiling faces and charming ways remembered. One rests happily, planning shining futures for the dears.

But here the analogy to the human nursery ends, for we cover our plant charges, not so much to keep them warm as to keep them cold; to shut out the prying rays of that old agitator, the sun, who, unless effectually hindered, would be poking the ribs of the small sleepers, nudging and whispering to them, causing their bed, the earth, to heave and expand and settle again, and otherwise disturbing their slumbers, so that when the proper time for awakening arrives, they lack the vigour and zest for life which is bought only with sound sleep.

A majority of the plants we grow in the rock garden are quite hardy; cold has no terrors for them in itself. What they find it hard to endure is the freezing and thawing and freezing again which is so much the rule of winter in our climate. Thus are the roots torn and mangled, crowns hoisted high and left flopping, little bulbs cast up and thrown aside as the earth answers to the will of the weather. Often, too, a mild "spell" in midwinter or very early spring will beguile some eager plant into growth, which is the height of indiscretion, for we may be sure that, if the south wind chances by with a caress, the north wind is hard on its heels with a frosty glower and snap that quickly put an end to young aspirations.

In the native homes of most of the plants we grow in the rock garden, a thick blanket of snow safeguards their rest almost from the fall of the leaf until it is safe for young buds and blades to be stirring again. But with us no such reliable provision is to be counted upon. We may have deep snow at times, but there are sure to be periods when the ground is bare and exposed to the caprices of the weather. And so we must use our wits to provide a serviceable substitute for this sunfast coverlet.

In the first place, we have to remember that winter damp and not winter cold is the enemy to be feared. It is a fact that we suffer more losses in a mild winter than in a cold one. To lie in a wet bed is death to many a plant that would withstand zero weather without flinching. And of course wet weather is to be expected; days, sometimes weeks, of corroding damp and mist, of beating rains. Under such conditions sensitive crowns rot, roots embedded in the mire become greatly debilitated if they do not succumb outright. After a mild, wet winter, it is made sadly plain to us whether or not we have so constructed our rock garden and mixed the soil as to provide sharp drainage.

A great many rock plants are evergreen, or evergray. The spring should find this special area well clothed in lovely verdure. Tufts of primrose, of pinks, of silenes, of armeria, mounds of aubrietia, of arabis, rosettes of androsace, of saxifrage, of lychnis, of lewisia, silver patches of anthemis, of achillea—all should appear, not worn and ragged, but quite fresh and pristine. And so they will if drainage sharp and sure be provided and sensible protection.

We do not cover the rock garden, as a rule, until after freezing weather, the intention being to keep the plants safely frozen in and passive until spring. But before this final act of the garden year is performed, the whole area should be put in apple-pie order, and each member of the community brought under a scrutinizing eye and given any attention that seems required. Even though the rock garden has been well looked after all summer, plenty will be found needing to be done. Always a few restless ones will have worked themselves free of the soil and have to be pressed back and tucked in; always there are weak or straggling branches to be cut off so that the plants will present a neat and thrifty appearance; always there are spent flower stalks or seed pods to remove, faded labels to replace, a few last determined weeds to tweak out, and small alterations to be made in the construction. The more scrupulous the care bestowed upon this last setting to rights of our little community, the fewer will be our losses over the winter and the more time shall we have to enjoy the surpassing beauties of the spring, as well as to meet the inevitable unexpected demands made upon our time by that exacting season.

To safeguard the drainage situation at this

late date we should go over the rock garden with a basket of stone chips making sure that all plants of suspected sensitiveness to damp have a wide collar of the chips drawn up closely about the neck so that the leaves and stems will not come in contact with the bare earth. Gray-leaved or woolly-leaved plants are always suspect; damp is anathema to them, and it is sad indeed when we lift the blanket in the spring to find, instead of the silver spread of achillea or androsace that had been our pride, a dreadful blackened mass. The mossy saxifrages should be looked after in this respect, too, and the alpine primulas, *Armeria caespitosa, Draba bruniaefolia;* the California lewisias, the small erodiums and geraniums, ramondia, wahlenbergias, the smaller pinks such as *Dianthus alpinus, D. neglectus, D. callizonus, D. freynii,* and *D. glacialis; Onosma tauricum, Campanula barbata, C. excisa, C. lanata, Alyssum pyrenaicum,* and many more. If chips are not at hand or easily procurable, flat stones drawn up closely about the crown of the plants will serve. Where possible, it is a wise and comfortable provision to top-dress the whole rock garden with stone chips mixed with a little leaf soil. One never knows where weak constitutions will develop or when we are in for an especially mild and wet winter.

In the milder climate of England, where there is less snow and a good deal more rain than afflicts us here, plants of known sensitiveness to damp are covered during the winter with glass. This precautionary measure, while not so generally necessary with us, may be resorted to in the case of any plants that have shown themselves especially unable to survive winter damp. To keep these dry, sheets of glass may be supported on four stones or, where the plant to be protected is growing against a rock, simply rested against this so that a tentlike shelter is formed.

In our climate, where we cannot depend upon a blanket of snow the winter through, I believe the most effective protection for rock plants is furnished by salt hay. This material, which can be bought by the bale in most neighbourhoods, is so light and fluffy in texture that it does not get sodden and settle down heavily upon the plants, preventing a free circulation of air and causing them to rot as do ordinary hay, straw, or soft leaves. It is much more easily applied and removed, also, than are leaves, which are blown hither and yon by the wind and must often be literally hand picked from among the little plants and bushlings. If leaves must be used, however, those of the oak are far preferable to elm or maple leaves. Oak leaves are hard and crisp and remain so over the winter, so do not make too close a covering. In any case where leaves are used, it is a good plan to strew little twigs and branches over the rock garden before the blanket is applied in order that it shall not rest too smotheringly upon the plants.

Manure should never be used. It makes far too stuffy and hot a blanket for our hardy little mountaineers; and an airless sleeping chamber with rich food upon arising is quite as bad for them as it is for the rest of us.

I sometimes think when going over the rock garden for the last time that at no other season is its peculiar charm so plainly manifest. Few I think would be blind to the beauty of the closely woven fabric that is wound among and about the gray rocks. Here, seemingly, are every tint and tone possible to green, to gray, or to red, and every leaf form that is lovely. Now, without the sparkling blossoms to beguile all our attention, there is opportunity to note the exquisite economy of the little tight rosettes and tufts, some overlaid with silver, others with frosted edges, some bronze-coloured, some emerald-green; to enjoy the fragrance and the texture of the velvet meadows of thyme, the hoary forests of sun rose, the lacelike pattern cut in silver of the seedlings of the caucasian poppy, *Papaver caucasicum* [*P. fugax*], the rich gloss on the leaves of some of the alpine primulas; to delight in the enchanting way of trailing plants with rocks, in the deft manner in which tufts have established themselves in unlikely clefts and spread out exuberantly over the rock face, in the steel-blue colour of some of the little aethionema bushes and the beaded mounds of *Sedum dasyphyllum*. Most of the crane's-bills assume rich tones in the autumn, as do the small coton-

easters, barberries, and huckleberries, and many of them are strung with brilliant fruit. Always, too, there is the sparkle of a few blossoms that have no mind to be put to bed. The Spanish poppy blooms defiantly to the last, all sorts of violets make their modest protests; one can always find a nosegay of primroses, a golden star amid the green tangle that is *Hypericum reptans*, a few lovely verbena-like blooms of *Androsace lanuginosa*, plenty of white strawberry blossoms among the dusty leaves of *Potentilla alba*.

Probably, too, in this last scrutiny one finds that some rare plant has seeded itself and is raising up a family of promising youngsters. This is always matter for great gratification, for it is a sure sign that the plant has made itself at home. One lingers, not in any great haste to close the door upon the scene of so much that has been pleasant and companionable for so many months. But after the first conclusive freeze the blanket should be laid on without delay. If oak leaves are used, they should be held in place with light brush, or failing these, the long stalks of plants cut down in the herbaceous borders, their seed heads removed, will do.

Blue Flowers for the Rock Garden

THERE SEEMS little doubt that blue is the favourite flower colour among gardeners and flower lovers generally. Few can resist the appeal of a blue blossom, however simple and common it may be. The modest cornflower has held its own without improvement or advertisement among far more resplendent flowers since long before the day of that great gardener of the Seventeenth Century, John Parkinson, who included it among the "chiefest choyce of nature's beauties and delights." We feel almost as warmly toward it, though its form is not of great beauty, nor does fragrance add to its charm. In its gentle blue colour lies the secret of its perennial popularity.

Those who walk in the woods in spring gather with especial enjoyment the bluest of the hepaticas. We strive for a "true blue" iris and welcome the "blue" primroses as gifts from Heaven. Among herbaceous plants the delphinium holds the eye of the gardening world with its azure aspirations, and blue borders and whole blue gardens have sprung up around the accent points of its slim cerulean spires.

And so it is among the eminences and royalties of the rock garden—those dyed with this gentle hue seem to lay an especial claim upon our affections; and never do the hills and valleys appear so radiant as when blue flowers predominate in their furnishings. Moreover, some of the rarest and most coveted alpines wear the celestial hue, among them the gentians, the finest of which are blue—a blue of such extraordinary strength that the beholder marvels that things so inconsiderable should burn with such fierce intensity.

In the following notes, however, my desire is not by any means to inspire the creation of blue rock gardens. Rock gardens devoted to plants of a single colour would be absurd and without point or interest. My aim is simply to give to those who care for blue flowers especially a choice among the best of them.

First, of course, come the blue-flowered bulbs of spring—scilla, hyacinths, chionodoxa, and muscari. Of these the earliest to bloom, following close upon the cold little snowdrops and often mingling with them, are *Scilla bifolia, S. sibirica, Hyacinthus azureus* [*Muscari azureum*], *Chionodoxa sardensis,* and *C. luciliae.* Then come the grape hyacinths (muscari) with their beaded blue spikes. Muscari 'Heavenly Blue' is a bit too rampageous for small rock gardens, and its autumn growth too untidy to be tolerated, but it should always be near by where its superb colour will count in the general effect of the rock garden and its delicious fragrance regale us as we prowl about. The English bluebell, *S. festalis* (*nutans*) [*Hyacinthoides non-scripta*], with its bell-hung shepherd's crook, and *S. campanulata* (*hispanica*) [*Hyacinthoides hispanica*], the Spanish bluebell, bloom in May. They are not so richly endowed with blue pigment as are the bulbs of the earlier year, but are delightful none the less.

Latest of the scillas to bloom is *S. italica* [*Hyacinthoides italien*]. *Hyacinthus amethystinus* also blooms late, a charming little plant and yet little grown; it has slender arched stems hung with small sapphire bells. A closely planted colony of them makes a fine patch of blue colour at a season when we have almost given up looking for beauty from the smaller bulbs. All these bulbs will grow cheerfully and increase in the soil of the rock garden either in sun or partial shade; the scillas, indeed, will stand quite heavy shade. They all appear at their best when planted in close colonies rather than scattered about.

Before the blue-flowered bulbs have retired from the scene, herbaceous plants in the same delightful livery begin to make themselves felt. Happily, there are many of these, for blue is an ardent peace-maker and enables many a fiery little mountaineer to live on amicable terms with his no less belligerent neighbour. It is here possible to speak only of the most outstanding beauties, but at the end of this chapter is a more comprehensive list of blue flowers. The intention has been to keep fairly strictly to varieties that might justly be characterized as true blue, avoiding the pure lavenders and purples or violet-blues. But the borderland is misty, and exactness in this matter of no especial benefit.

The most prolific contributor to our azure delight is the borage tribe. From this great stock we derive plants whose flowers are of the purest and most exquisite blue—omphalodes (navelwort), cynoglossum (hound's tongue), borago, anchusa, pulmonaria (lungwort), myosotis (forget-me-not), mertensia (American lungwort), and lithospermum (gromwell).

Of the navelworts we have three species designed to warm the heart of any rock gardener. *Omphalodes verna,* known affectionately as blue-eyed Mary, is the most amiable of the family. It has rambling propensities and loves to spread about among stones in a partially shaded place where the sprays of blue stars shine with incredible brilliance. *O. cappadocica* grows in a neat little tuft and sends aloft in early summer and onward for several weeks airy sprays of blue flowers like large forget-me-nots. *O. luciliae* is a bit of a miff. It loves lime and a crevice and sometimes then will take itself off for no accountable reason, but when it tarries there is reward enough for any trouble expended upon keeping it.

Cynoglossum amabile is perhaps a bit large for the rock garden, though it is in the spirit of things grown there. *C. nervosum* is reported, however, as growing but a foot tall with hairy stems and leaves and a great shower of large intensely blue flowers. *Borago laxiflora* [*B. pygmaea*] is a bit coarse and sprawling and has not with me proved of iron hardiness. But some in milder climates will care to grow it for the sake of those constellations of blue stars that terminate the lax branches.

Of the anchusas, *A. myosotidiflora* is the only one suitable for the rock garden. It grows eighteen inches tall and bears in early spring great sprays of forget-me-not-like blossoms that continue for more than a month. In the summer, the leaves grow large and lush and must often be cut off to save the life of some more fragile plant. This lovely alkanet self-sows with enthusiasm once it is happily established and for all its good qualities may easily become a menace in a small rock garden.

Earlier still, often by the first of April, flowers the lungwort, *Pulmonaria angustifolia* (*azurea*), with pink buds and large, round, clear blue blossoms. This plant loves a sunshade but seems not to mind whether the ground in which it grows be dry or moist; and it increases so rapidly as to invite frequent division, thus providing easily for wider and wider stretches of its heavenly colour. It is one of the best of spring-flowering plants for border or rock garden, yet it seems little known or grown.

Mertensia virginica, with its pendent turquoise blossoms and bright pink buds, is a native plant enjoyed in most gardens. It is somewhat large where the rockwork is of no great extent, and it is gratifying to find that there are dwarf-growing mertensias that repeat the grace and the especially ravishing colour of this beautiful plant. *M. lanceolata* from the plains and open hills of Colorado and Wyoming is a delightful small thing. *M. echioides* and *M. primuloides* are enchanting exotics from the high Himalayas that, like all mertensias, may easily be raised from seed.

Owing to the machinations of the Plant Quarantine, one of the most splendid of blue-flowering plants, *Lithospermum prostratum,* is now so scarce among us as hardly to be found at all. Let us hope that anyone so lucky as to possess this plant will endeavour to work up a stock of it in order that it may once more illumine the declivities of our rock gardens.

From the West come two plants of inestimable worth that thus far are little known. These are *Synthyris rotundifolia* [*S. reniformis*] and *S. reniformis*. They are charming tufted things blooming very early in the year, with rounded, leathery leaves and spikes of fluffy blue blossoms, pale and deep blue respectively. They like fairly cool conditions and a soil rich in leaf mould. Otherwise they are no trouble.

American, too, are the polemoniums (Jacob's ladder) with their pale bells and golden stamens. *P. reptans* is wild in woodsy places of New York and other Eastern states, and there are numerous fine species to be had out of the West. Of these *P. confertum* [*P. viscosum*] is probably the choicest jewel, but not one to be treated lightly. It has proved with me a difficult subject, though it is as easy to raise from seed as any pink. Hope is not yet abandoned, however. Continued experiment will some day find a way to make it happy. Quaker ladies or bluets (houstonia) must ever be found where blue flowers are beloved, and what others are more dainty and engaging. But do not be satisfied to know the familiar little *H. caerulea* alone. Make the acquaintance as well of *H. serpyllifolia* whose creeping stems and tiny leaves reach over the ground to form a close green mat from which spring the larger flowers of a deeper blue on threadlike stems. These plants love a slightly moist situation, and if the soil be a bit sourish, so much the better.

Among American plants, however, the cerulean possibilities of the penstemon family make the lover of blue flowers fairly dizzy. It is a vast race rising to heights of inspired beauty but descending to depths of no-account weediness as well. The best of them live in the West—in the mountains, foothills, and plains of Colorado, Utah, Wyoming, Idaho, Montana, Arizona. Thus far they are little seen in gardens save those of collectors or specialists;

few are listed by the trade, and their nomenclature is in confusion. Nevertheless, they are dawning upon the horizon of the gardening world. Seeds of them are to be had in one way and another, and plants of several kinds. *Penstemon alpinus* and *P. coeruleus* (*angustifolius*) are of quite transcendent beauty. It is a pity that any gardener should not know them. Penstemons are for the most part summer blooming and require a light, perfectly drained soil in full sunshine.

The veronicas, too, belong to the long blue days of summer—a vast host of them, mostly prostrate, with spikes of small blossoms ranging over all the scale of blue. And campanulas bring many blue flowers to the summer garden. The quality of their colour is cool—always with a suggestion of gray—but the range is wide, from pale to a fairly strong lavender-blue that is very satisfying in the heat of summer suns.

From the flaxes (linum) we derive the deep pure blue of summer skies. *L. alpinum* is the best for the rock garden, as its stature is low, but all are charming where there is sufficient space. They self-sow with freedom, and though they are short-lived in some gardens, keep themselves going by this means.

Forget-me-nots are multitudinous in any garden once they are established, for they are all joyous self-sowers and, if not rooted out by over orderly souls, establish themselves along path edges, under and around the little shrubs, and in all sorts of places. A word concerning the different kinds may be of interest. *Myosotis alpestris* is an alpine of tight tufted habit with a huge head of blossoms down close to the tuft. It has given rise to many fine varieties much used for bedding. If these plants are to be left outside over the winter they require to be given rather high and well-drained situations. *M. dissitiflora* is also an alpine and the earliest to flower. It is a charming kind, low and tufty with a delightful spraylike flowering. *M. sylvatica*, the wood forget-me-not, once planted, will always be a present delight along the shaded ways of the rock garden or in the adjoining wood or shrubberies. It is taller and looser in habit than those before spoken of. *M. palustris* is the water forget-me-not, delightful to plant between stones along the pool or stream where it soon makes fine masses; its variety *semperflorens* is ever-blooming, low and prostrate, a lovely plant for shaded places and a reliable perennial. *M. azorica*, whose dark rich blue blossoms appear later in the year, should be planted by gardeners whose climatic conditions are less severe than those that obtain in the neighbourhood of New York City. It is a little tender, but quite lovely.

The latest blue flower to light the garden—and this takes us almost to November—is *Ceratostigma plumbaginoides,* formerly known, only slightly less tongue-twistingly, as *Plumbago Larpentae*. It is a gorgeous plant and in full sunshine spreads most satisfactorily. Its display makes a fitting end to our pageant of blue flowers.

A list of blue-flowered plants for the rock garden (Those marked * are suitable for use in small gardens.)

Ajuga genevensis brockbanki
     "   metallica crispa
*Allium cyaneum
Anagallis caerulea [*A. arvensis* var. *caerulea*] (annual)
Anchusa myosotidiflora [*Brunnera macrophylla*]
*Anemone apennina
*   "   blanda
*   "   nemorosa robinsoniana
*Aquilegia caerulea
*Asperula azurea setosa [*A. orientalis*] (annual)
*Bellis rotundifolia caerulescens
     [*B. caerulescens*]
Borago laxiflora [*B. pygmaea*]
*Brodiaea laxa [*Triteleia laxa*] (California bulb)
*Campanula barbata
*   "   caespitosa
     "   carpatica
*   "   cenisia
*   "   garganica
*   "   pusilla [*C. cochleariifolia*]
*   "   raddeana
*   "   rainerii
*   "   rotundifolia
*   "   tommasiniana
*Catananche caerulea
Ceratostigma plumbaginoides
*Chionodoxa gigantea (bulb)
*   "   luciliae (bulb)
*   "   sardensis (bulb)
Collinsia grandiflora (annual)

*Crocus speciosus (bulb)

Cynoglossum nervosum

Delphinium azureum [*D. carolinianum*]

       "   bicolor

       "   brunonianum

       "   carolinianum

       "   caucasicum [*D. speciosum*]

       "   coelestinum [*D. formosum*]

       "   caeruleum

       "   grandiflorum

*Eritrichium nanum

Eryngium bourghati

       "   glaciale

*Gentiana acaulis

  *   "   affinis

       "   andrewsi

       "   asclepiadea

       "   crinita

  *   "   Farreri

  *   "   Freyniana [variety of *G. septemfida*]

  *   "   lagodechiana

  *   "   linearis

       "   pneumonanthe

       "   saponaria

  *   "   septemfida

  *   "   verna

Geranium grandiflorum

*Globularia bellidifolia

  *   "   incanescens

  *   "   nana

  *   "   nudicaulis [*G. vulgaris*]

  *   "   trichosantha

*Houstonia caerulea

  *   "   serpyllifolia

*Hyacinthus amethystinus

  *   "   azureus [*Muscari azureum*]

*Iris cristata

    "   foliosa

    "   lacustris

    "   pumila caerulea

    "   verna

*Jasione humilis

*   "   perennis [*J. laevis*]

*Linum alpinum [*L. perenne* ssp. *alpinum*]

    "   perenne

*   "   hirsutum

*Lithospermum prostratum [*Lithodora diffusa*]

Lobelia siphilitica

Mertensia ciliata (siberica)

*   "   echioides

*   "   elongata

*   "   lanceolata

*   "   papillosa

*   "   primuloides

    "   virginica

*Muscari botryoides (bulb)

    "   'Heavenly Blue' (bulb)

    "   heldreichi [*botryoides* var. *heldreichii*]

    (bulb)

*Myosotis alpestris

    "   azorica

    "   dissitiflora

*   "   palustris semperflorens

*   "   rehsteineri

    "   sylvatica

*   "   welwitschi (annual)

Nemesia dwarf blue gem (annual)

*Nemophila insignis (annual)

*Omphalodes cappadocica

*   "   luciliae

*   "   verna

Orobus cyaneus [*Lathyrus cyaneus*]

Oxytropis Richardsoni (splendens)
*Penstemon alpinus
        "   brandegeei
✻   "   caeruleus (angustifolius)
        "   cyananthus
✻   "   glaber
        "   heterophyllus
        "   secundiflorus
Phacelia campanularia (annual)
*Phyteuma scheuchzeri
Polemonium caeruleum
✻   "   confertum [*P. viscosum*]
        "   grandiflorum
        "   lanatum
        "   lemmonei
        "   pulcherrimum
✻   "   reptans
*Primula vulgaris caerulea and
   P. muscarioides
*Pulmonaria azurea (angustifolia)
*Puschkinia libanotica [*P. scilloides* var.
   libanotica] (bulb)
*Scilla bifolia (bulb)
        "   campanulata [*Hyacinthoides hispanica*]

        (bulb)
        "   festalis [*Hyacinthoides non-scripta*]
        (bulb)
        "   italica [*Hyacinthoides italien*] (bulb)
✻   "   sibirica (bulb)
*Sedum caeruleum (annual)
Sisyrinchium angustifolium
*Synthyris renformis
✻   "   rotundifolia [*S. reniformis*]
*Veronica allionii
        "   austriaca (prenja)
✻   "   caespitosa
✻   "   canescens
        "   incana
✻   "   pectinata
        "   prostrata
✻   "   repens
✻   "   rupestris
        "   satureioides
✻   "   saxatilis [*V. fruticans*]
✻   "   teucrium dubia [*V.*
   austriacateucrium]
✻   "   thymifolia

CHAPTER XXV

Yellow Flowers for the Rock Garden

Nature is lavish with yellow pigment when she deals with flowers, but it cannot be said she often employs it in colouring her choicest treasures. For these she dabbles in azure, in high scarlet, in violet, and the greater number she leaves with no colour at all save a brush of golden stamens or delicate lines or flushes of colour. But yellow and magenta she spills abroad in full-handed and unthrifty mood.

For use in the rock garden, yellow flowers are many and of great diversity, and one thing may be almost universally said in their favour: the greater number of them are easy to grow. When one hears of a dwarf yellow-flowered plant, unless it be some stand-offish primrose, or such as the illusive golden drop (*Onosma tauricum*) it is, in nine cases out of ten, safe to say, "Ah, here is a kindly soul who will bring light to my hill country and give me no trouble at all." Of course, it may happen to be one of those weedy and all too willing sisters that abound (along with the most eminent worthies) in the great yellow-flowered races—the euphorbias, the drabas, the potentillas, the oenotheras, the sedums, and others—in which case they may give a great deal of trouble with their wild seeding, their pushing ways, and stalwart floppings. Undoubtedly, we must choose our yellow flowers with care, but having thus chosen we shall have acquired some of the brightest and most indispensable of rock garden ornaments. It is a happy fact that most yellow flowers love to grow in full sunshine, for it is in its glow that they appear to best advantage.

Yellow is a favourite, perhaps one might say *the* favourite colour of the spring. White flowers are very much in evidence at that season, as at all others, but for colour the aureate hues have it, from primrose and cream and citrine on to fuller and deeper tones, all in delightful accord with the tender yellow-green of the leafage just coming into being and gleaming like fine gold ornaments in the shy vernal sunshine.

One of the first of them is the winter aconite (*Eranthis hyemalis*) that comes up from a little tuber and, when planted generously in shaded places, makes a pleasant glow against Spring's brown breast. With incredible speed then is thrust up the stout stalk of the adonis flower, *Adonis amurensis,* holding a foot in air its great suns of green-gold light. Nothing is so exciting at this time of year as this plant which is so little seen. Its relative, *A. vernalis,* which blooms nearly a month later, is desirable as well, but lacks the spectacular suddenness and brilliance of the earlier flowering species. And while we are admiring the great adonis come the splashes of hot colour made by the cloth of gold crocus, *C. susianus* [*C. augustifolius*], one of the hardiest and most indestructible of its kind. There are other yellow crocuses, but these with the little daffodils have had a chapter to themselves and so no more of them now. Several yellow-flowered wild tulips are very gay in the spring, among them the wild British tulip, *T. silvestris, T. persica, T. australis, T. batalinii,* the primrose form of *kaufmanniana,* and *T. kolpakowskiana,* that sometimes has a reddish flush.

One of the earliest herbaceous plants to bloom is *Corydalis cheilanthifolia.* Its broad tuft of beautiful fernlike leaves would adorn any garden, even lacking the sheaf of stiff little spikes close set with yellow flowers. It comes with the daffodils but is best not set near them because of its greenish cast. It is a fine subject for walls, whether in the crevices or at the top, and thrives in the shade seeding itself about but never becoming a nuisance. *C. lutea* is a filmy mass of delicate foliage and slender stems out of which spring loose clusters of yellow flowers all through the season until fall. It is not at all a plant for borders, but finds itself at home in crevices of walls or steps, which it veils in a charming manner. If it is not hardy in your neighbourhood be not discouraged, for it will reappear year after year from its own sowing.

The drabas, although many of them are true alpines, would seldom, I think, be called choice. They belong to a vast race among which flourish many undoubted weeds; but search among them will reveal a number of not very striking but good and amiable little rock plants. *Draba aizoides* blooms in April, its tiny hillocks of spiky bright green rosettes stuck over with threadlike stems carrying heads of bright yellow flowers, the whole very small and neat. Other worthy kinds are *D. aizoon* [*D. lasiocarpa*], somewhat like, but fatter and slightly taller than the last; *D. olympica* [*D. brunifolia olympica*], and its variety or close kin *brunifolia,* spread out into little green mats pricked over with yellow flowers on short stems; *D. repens* "from grassy slopes of the Caucasus" is rather a weed but an ingratiating one. All these are so small as to require a ledge or a little slope to themselves lest they be entirely outshone and overcome by their bolder neighbours. They all love lime and sunshine and dry feet.

Lovely and more showy are the alyssums, and they are early-flowering, too. That generous friend, the old basket of gold (*Alyssum saxatile compactum* [*Aurinia saxatilis 'Compacta'*]), is seen in most gardens, but its pale sister, citrinum, so much more lovely in its delicate Naples yellow colouring, is seldom seen. It cannot be said that this superior plant is so perfectly steady-going and reliable as the older form, but it is easily to be had from seeds, and it is well worth the high and dry position in full sunshine that seems most likely to insure its permanence. A fascinating trio of smaller alyssums are *A. alpestre, A. serpyllifolium, A. montanum*. These are no more than three or four inches high and must be given very well-drained positions in sandy soil where the sun shines continuously. These, too, may be easily had from seed, but thereafter the dryness of their feet must be a constant care.

The hypericums boast some real aristocrats for the rock garden. Nor are they generally difficult to grow in sunny, rocky places in well-drained soil, though I have known one and another of them go off in the pride of its luxuriance for no accountable reason. They are especially sensitive to the searing winds of early spring and should be kept covered with wisps of salt hay for some time after the heavier blanket has been removed. They are late spring and summer blooming, and a number of them continue on into the fall. The blossoms are gorgeous shining suns, large for the size of the plants. *H. coris* is an appealing gray-blue bushling perhaps six inches tall, the foliage heathlike, with corymbs of pale gold blossoms. *H. reptans* is a prostrate desirability from the Himalayas that veils the rocks about it in a dense mat of bright green shoots clothed in small evergreen leaves, upon which sit the great aureate blossoms. *H. olympicum* has shrubby stems and small glaucus evergreen leaves and the characteristic large golden blossoms borne over a long season.

When we come to the euphorbias, we are very close to the doubtful company of weeds; yet *E. myrsinites*, with its fleshy gray branches and green-gold flower heads, spreading over a rock is really effective and its crop of self-sown seedlings is always carried away gladly by visitors. *E. epithymoides* and *E. polychroma* [*E. epithymoides*], though often offered as individuals, seem to me one and the same thing. They—or it—are nice for a high, roomy situation in the rock garden or a front place in dry, sunny borders. The little cypress spurge, *E. cyparissias* is definitely on the weed list, I am afraid, yet I dare say most of us are winking at the presence of this small vandal in some out-of-the-way corner of our gardens.

Erysimum gives us several easily grown and delightful rock plants, two of which should be mentioned here. The little hedge mustard, *E. pulchellum* (*rupestre*) is such a pretty and fragrant and easy thing that it finds a place in most rock gardens. It is a cousin of the wallflowers and resembles them, with its heads of soft-yellow flowers and pleasant scent. With me it is not long-lived, and may be a biennial, but it self-sows and is always on hand. A very lovely and much more rare species is *E. pumilum,* found in high places in the European Alps. After the true manner of alpines, stems a few inches tall spring from a small rosette carrying heads of yellow blossoms so large as to be out of all proportion to the size of the plant. It must be given a high place, dry and well drained, or it will grow out of its tufted neatness and so lose much of its charm.

In potentilla we find innumerable yellow-flowered plants, many of them the commonest weeds, but out of the vast aggregation emerge a few veritable treasures. A conservative choice among them would be: *P. nevadensis,* a dweller in our high Sierra Nevada, where it forms neat tufts of gray-green leaves emitting short stems carrying large blossoms of a full fine yellow; *P. calabra,* which Mr. Farrer calls a "dullness of little value," but which I enjoy for the sake of its ample tuft of silver leaves; *P. verna* is well worth while, and its diminutive form, *nana,* is a real treasure. This type makes flat mats of charming leaves with many yellow blossoms. A few yellow-flowered potentillas are enough for any rock garden, as they do not offer great variety. There are some good white-flowered forms, and the pink *P. nitida* is a real sensation. Most of the race offer little difficulty in the way of cultivation. They are usually satisfied with sunshine and a well-drained situation.

Cheiranthus allioni [*Erysimum allionii*] is one of the most splendid of yellow-flowered plants and should be grown in quantity, though it is only a biennial. Its colour approaches orange, indescribably rich and glowing, and it is very striking used among the early-flowering tulips, forget-me-nots, and their contemporaries. Seed of it may be started any time in the late spring and the plants will be ready to be put in their appointed places by September. If allowed to go to seed there will be plenty of young hopefuls to gather up and distribute where they are needed. This fine member of the wallflower family blooms nearly all summer if kept from seeding. It has a pleasant fragrance.

The little European buttercup, *Ranunculus montanus,* is a fine tufted plant with golden yellow blossoms borne generously in the late spring. From inula and oenothera and sedum we derive numerous plants for the rock garden that flower in the summer and autumn. A selection will be found in the following list:

Rock plants with yellow flowers
(Those marked * are suitable for small rock gardens)

Achillea—*A. tomentosa.* Like a dwarf, neat field yarrow. Light soil, sun.

Adonis—*A. amurensis.* Gorgeous suns opening in March. *A. vernalis.* Later to flower. Give a warm exposure and lime.

Allium—A. moly. Quick-spreading little Spanish onion for light shade.

Alyssum—A. alpestre. Three inches tall, gay, compact, and hoary of leaf. *A. montanum.* An elfin plant with flowers smelling like wallflowers. *A. serpyllifolium.* A quaint gray midget for a high and dry spot. *A. saxatile compactum.* A plant for everybody. *A. saxatile citrinum* [*Aurinia saxatilis 'citrinum'*]. Infinitely more lovely as to colour.

Anemone—**A. ranunculoides*. A modest windflower for a shaded corner.

Anthemis—*A. montana*. Gray lace leaves and creamy daisies. Sun.

Anthemis—*A. cupaniana*. Much the same.

Aquilegia—*A. chrysantha*. A lovely plant for a large rock garden.

Arnica—*A. montana*. A mat of flat leaves, orange flowers on foot-high stems.

Artemisia—Numerous kinds with soft gray foliage.

Calochortus—**C. Benthami* [*C. monophyllus*]. Try these lovely California bulbs. Sun and sand. **C. citrinum* [*C. weedii*].

Cheiranthus—**C. allioni* [*Erysimum allionii*]. A foot-tall biennial of great beauty. *C. (Erysimum) ochroleucum*. Of less worth but good. Biennial.

Chrysogonum—**C. virginianum*. A modest native with gay flowers borne in July.

Coronilla—*C. iberica* [*C. orientalis*]. A lovely prostrate plant with gray foliage. Summer.

Corydalis—**C. cheilanthifolia*. From western China. *C. lutea*. For old walls and crevices in shade. Invaluable.

*Crocus—*C. aureus* [*C. flavus*], *C. chrysanthus*, *C. korolkowii*, *C. olivieri*, *C. susianus* [*C. augustifolius*].

Cypripedium—**C. parviflorum* [*C. calceolus* var. *parviflorum*]. Most easily grown of its race. Shade.

Cytisus—**C. ardoinii*. Lovely little broom of creeping habit. Five inches. *C. hirsutus*. A foot tall. All the brooms are easy from seed.

Dianthus—**D. knappii*. Compact heads of clear yellow flowers.

Digitalis—*D. ambigua* [*D. grandiflora*]. A fine yellow-flowered perennial foxglove.

Draba—**D. aizoides*. A nice little plant for a sunny spot.

Doronicum—*D. caucasicum* [*D. orientale*]. A fine upstanding plant blooming early in spring.

Dryas—*D. drummondii*. A prostrate plant with golden nodding flowers.

Epimedium—*E. pinnatum*. Most lovely with forget-me-nots.

Eranthis—**E. hyemalis*. The little winter aconite of the spring garden.

Erysimum—*E. pulchellum*. For any sunny spot where the soil is drained. **E. pumilum*. Rarer and more lovely.

*Erythronium—*E. grandiflorum, E. giganteum*, and *E. hendersonii*, all fine.

Euphorbia *ephithymoides*. Showy and handsome where there is room for it. *E. polychroma* [*E. epithymoides*]. Much the same. Chrome-yellow flowers; 2 ft.

*Genista—*G. dalmatica* [*G. sylvestris*], *G. hispanica, G. pilosa, G. germanica, G. prostrata, G. sagittalis*.

Geum—**G. montanum*. Dwarf and compact with many golden flowers. Sun. **G. reptans*. Rare and lovely. Soil composed of stone chips and mould.

Helianthemums—Nice bushlings for sunny places in well-drained soil. *H. vulgare* [*H. chamaecistus*] and numerous hybrids.

Hypericum—*H. coris*. Fairy St. Johnswort

from Maritime Alps. *H. reptans.* Flat sheets of green with brilliant blossoms.

Inula—*I. acaulis.* Large flowers flaunted on 6-inch stems. Robust and easy. *I. ensifolia.* Compact; many daisylike flowers in summer.

Iris—*I. arenaria.* Very dwarf with large yellow blossoms. Sandy soil; sun. *I. lutea.* Taller and not a clear yellow. *I. Orange Queen.* A better colour than the last.

Linum—*L. capitatum, L. capanulatum,* and *L. flavum* are all fine yellow-flowered flaxes for sunny well-drained positions.

Lithospermum—*L. canescens.* Gray leaves, flowers in leafy cymes. Native.

Narcissus—*N. cyclamineus, N. minor, N. minimus* [*N. asturiensis*], *N. gracilis* [*N. tenuior*], *N. tenuior, N. juncifolius* [*N. assoanus*], *N. bulbocodium.*

Oenothera—*Oe. brachycarpa.* Four-inch tufted evening primrose. Dry situation. *Oe. missouriensis.* Brilliant but needs space. Late summer. *Oe. pumila.* Inconspicuous biennial that sows itself about.

Onosma—*O. tauricum.* The golden drop must be secured against all dampness.

Papaver—*P. kerneri.* A form of the alpine poppy. *P. pyrenaicum.* The same.

Polemonium—*P. pauciflorum.* Pale tubular flowers, nice foliage. Native.

Potentilla—*P. ambigua* [*P. cuneuta*], *P. apennina, P. calabra, P. fruticosa* (shrub).

Primula—*P. auricula.* The fragrant old Dusty Miller. Good soil and sun. *P. bulleyana.* Golden-yellow with soft orange. Shade and damp. *P. elatior.* Oxlip, umbels of yellow flowers. *P. helodoxa.* Biennial; whorls of lovely yellow flowers. China. *P. luteola.* Tall with whorls of blossoms. Deep loamy soil. *P. sikkimensis.* Moisture loving. Pale clusters of fragrant flowers. *P. veris.* The cowslip. *P. vulgaris.* The English primrose.

Ranunculus—*R. montanus.* Cheerful little buttercup.

Saxifraga—*S. aizoon lutea* [*S. paniculata lutea*]. Lovely little plant for a choice place.

Sedum—*S. acre, S. altissima* [*S. sediforme*], *S. kamtschaticum, S. rupestre* [*S. reflexum*], *S. spathulifolium,* etc.

Tulipa—*T. australis, T. batalini, T. kaufmanniana, T. persica, T. silvestris.*

Uvularia—*U. grandiflora.* For woodland; slender plant with drooping bell.

Viola—*V. biflora.* Small plant with creeping roots and twin flowers. *V. glabella.* Handsome Western species easily raised from seed. *V. lutea.* A European mountain violet with stems 6 ins. high.

CHAPTER XXVI

White Flowers for the Rock Garden

W HITE FLOWERS are so numerous that nothing would be easier than to plant an entire rock garden with them alone. But despite the fact that many of them are not quite as the driven snow, numbers tending toward cream, or green, or gray, or a faint flush, and still others being flecked or etched or stained with colour, it would be, on the whole, I think, a chill and uninviting region. We should sadly miss the glowing hues and the exciting points of brilliance we delight to find in our rock gardens. But, in any case, we cannot do without a great many of the candid sisterhood, for among them are not only some of the most reliable of the standbys, such as arabis, hardy candytuft, and the like, but many of the daintiest and most lovely treasures.

The white-flowered bulbs of spring are especially virginal and beautiful. The snowdrop; the snowflake, like a giant snowdrop, which, because of its delightful fragrance was of old styled the bulbous violet; white forms of scilla, chionodoxa, crocus and muscari; the white and creamy troutlilies and the shining stars of Bethlehem, so often neglected, but always charming seen in clumps in some half-shaded place among the unfolding fronds of ferns. The white-flowered checker lily, *Fritillaria meleagris alba,* is one of the most engaging of spring bulbous flowers. Its large, drooping pale flower faintly checkered over with green is most quaint and attractive. It likes a partially shaded place, not too dry.

Many of our most charming native woodland flowers are white: among them the wood anemone and its almost invariable companion the rue anemone; the bloodroot, with its pearly buds

and starry flowers; the quaint Dutchman's breeches; the sprightly little Canada mayflower (*Maianthemum canadensis*); *Trillium grandiflorum*, which shows in green glades like a shy wood nymph; the foamflower (*Tiarella cordifolia*), so lovely seen flowing down a rocky declivity and, among many others, the violets, among which none are so cherished as the white ones. There are *V. blanda* with its fine fragrance; *V. canadensis*, that blossoms all the season until frost; *V. lanceolata*, sprightly and for a dampish place, and *V. striata*, creamy flowers etched with dusky colour. This is a most floriferous and delightful sort. Rare and exquisite among white-flowered violets is the albino form of the bird's-foot. Like its purple prototype, this scarce treasure must be given the acid soil (rotted oak leaves, pine or hemlock needles, rotted material from old stumps or logs and white sand in mixture) in which alone it will thrive.

The mention of acid soil reminds us that a bed of it will enable us to grow still other lovely natives that we should be sad to do without. Make this bed in a half-shaded situation, putting the acid soil mixture in at least eight inches deep, and enjoy the beauty of *Shortia galacifolia*, whose thick and shining foliage and lovely five-cleft bells are found very locally in the high mountains of Carolina. They are usually found in the company of *Galax aphylla*, pyrolas, and chimaphilas, all of which may be grown happily in a rock garden if the accustomed soil be faithfully reproduced.

Among other plants with white flowers, some of the most conspicuous and easily grown belong to the tribes of arabis, iberis, phlox, and cerastium, but a danger signal should be set beside each one of them, especially where a small rock garden is under consideration. Beautiful they are, to be sure, and ready to spread great drifts of snowy whiteness wherever they are given a foothold; indestructible, willing, or perhaps one should say insistent, they soon take possession of the entire rock garden, advancing inexorably each after the manner of its kind—by recklessly flung seeds, by sneaking underground tentacles, by quick-rooting branches, until wide areas are within their grasp. If splurge and splash are all that is wanted, these plants with the golden alyssum and one or two other such depredatious—I trust the word is in the dictionary—spirits will give it in full measure. But if you cherish at heart the ideal that a rock garden should be a treasure house of choice and restrained beauties, grow these others by all means, but give them a mountain to themselves, or make up your mind to spend much time and back-breaking labour in keeping them within bounds. The white dead nettle, *Lamium album*, is another that will bear watching, though not so great a spreader as the blue form, than which it is far more beautiful. Indeed, its spikes of creamy blossoms are among the favourites of the summer, but I am able to enjoy them only by so placing the plant that it can do no harm.

On the other hand, there are many conspicuously beautiful white-flowered plants that will give no trouble at all. A very fine and useful one is *Veronica rupestris alba*. It is easy to grow, gracious in its response to kindly treatment, and of a most exquisite whiteness; but, within reason, it remains where it is put, and no small treasure is endangered because of it.

Arenaria montana also stands forth as one of the showy white-flowered plants which yet does not constitute a peril to smaller loves. It makes a tangle of lax branches set off by grayish leaves and a wild profusion in May of large white flowers. Raise it from seed if you can get it in no other way. *Arenaria (Sagina) caespitosa* [*Sagina subulata*] is like a little moss that once a year, in spring, forgets its green tradition and becomes a mist of tiny white stars. A fine little plant for a shaded place where it may spread over and among stones, or line the joints of steps or old walls (in shade) with its emerald verdure.

Achillea and anthemis both offer attractive and easily grown plants with silvery or hoary foliage and white, cream, or yellow flowers. They like a sunny situation and a soil that is thoroughly well drained. Like most gray-leaved plants, they detest standing moisture, whether in the earth or saturating the air. *Achillea serbica* is satisfactory and easy. Its narrow, hoary leaves are pretty and its many white daisylike blossoms are attractive in the early summer. The foliage of *A. umbellata* is silvery and finely cut. It is a desirable sort. *Anthemis montana* makes a fine spread of gray lace leafage out of which arise creamy daisies on long lax stems. *A. aizoon*[1] is a smaller and choicer plant, worth

---

[1] *Achillea ageratifolia.*

supplying with a comfortable niche between stones where its feet will be dry and its head in the sun. These plants though spreading in habit are all quite dwarf in stature.

Potentilla alba is flowery the season through, though it is one of the first rock plants to venture its blossoms. Any situation will suit it. *Nierembergia rivularis*, from the La Plata River, makes thickets of soft leaves among which are borne exquisite white cups over a long season. This is a lovely thing. The white-flowered thyme, *Thymus serpyllum albus* weaves a close-fitting mantle over earth and stones and presently, almost in the twinkling of an eye, changes it to one of tiny white blossoms. This is one of the most precious of plants, delightful for spreading over the lower reaches of the rock garden, and its sharp fragrance is invigorating. The creeping chalk plant, *Gypsophila repens*, is happily well known, and may be easily grown in any sunny dry situation, though it prefers one where lime is present in the soil. It is seldom wholly out of bloom, and so its value is great. A good clipping in spring or fall will keep it tidy. Not so often seen is a little species from the mountains of Kashmir and Sikkim. This is *G. cerastioides* with thickish hairy leaves and lovely large white blossoms etched with purple. It is not a rapid grower, but in a year or so makes nice little compact mats that are ornamental in or out of bloom.

Very pretty, too, and kindly is blue-eyed Mary's pale sister, *Omphalodes verna alba*. In half shade and a nice vegetable soil it spreads into close mats, and many round-eyed snowy blossoms appear in April amidst its pleasant greenery. In the same situation might grow epimediums, of which the white-flowered ones are especially dainty and pleasing, and their airy and fluttering leafage an added beauty anywhere. *Asperula odorata*, the sweet woodruff, for later bloom among these two would be delightful.

The blossoms of the greater number of saxifrages are white but they are usually enlivened by flecks or spots of red or other colour. These are among the rock garden's most glorious furnishings; indeed, according to Mr. Farrer, who was their most ardent admirer, without them a rock garden can boast no glory at all. Here, in America, it is not easy as yet to obtain any but a few of the vast number of species. Gardeners and nurserymen alike seem imbued with the notion that they are all of a like ungraciousness and perversity. As a matter of fact, numbers of them grow far more easily and with less consideration and attention than many a plant we attempt without a thought. A great many of what are known as the silver or encrusted saxifrages are perfectly amiable and enduring, and given only fair conditions will grow into supremely gratifying hummocks of beautiful gray or bluish, thick-leaved rosettes from which arise in due time the perfectly airy and exquisite sprays of starry flowers on graceful, swaying stems. These encrusted saxifrages love sunshine, but I have found in our climate where, while giving them plenty of sunshine, we also treat them to long spells of drought, it is well to put a rock between them and the afternoon sun. Thus considered, there is no trouble in growing many of

them in the gritty, loamy soil among the stones of the rock garden, with or without lime. They do require, however, to be occasionally top-dressed with loam and sand where they have worked themselves out of the soil. Of these encrusted saxifrages, some that I have found to be easily grown are the following: several forms of *Saxifraga aizoon* [*S. paniculata*], including *La Graveana*, *lutea*, *rosea*, and others; *S. cochlearis* with heavily silvered blue-green rosettes; *S. cotyledon*, with huge green rosettes, *S. lingulata* [*S. callosa*], leaves long and narrow and well silvered; *S. longifolia*; *S. macnabiana*, one of the easiest; and several others.

The mossy saxifrages make enchanting hills and hummocks (a few inches high) of the most perfect emerald green little rosettes which in May are almost lost beneath a forest of fragile stems carrying exquisite blossoms, white, pink, rosy. *S. wallacei* is one of the loveliest, *S. hypnoides* a delightful white-flowered species; *S. dicipiens* [*S. hypnoides*] with white flowers and rosettes that turn a nice crimson in winter. These are but a few. The mossies have a disconcerting way of suddenly beginning to turn brown. Sometimes a little good soil worked in among the growths will stop the trouble, again a stone dropped in among them seems to have a heartening effect, causing the green rosettes to huddle against it and cease their pining and dying. And often it is best to dig up the plant and pull it gently to pieces, replanting the little growths in moist gritty soil in a half-shaded place until they are well rooted.

The mossies succeed in a light gritty soil

and in situations where the sun falls upon them for but part of the day, and they must be watered in times of drought. They seem to delight to grow among largish stones between which they hump their green mounds in apparent comfort. *S. ceratophylla* [*S. trifurcata*] is also a "mossy" and of the easiest culture—a plant for any rock garden not hopelessly sour or overhung by trees. London Pride, *Saxifraga umbrosa*, requires a cool and damp situation. There is no reason why any careful gardener should not grow a collection of saxifrages, and he misses a good deal if he does not.

A selection of white-flowered plants for the rock garden

Achillea—*A. huteri*. Delicate silver leaves, white flowers. 4 ins. *A. serbica*. Easy and enduring. All achilleas are easy from seed. *A. umbellata*. Top-dress or divide frequently. Lovely.

Alyssum—*A. spinosum*. Gray bushling for dry, sunny situation.

Androsace—*A. coronopifolia* [*A. lactifolia*]. Dainty little self-sowing biennial. *A. lactea*. A 4-inch mite with milky flowers.

Anemone—*A. canadensis*. For outlying districts in shade. A wily spreader. *A. sylvestris*. From German woods. Also a wily spreader.

Anthemis—*A. aizoon*. Silver leaves and neat habit. *A. montana*. Spreading silver lace leaves and creamy daisies.

Aquilegia—*A. flabellata*. A 6-inch Japanese with ivory-white blossoms.

Arabis—*A. albida fl. pl.* [*A. caucasica fl. pl.*]. Beautiful double form of the common arabis. *A. kellereri*. Choice little rock plant. *A. sturii*.

Very dwarf, distinct, and pretty. *A. procurrens*. Flat, advancing rosettes. Spreads rapidly.

Arenaria—*A. balearica*. An emerald covering for shaded rocks. *A. caespitosa* [*Sagina subulata*]. Invaluable little green moss. *A. montana*. One of the best of rock plants.

Armeria—*A. maritima alba*. White form of the charming common thrift.

Asperula—*A. odorata*. Give it space and a shaded corner and enjoy it.

Campanula—*C. carpatica alba*. Requires space but is very lovely. *C. hosti alba* [*C. rotundifolia* var. *hostii*]. A beauty for half shade. *C. pusilla alba* [*C. cochleariifolia*]. Dainty 2-inch ramper hung with many bells. *C. rotundifolia alba*. White form of our native harebell.

Cerastium—*C. tomentosum*. Too easy to be safe among choice plants.

Chrysanthemum—*C. arcticum*. Thick leaves and many daisies in October.

Dianthus—*D. arenarius*. Dark narrow leaves, fringy sweet blossoms. Delicious. *D. alpinus albus*. Rare and not easy. Half shade. Vegetable soil. *D. deltoides albus*. Easy and pretty for an outlying place. *D. fragrans*. Easy to grow and deliciously sweet. *D. integer*. A charming dwarf for a choice place in sun.

Dryas—*D. octopetala*. Glorious for a high exposed place in the rock garden.

Erinus—*E. alpinus albus*. Shelter and protect from spring winds. Pretty.

Erodium—*E. amanum*. A choice storksbill for a sunny spot. Silver leaves.

Fritillaria—*F. meleagris alba*. One of the choicest spring flowers.

Funkia—*F. minor* [*Hosta minor*]. Quaint little prototype of the giant *F. subcordata* [*Hosta subcordata*]. A gem.

Gypsophila—The dwarfs of this family love sun and drought.

Helianthemum—*H. apenninum*. Very lovely.

Helleborus—*H. niger*. The white Christmas rose of chill December days.

Hutchinsia—*H. alpina* [*Pritzelago alpina*]. A nice little bunch of green leaves and white blossoms.

Iberis—*I. sempervirens*. Sheets of snow. Robust. More compact forms are little gem and snowflake.

Iris—*I. cristata alba*. Rare and exquisite. *I. pumila alba*. Small and dainty. *I. tectorum alba*. Perhaps the most beautiful iris that grows.

Leontopodium—*L. alpinum*. The edelweiss. Easy but fears damp.

Leucocrinum—*L. montanum*. The sandlily of the Rockies. Lovely.

Leucojum—*L. vernum*. Do not miss having this in your garden. *L. aestivum*. Summer-flowering.

Linaria—*L. cymbalia alba*. A 2-inch treasure for paved paths and walls.

Lychnis—*L. alpina alba*. A wee little plant, easy to raise from seed.

Mitella—*M. diphylla*. For shade and leaf soil.

Myosotis—White forget-me-nots are especially dainty and sweet.

Nierembergia—*N. rivularis*. Its large cups are borne in the late summer. Give light soil and sun.

Oenothera—*Oe. caespitosa*. Thrilling but a notable spreader. *Oe. speciosa*. Enjoy this in another's garden. Ineradicable.

Ompahlodes—*O. verna alba*. A friendly and lovely plant for shade.

Phlox—*P. subulata* 'Nelsonii.' Beautiful and more compact than subulatas generally. *P. divaricata alba*. Exquisite and not often seen.

Polygonatum—*P. giganteum* [*P. biflorum*]. A striking woodland plant.

Potentilla—*P. alba*. Indefatigable in blossoming. Low-growing and easy.

Primula—*P. vulgaris* (Harbinger of Spring). Exquisite and early flowering. Other white-flowered sorts are *japonica alba, denticulata alba, involucrata, chionantha,* and *hirsuta alba*.

Saponaria—*S. ocymoides alba*. Useful and not often seen. Trailer.

Saxifrages—Many and various. Be sure to know a few.

Sedum—*S. album, S. ternatum, S. nevii,* and *S. glaucum*.

Silene—*S. alpestris*. Useful and charming. Dark leaves. *S. maritima*. Rather sprawling, but pretty.

Thymus—*T. serpyllum albus*. Spreads a veil of fragrant green.

Tiarella—*T. cordifolia*. Loves woods soil and shade. Lovely.

Trillium—*T. grandiflorum*. Happy under the same conditions.

Veronica—*V. rupestris alba*. Indispensable. *V. saxatilis alba* [*V. fruticans alba*]. Dwarf little trailer of great charm.

Violets, of many kinds.

CHAPTER XXVII

Pink Flowers for the Rock Garden

PINK FLOWERS, devoid of a more or less strong ad-mixture of blue or violet, are not very numerous. The magenta sisterhood is legion-strong and many of them are lovely; but they are in bad repute, and the effort here is to make note of a few plants whose flowers, save in a few favourite and not very grievously sinning cases, follow a gay and dainty scale from blush to pure carmine-pink. Choice bits of finery, these, for the ornamentation of our rock gardens.

Among the spring-flowering bulbs are very few that come within the scope of our present interest. Perhaps the very prettiest are the two California troutlilies, *Erythronium Jonsoni* [*E. revolutum* var. *jonsonii*] and *E. revolutum Pink Beauty*. The one has bright, candy-pink, smartly reflexing petals, and the flowers of the other are shell-pink with a central zone of gold. Both of these are delightful additions to the spring rock garden and bloom early.

There are, of course, many hyacinths decked in the most luscious tones of pink, but these rotund and sophisticated beings have no place among our small mountain citizenry. Both Spanish and English bluebells, however, have pink varieties that rightfully find a place in the rock garden. *Scilla campanulata* [*Hyacinthoides hispanica*] *Rosalind* carries full heads of blush-coloured bells, while *S. nutans (festalis)* [*Hyacinthoides non-scripta*] *Blush Queen* hangs its curving stalk with smaller shell-pink chimes. There is a form of *S. nutans* called *rosea* whose deeper-toned blossoms approach the magenta danger zone but are not frank enough about it to be of definite value. I will mention here a little autumn-blooming squill

called *Scilla chinensis* that produces a six-inch stalk of bright rose-coloured flowers, not a very good tone of pink, but admissible because of the season.

Among botanical or wild tulips we have: *T. saxatilis*, pale pink with a splash of yellow at the centre; the lady tulip, *T. clusiana*, with crisp stripes of bright carmine-pink and white; the waterlily tulip, *T. kaufmanniana*, whose creamy petals are boldly flashed with carmine. All these give their blossoms at a very early season and are of the greatest charm and value in sunny, sheltered places in a sweet, well-drained, and limy soil. A summer-flowering bulb of great attraction is *Zephyranthes carinata* [*Z. grandiflora*], that our English cousins call flower of the west wind. The colour of the large crocus-like blossoms is a fine pink. Its relative, *Z. rosea*, blooms in the late summer and autumn. Being natives of Mexico and other beneficent climes they are a bit tender, and persons living north of Washington must take them up and store them in a frost-proof place at the approach of winter—preferably, say the wise ones, in damp sand.

Some of the hybrids of the Lenten rose, *Helleborus orientalis*, have delightful pink blossoms, and as they are borne in March on long stiff stems, it is very pleasant to have them. The true Christmas rose, *H. niger*, is pure white of the most glistening quality, but *H. altifolia* [*H. niger*]—often sold for it—has blossoms that open pale blush and gradually turn a quite bright pink on the under sides of the petals. They bloom in November and December. If small frames are put over the clumps the waxen blossoms will be preserved from injury by storms and frosts. They are shade-loving plants and consort well with hepaticas and ferns and wood hyacinths where the soil is deep and rich.

Of familiar native early-blooming plants whose pink blossoms would grace any rock garden there are a number. There are dainty pink hepaticas to be gathered from any woodland assemblage; there is the spring beauty (*Claytonia virginica*); the exquisitely fragrant trailing arbutus (*Epigaea repens*), whose soul is satisfied only with a definitely acid soil—one made up of rotted oak leaves, pine or hemlock needles, and white sand—and which should be lightly covered with leaves and needles for at least a year after planting. Then there are the graceful trilliums *T. stylosum* [*T. catesbaei*] and *T. cernuum*, loving shade and a fat woods soil, and the rare pink form of *T. grandiflorum*—born pink, not merely flushing as the flower ages. The pink lady's slipper, *Cypripedium acaule*, will come a bit later and enjoys the same soil prepared for arbutus.

One of the very best pink-flowered rock plants is *Silene pennsylvanica*, which decorates the rocky hillsides of many parts of the East. In different localities the colour varies, and it is found from pale pink to quite a bright rose-carmine. It is a most kindly plant, spreading by self-sowing where it is happy, but it is safe to say that it is not happy where lime is present in the soil. As we turn to the Far West, we find its beautiful relative, *S. hookeri*, a low plant with a rather fleshy stock that bears very large pink blossoms of a pure tone. At alpine heights grows *S. acaulis,* a mosslike little plant that covers itself with bright pink blossoms in its native haunts, but when brought into captivity often refuses to bloom, though its small greenery spreads into nice little mats. I should be glad to hear from any who have been successful in flowering *S. acaulis.*

And while we are considering Western plants with pink blossoms, we should speak of the spectacular lewisias. These are as yet little known in Eastern gardens, but they are extremely attractive and handsome. They form fine rosettes of shining, fleshy leaves from which arise on short stems clusters of distinctive flowers. I have grown a number of them on a rocky slope of the rock garden facing due East, with some protection from the southern sun, and they have lived and blossomed for several years. The soil they seem to like is deep and sandy and full of leaf mould. The handsomest variety is *L. tweedyi,* but *L. leeana* and *L. Howelli* [*L. cotyledon howelli*] are also lovely, and the bitterroot, *L. rediviva,* is one of the prettiest. It dies away after giving its large pink satin blossoms, but the spot where it grows should be marked, for it will again rise with the coming of the new spring.

Among the foreigners, few families give us more enchanting pink flowers than do the aethionemas. These are little low bushlings, their small leaves often gray or bright blue-green, which harmonize delightfully with the heads of pink flowers that finish the little branches. All of them love the fullest sun and a soil gritty and well-drained and impregnated with lime. They are charming for a wall, a cliff, or any high place in the rock garden. After flowering, they should be clipped over to keep them from growing leggy. They are easily raised from seed and will self-sow themselves when happily situated.

The alpine pinks, of course, are rich in flowers of the hue under consideration. These, too, are most easy to raise from seed and the greater number of them may be comfortably housed on any sunny, properly constructed rock garden. One of the best of all is *Dianthus neglectus* [*D. pavonis*], the undersides of whose bright pink blossoms are buff-coloured.

The arabis tribe we think of largely as white-flowered, but there are two very pretty pink kinds that are decidedly worth growing. *Arabis albida rosea* [*A. caucasica rosea*], with shell-pink blossoms, is very lovely and often blooms during March. *A. aubrietioides* is more compact and smaller all through, and the blossoms are a delicate mauve-pink. These plants also are the better for a good clipping after flowering, and division every few years keeps us well stocked with compact and sturdy plants.

Phlox subulata Vivid gives us one of the handsomest spreads of delicious pink colour available; and both *P. amoena* and *P. pilosa splendens* are good. The helianthemums (sunroses) are attractive little bushes, many having hoary leaves, among which we find numerous pink-flowered sorts. They may be grown with the greatest ease in a sunny situation where the soil is well drained. They are especially effective where they have a large stone to spread over. After flowering, the bushes should be well cut back in order to maintain a shapely outline.

Lissadel seedling is one of the prettiest forms I have seen, displaying several lovely tones of pink and old rose. Helianthemums are easily raised from seed. The thrifts (armeria) are an altogether pink-flowered family, save for an occasional albino. They run a delightful scale from pale blush to striking rose-carmine, and are the pleasantest and most useful little plants imaginable. All save *A. caespitosa* may be raised from seed and grown in any sunny well-drained position with the greatest ease. This diminutive treasure is safest in a more or less vertical crevice with a good depth of sandy soil behind and its face in the sun. It forms a huddle of little spiky rosettes stuck all over in late April with rounded heads of pink flowers.

From both geraniums and erodiums we derive a few dainty pink-flowered species for the rock garden, some of which have the added beauty of gray or silvered foliage to set off the frail pink blossoms. *Geranium argenteum* is said by an enthusiast to be one of the loveliest things in Nature, with its glistening silver foliage and its "great dog-rose blossoms." *G. cinereum* is only a little less lovely, because its blossoms are not so pure in colour nor its leaves so silvery. These two do not much exceed six inches in height, and with the little four-inch spreading *G. sanguineum lancastriense,* make a trio that should be found in every rock garden where dainty and exquisite things are prized. The most enchanting of the erodiums is *E. supracanum,* with richly silvered fernlike leaves and blossoms like fluttering pink butterflies. Both geraniums and erodiums are very easy to raise from seed. They enjoy a high position on the rock garden and sunshine for the greater part of the day. A light sandy soil and a deep root run please them. They dislike disturbance and should be moved while very small.

And then we have the androsaces, typical high mountain plants, many of which, however, will come to our lowland rock gardens and thrive with the most gracious luxuriance. *A. lanuginosa* is a rarely lovely trailer with soft gray stems and leaves and masses of sprightly verbena-like blossoms on short stems borne almost through the season. Its home is in the Himalaya Mountains. A warm sandy slope with outcroppings of rock makes a happy situation for it. *A. sarmentosa, A. chumbyi* [*A. sarmentosa* var. *chumbyi*], and *A. primuloides* are all delightful, with widely ramifying rosettes, hairy and gray, and gay little umbrellas of blossom most exuberantly borne in various tones of pink and rose. *A. sempervivoides* is smaller altogether, with green, fleshy rosettes, very neat and tidy, and bright rosy blossoms. It is the earliest to bloom and a nice little plant for a choice spot where it will not be disturbed by the encroachments of more sturdy neighbours.

Among the latest pink-flowered plants to bloom are *Silene schafta* and *Sedum sieboldi* [*Hylotelephium sieboldi*]. They are not capricious, and we are not critical of the quality of their rosiness at so late a season.

A selection of pink flowers for the rock garden

Aethionema—*A. armenum.* Gray-blue bushling of four inches. *A. grandiflorum.* The largest of the race; long prostrate branches. *A. jucundum* [*A. condifolium*]. The very loveliest; about three inches tall. *A. persicum.* Lovely and best for the beginner. *A. warley hybrid.* Brilliant flowers, low bushling.

Androsace—*A. carnea.* Tiny emerald-green rosette, small pink flowers. *A. Laggeri.* Much the same with deeper pink blossoms. *A. Chumbyi* [*A. sarmentosa chumbyi*]. Easy and satisfactory. *A. lanuginosa.* A charming trailer. *A. primuloides, A. sarmentosa. A. sempervivoides.* To be cherished.

Antennaria—*A. dioica rosea.* A good gray-leaved cover plant.

Arabis—*A. albida rosea* [*A. caucasica rosea*]. An early-flowering blessing. *A. aubrietioides.* Very attractive and compact. Likes shelter. *A. rosea* [*A. muralis*]. A biennial of little importance.

Armeria—*A. alpina.* Easy and useful. *A. caespitosa.* An undoubted treasure. *A. juncea* (*setacea*). Compact mat and bright rose-pink blossoms. *A. maritima.* The little friendly common thrift. *A. plantaginea.* Very brilliant.

Asperula—*A. cyananchica.* A mass of fine green threads and tiny pink blooms. *A. hirta.* A small treasure for a choice situation.

Aubrietia—*A. bridesmaid.* Has pale blush flowers.

Bellium—*B. minutum.* A tiny pinkish daisy from Greece.

Claytonia—*C. virginica.* Spring beauty.

Convolvulus—*C. incanus.* Clusters of gray velvet leaves and pink vases. 4 inches. A spreader.

Cypripedium—*C. acaule.* Pink lady's slipper.

Daphne—*D. cneorum.* Pink-flowered bushling for half shade and wood soil.

Dianthus—*D. alpinus.* All the rock garden pinks are delightful. *D. caesius, D. deltoides, D. neglectus* [*D. pavonis*], *D. silvestris.*

Dicentra—*D. formosa.* Pendant hearts and fernlike foliage. *D. eximia.* A more luxuriant plant from the West.

Epigaea—*E. repens.* The trailing arbutus.

Epimedium—*E. roseum* [*E. pinnatum roseum*]. A graceful shade lover.

Erinus—*E. alpinus.* A nice little plant but not overhardy. Shelter.

Erodium—*E. macradenum.* Pale pink with a dark blotch. *E. romanum. E. supracanum.*

Erythronium—*E. hartwegii.* Mauve-pink troutlily. Very good and lusty. *E. revolutum Johnsoni, E. revolutum Pink Beauty.*

Geranium—*E. argenteum.* Most lovely. *G. cinereum. G. sanguineum lancastriense.* The best to begin with.

Gypsophila—*G. repens rosea.* Blush-flowered trailer. *G. fratensis.* The best of the prostrate chalkplants. *G. muralis.* A small annual making a rosy cloud.

Helianthemum—*H. amabile.* Neat, hoary with rose-pink blossoms. *H. rhodanthe carneum. H. Lissadel Seedling.* Charming. *H. Rose Queen.*

Helleborus—*H. altifolia* [*H. niger* var. *altifolia*]. Pink-flowered Christmas rose.

Hepatica—*H. triloba.* Pink forms must be selected when in bloom.

Lewisia—*H. leeana. L. howelli.* Handsome crested leaves, pink flowers. *L. rediviva.* Satiny pink flowers of great beauty. Deciduous. *L. tweedyi.* Largest and most beautiful of the group.

Lychnis—*L. alpina.* A tiny tuft with magenta blossoms. *L. dioica* [*Silene dioica*]. A biennial self-sower. Pretty if you have room for it. *L. lagascae* [*Petrocoptis glaucifolia*]. Gay and distinctive but unreliable. Easy from seed. *L. viscaria.* An old friend, magentaish but kindly.

Myosotis—Pink forms of *sylvatica* and *victoria.* Charmingly dainty.

Papaver—*P. nudicaule* (pearls of dawn). Lovely and diaphanous.

Phlox—*P. amoena.* Easy and useful. *P. pilosa splendens.* Bright but not choice. *P. subulata vivid.* One of the best pink-flowering plants.

Primula—*P. cortusoides.* Magentaish but delightful. *P. farinosa.* Lovely for a dampish spot. *P. frondosa.* Much like it but not so fine a colour. *P. rosea.* For a damp spot. Startling rose-pink.

Saponaria—*S. ocymoides.* An old reliable trailer.

Saxifraga—*S. aizoon rosea* [*S. paniculata rosea*]. Silvered rosettes and pink blossoms. *S. dicipiens* (guilford seedling). A "mossy" with shell-pink flowers. *S. rhei superba.* A lovely pink-flowered mossy saxifrage.

Scilla—*S. campanulata Rosalind* [*Hyacinthoides hispanica 'Rosalind'*]. *S. Nutans* (*festalis*) [*Hyacinthoides non-scripta*] (*Blush Queen*).

Sedum—*S. pilosum.* A biennial of great beauty. Easily raised from seed. *S. sieboldi.* One of the latest flowers to grace the rock garden.

Silene—*S. acaulis. S. hookeri.* Lovely California mountain plant. *S. schafta.* Late-flowering and easy. *S. pennsylvanica.* Beautiful native plant for half-shaded situation.

Townsendia—*T. exscarpa.* A charming but elusive Westerner.

Trillium—*T. cernuum. T. stylosum* [*T. catesbaei*].

Tulipa—*T. clusiana* (the lady tulip). A warm, protected situation. *T. kaufmanniana.* Brilliant in the spring garden. *T. saxatilis.* Rare and lovely.

Tunica—*T. saxifraga.* A spry little plant for every garden.

Veronica—*V. pectinata rosea.* A nice carpet for small bulbs.

Viola—*V. arenaria rosea* [*V. rupestris rosea*]. Magentaish but beguiling. *V. bosniaca.* One of the finest of its race. Probably biennial. *V. cornuta rosea.* Easy and gay.

Zephyranthes—*Z. carinata* [*Z. grandiflora*]. *Z. rosea.*

CHAPTER XXVIII

Brief Hints on Construction

IT IS NOT possible to prescribe exact directions for the building of a rock garden. Each situation will require a different treatment, and every builder will cherish some idea of the effect he wishes to bring about. Often the conformation of the ground chosen for the rock garden settles the matter of what type is to be built—a high slope, a valley, a glen, each presupposing a definite type of construction. Again the kind and size of the stones at our command determine or restrict to a great degree what we are able to accomplish.

If the available situation happens to be a slope with natural outcroppings of rock nothing could be more fortunate provided the exposure is a genial one. In this case the work is half done and at a minimum of expense. On the other hand, if the only space to be had is perfectly level, then all the wit, the taste, the vision of the builder must be brought into play to make the finished garden appear like a stretch of naturally rugged landscape, harmonious and coherent in all its parts, and of a piece with its surroundings. Not at all is this situation to be regarded as hopeless, however, nor even exceptionally difficult; but it will take more labour and more material, and the builder must be able clearly to visualize the form he wishes his miniature landscape to take and to work patiently toward it. He will be doing all the work unassisted by nature, but he may, nevertheless, contrive a beautiful rock garden wherein homes for the choicest rock plants may be found. The greatest difficulty, perhaps, will be to reconcile it to its surroundings, so that it will not appear alien and out of place. But as Mr. Farrer wrote, if you want a beautiful rockery as well as beautiful plants, you must work

it out for yourself. And this is true. For the rest, here are a few general principles that will help make the world of the garden safe for our Lilliputian democracy.

The situation

Of course, the ideal situation does not fall to the lot of many of us. Indeed, I am not quite sure what the ideal situation would be; it depends, it seems to me, upon what one wants to do. But for growing a wide variety of sun-loving rock plants and alpines, and a lesser number of shade lovers—and this is the aim of most rock gardeners—I would choose a piece of sloping ground (not too steep) quite out in the open, away from buildings, hedges, fences, all formal adjuncts and artificial construction, and well out from under overhanging branches, where a free circulation of air is assured and plenty of sunshine. You can build in northern exposures and shaded hollows for such plants as crave them, but it is not possible to contrive sunshine, and this is the desire of the heart of most alpines.

That the fall of the rock garden should be from north to south is considered very desirable, this general slope providing many planting sites having easterly and westerly exposures. A fall from south to north is much less available from the point of view of growing alpines; even a slight slope to the north creates a cold exposure, and while this is satisfactory to a number of plants, it is not for the great majority.

North of the rock garden, it is a wise provision to mass evergreens and early-flowering shrubs and small trees as a protection from the bitter winds of winter, and if there are a few tall trees away to the east, the frozen leaves and blossoms of the early spring will be saved the kiss of the morning sun which is so often fatal to them. Care should be observed that the setting of trees and shrubs usually necessary to tie the rock garden into the surrounding landscape should not be of a character or proximity to shut off light and air from the plants. For the most part, the surrounding shrubs and trees should be dwarf of stature with a few taller subjects for accent. Evergreen and deciduous things should be equally resorted to, but simple groupings of a few kinds are more effective than conglomerate assemblages. A few early-flowering deciduous shrubs in the neighbourhood of the rock garden add greatly to the modest display made by the early rock plants. A selection might be, if the garden is of fair size, the spring witch-hazels, *Hamamelis mollis* and *H. japonica, Daphne mezereum, Chaenomales (Cydonia) japonica* or Japanese quince in several lovely colours, spice bush, *Cornus mas, Magnolia stellata,* corylopsis of several kinds, Japanese cherries, peaches, and crabapples.

It has already been pointed out that a piece of sloping ground obviates much labour and makes easily possible a delightful type of rock garden. But, failing this, almost any site may be contrived into an effective bit of landscape and a happy home for a great variety of plants. A possible situation often overlooked is a grassy bank, in most instances difficult to keep tidy and usually ragged in appearance. By removing the sod and cleaning the place thoroughly of grass roots and digging in a little good earth and sand, then planting the stones so that each lies a little farther back than the other, leaving between them crevices and niches wherein all sorts of little tufts and bulbs and tiny shrubs may be inserted, a most gay and interesting rock garden may be materialized where before was a dull expanse of no interest whatever.

Assuming that the site chosen for the rock garden lies on the level or on a gentle slope, the first thing to do is to mark off the area that is to be brought under treatment. Whatever its size, let the outline be broadly irregular, not fussily broken up or evenly scalloped. Stakes may be used to define the boundaries, or a small trench dug to mark the outline more clearly. When the size and shape have been determined, the earth should be dug out to a depth of at least a foot—more if the situation is low and apt to be damp. This is to insure drainage, but, of course, if the slope is steep, almost no artificial drainage will be required. Into the excavation should go broken stones, clinkers, pieces of rock, anything that will insure the ready draining away of superfluous moisture which is so unwholesome for many rock plants. On top of the drainage material a layer of sods, grass side down, should be placed, to prevent the soil from percolating through the loose material. Over the sods, several inches of coarse soil may be thrown, and the foundation is then ready.

The stones

The chief end of a rock garden, it should be understood, is not the stones. Their mission is simply to provide safe and comfortable quarters for a wide variety of plants. The aim is not a garden of rocks, as would sometimes seem to be the case, but a great number of delightful plants flourishing in a rocky situation. But we should, nevertheless, make the most of our stones, considering them carefully when they are assembled, and setting aside the best pieces, those that are fine in shape and nicely weathered, for the most prominent positions. The beauty of the rock garden is largely dependent upon the beauty and suitableness of the stones. Often, of course, we must use just what comes to hand or what is the most easily to be got at, but even among these there will be a choice, and it pays to make it with care. The poorer pieces may be buried as the construction rises and the finest kept for showing above ground.

It is preferable, where possible, to make use of one type of stone throughout the construction; this is the first step toward making it a harmonious whole. Sandstone or limestone are the best types to use, both from the point of view of the comfort and health of the plants and of the appearance of the rock garden. Freshly quarried stone or cut stone is rather too new and raw to create a happy effect, but, on the other hand, the square or rectangular forms often taken by such stones make building very easy, and very soon the small creepers and mantling shrubs, assisted by the kindly finger of time, blur the raw surfaces, and the effect is not so bad. The poorest to use are rounded field stones. With these it is impossible to make a stable construction; they are apt to turn over if stepped on, frost easily dislodges them, and it is impossible to pack earth about them in such a way that it will not presently come sifting out. Stones that are more or less absorbent are enjoyed by the plants, their searching roots clinging about them and finding moisture in the crevices. Very soft stone is unsatisfactory for the reason that it is apt to disintegrate under heavy frosts, undermining our constructing and often bringing our careful work to ruin. Tufa[1] is a calcareous water deposit "rock," in the fissures and indentations of which many small plants find most felicitous homes. It is too spectacular and artificial in effect to use freely, but pieces may be incorporated in the rock work and used to accommodate certain small saxifrages, tiny pinks, and the like. Granite is hard and unsympathetic, but if you are under the necessity of making use of just what is at hand, this or any other stone can be made to do.

The construction

It is of the first importance before beginning to build to have all the material on the spot. This greatly facilitates building. A few very large rocks add immensely to the dignity and nobility of the scene, so an effort should be made to secure a few. These should not be placed low down in the construction, as is often done, but should lie along the heights as

they would in nature. The massive outcroppings of rock appear naturally at the summit while smaller stones and broken stuff are found at the bottom. A reversal of this natural arrangement creates a weak and unconvincing effect.

From the first, one should set out to create beauty quite apart from the plants. "When the compilation is finished," wrote Mr. Farrer, "it ought to look established, harmonious and of a piece, long before a single tuft has been put in place." This is the ideal to work toward. Begin by scrutinizing the staked area attentively, trying the while to realize its possibilities. Then endeavour to form a mental picture of a natural scene that might be materialized within its boundaries—a little range of hills, irregular in outline, but never spectacular, or if the rock garden is to be very small, a single mountain, broad and irregular and sloping gently from the summit, not after the manner of a successful pudding, but thrusting out massively and unevenly, forming bays and gorges as a proper mountain would.

When the picture is clear in the mind, the main paths should be laid out. These should be narrow and pleasantly meandering and designed to reach all parts of the construction. Flat, irregularly shaped stones make the best paths, but simple earth paths are quite in keeping. Bluestone, gravel, or turf appear too artificial to fit into the picture. To increase the natural appearance of the construction, it is effective to build out a rocky shoulder or place a large stone where the paths make a turn to

---

[1] *"Tufa is a calcareous deposit of rather porous character precipitated from solution by lime-charged waters," and not to be confused with the volcanic "tuff."*

create the illusion that the divergence was necessary. When the compilation is completed, stepping stones may be placed here and there over the hills to facilitate getting about.

To start the construction, the earth from the excavation may be mixed with broken stone, large and small, and piled in along the paths to form the foundation of our little hills, or whatever form the construction is to take, the paths taking their places in the scheme as valleys winding between the hills. Then begin building at the bottom, piling up the earth and stones as nearly as possible in the likeness of the picture conceived, covering some stone entirely to strengthen the construction, allowing others to thrust out of the earth to form massive abrupt shoulders, ledges, terraces, sheer declivities, in the clefts of which many a small plant will delight to grow. Each stone should appear as much as possible as if it belonged to some great underlying ledge of rock. "See that your rock work is not disjointed in effect, but so ordered that each rock looks as if it belonged to the next, and had been its bedfellow since the foundations of the hills were made." To this end, here are a few unalterable laws to be followed:

Do not cast stones haphazard over a mound of earth; each must be firmly set with method and intention.

To insure permanent stability, each stone should be buried at least a third in the earth.

Each stone should lie upon its broadest base, as it would in nature; never should it be stood on end. The spike rock garden had quite a vogue at one time, but it is a vulgar travesty upon nature and a most unlikely home for plants.

Each stone should slope back toward the bank behind it in order that moisture may be directed toward the roots of the plants instead of away from them.

The construction should not overhang at any point, as plants growing at the base would be cut off from the rainfall.

See that the earth is thoroughly rammed about every stone. This is all-important, for air pockets are death traps for prowling roots, and it is impossible to remedy this serious defect when once the construction is finished.

If the rock used is stratified, it will add immensely to the realistic beauty and reposefulness of the garden if the lines of stratification are matched.

To increase the apparent difference in height between hill and valley, we may resort to planting. For the most part, plant high on the heights; a small evergreen or little deciduous shrub, or some hardy plant whose stems aspire, such as Iceland poppies, columbines, the medium-sized penstemons, will greatly aid illusion. A little tree used in such a situation should be of spreading form, crooked, and as if contorted by the fury of many storms in an exposed position. Bushy, spreading plants are most effective near the base with the higher regions reserved for the smaller, choicer things. Thus, in nature, we leave behind the coarser growths as we climb the mountain, finding the smaller treasures higher up.

Early autumn is a good time to build a rock garden, and it should be allowed to stand over the winter unplanted in order that it may have a chance to settle and mould itself into its ulti-mate form. The canny builder chooses the site of his rock garden where it may be added to, for one of the first things he will realize when it is completed is that it is far too small.

INDEX

Abelia chinensis, 114
Achillea: argentea, 107;
huteri, 107, 163; kellereri,
107; serbica, 107, 161,
163; tomentosa, 156;
umbellata, 107, 161, 163
Aconite, 16; winter, 48, 135
Aconitum uncinatum, 134
Actea alba, 134
Adder's Tongue, 53
Adiantum pedatum, 139
Adonis: amurensis, 109,
134, 154, 156; vernalis,
134, 154, 156
Aethionema, 122, 167;
armenum, 108, 168;
condifolium, 108, 168;
grandiflorum, 168;
jucundum, 108, 168;
persicum, 169; Warley
Hybrid, 169
Ajuga: genevensis
brockbankii, 134, 149;
metallica crispa, 149
Allium: cernuum, 121, 134;
cyaneum, 121, 134, 149;
moly, 134, 156; stellatum,
121, 134
Alpine anemone, 59
Alpine plants, defined, 2-3
Alyssum, 122; alpestre, 155,
156; Golden, 4, 5;
montanum, 155, 156;
saxatile, 106, 107, 109; s.
citrinum, 157; s.
compactum, 155, 156; s.
citrinum, 109;
serpyllifolium, 155, 156;
spinosum, 108, 163
American lungwort, 146
American pasque flower,
59
American shooting star,
135

American twinflower, 138
Anagallis: arvenis var.
caerulea, 149; caerulea,
149
Anchusa, 146;
myosotidiflora, 109, 134,
147, 149
Andromeda polifolia, 115,
137
Androsace: carnea, 134,
169; c. var. laggeri, 134;
chumbyi, 3, 109, 168,
169; coronopifolia, 13,
163; lactea, 163;
lactiflora, 13; lactifolia,
163; laggeri, 134, 169;
lanuginosa, 108, 134,
144, 168, 169;
primuloides, 106, 168,
169; sarmentosa, 108,
134, 168, 169; s. chumbyi,
3, 108, 109, 168, 169;
sempervivoides, 168, 169
Anemone: alpine, 59;
apennina, 60, 134, 149;
blanda, 60, 134, 149;
canadensis, 58, 163;
cañon, 59; deltoides, 59;
drummondii, 59;
globosa, 59; hepatica,
58; japonica, 60;
multifida, 59; nemorosa,
60, 134; n. alba, 61; n.
flore-pleno, 61; n.
robinsoniana, 149;
occidentalis, 59;
parviflora, 59; patens
nuttaliana, 59; pulsatilla,
59, 60; quinquefolia, 57,
137; ranunculoides, 61,
157; robinsoniana, 60,
134; rue, 136;
sphemophylla, 59;
sylvestris, 134, 163;

syndesmon
thalictroides, 58;
vernalis, 60; virginiana,
58; wood, 58; yellow
wood, 61
Angel's Tears daffodil, 26
Antennaria dioca rosea,
169
Antennarias, 107
Anthemis: aizoon, 108, 163;
cupaniana, 157;
montana, 107, 157, 161,
163
Aquilegia: caerulea, 149;
chrysantha, 157;
(columbine), 134;
flabellata, 163
Arabis, 5, 122; albida, 106,
107, 109; a. flore pleno,
107; a. rosea, 70, 109,
167, 169; albida fl. pl,
163; aubrietoides, 169;
caicasoca rosea, 167;
caucasica, 106, 107; c. fl.
pl., 163; c. rosea, 109; c.
rosea, 169; common, 4;
kellerei, 163; muralis,
169; rosea, 169; sturii,
163
Arbutus, trailing, 137, 166,
169
Arenaria: balearica, 133, 134,
163; caespitosa, 133, 134,
161, 163; montana, 45,
122, 134, 161, 163
Armeria: alpina, 169;
caespitosa, 168, 169;
juncea, 169; maritima,
169; m. alba, 163;
plantaginea, 169;
setacea, 169
Arnica montana, 157
Artemisia, 157; campestris
borealis, 107;

canadensis, 107; frigida,
107; pedemontana, 107
Asarum: canadense, 134;
hartwegii, 134
Asperula: azurea setosa, 13,
149; cyananchica, 120,
169; hirta, 169; odorata,
134, 162, 163; orientalis,
13, 149
Aspidium: aculeatum
braunii, 139; cristatum,
139; spinulosum, 139
Aspidum aculeatum
braunii, 139
Asplenium: ebenum, 139;
platyneuron, 139;
rhizophyllum, 139
Aster liniariifolius, 110,
120-21
Athemis montana, 109
Aubrietia, 107, 122;
bridesmaid, 169;
deltoidea, 45
Aurinia: saxatilis, 106, 107,
109; s. citrinum, 107,
109, 157; s. Compata, 155
Autumn, seeding in, 124
Azalea, 137; binodigiri,
114

B

Baneberry, 134
Barberry: hedge, 113;
stenophylla, 113;
thumbergii minor, 113;
verruculosa, 113
Beech fern, 140
Bellflower, 93, 134
Bellis: caerulescens, 121,
149; rotundifolia
caerulescens, 149
Bellium minutum, 169
Bellwort, 136
Bird's Eye primrose, 37

· 177 ·

Index

Rock gardens:
construction of, 174-76;
covering, 142-43;
drainage in, 142-43;
ground conditions, 171;
orientation of, 172;
situation for, 172-73;
stones for, 173-74;
uncovering, 10; weeding,
10

Rock plants: for acid soil,
137-38; blue-flowered,
149-51; defined, 2-3;
effects of moisture on,
141-42; effects of
temperature on, 141-42;
ferns, 138-40; for
ordinary soil, 134-37;
pink colored, 165-70;
raising from seeds, 123-
29; salt hay for, 143; for
shade, 131-40; white-
flowered, 159-64;
yellow-flowered, 153-58

Romanzoffia sitchensis,
136

Rose: Christmas, 135, 164,
166; Lenten, 135, 166

Rosemary, marsh, 115

Royal fern, 140

Rue anemone, 136

Rusty woodsia, 140

S
Sagina subulata, 133, 161,
163

Salix: arenaria, 115;
bracycarpa, 115;
glaucops, 115; repens
argentea, 115

Salt hay, for rock gardens,
143

Sand iris, 71

Sandlily, 164

Sand myrtle, 114

Sanguinaria canadensis, 136

Santolina:
chamaecyparissus, 107;
incana, 107

Saponaria: ocymoides, 170;
o. alba, 164

Saponaria cymoides, 122

Saxifraga, 164; aizoon, 107,
162; a. lutea, 158; s.
rosea, 170; callosa, 108,
162; ceratophylla, 136;
cochlearis, 108, 162;
cotyledon, 162;
dicipiens, 162, 170;
fortunei, 121, 136;
granulata, 136;
hypnoides, 162; La
Graveana, 162; lingulata,
108, 162; longifolia, 108,
162; lutea, 162;
macnabiana, 162;
paniculata, 162; p. lutea,
158; p. rosea, 170; rhei
superba, 170; rosea, 162;
rotundifolia, 136;
trifurcata, 136; umbrosa,
136; wallacei, 162

Scabiosa pterocephala, 119

Scarlet larkspur, 137

Scilla: amoena, 50;
atrocaerulea, 50; bifolia,
50, 146, 151; b. taurica,
50; campanulata, 50, 151,
165; c. (hispanica), 146;
c. Rosalind, 170;
chinensis, 166; f. alba
major, 50; festalis, 50,
109, 151; f. Blush Queen,
165; f. (nutans), 146;
italica, 51, 146, 151;
nutans, 50, 165; n.
(festalis), 170; sibirica,
50, 65, 109, 146, 151;
Spanish, 106

Scotch bluebell, 96

Sedum: acre, 101, 136, 158;
album, 101, 164;
altissima, 158;
altissimum, 100;
anglicum, 102, 136;
brevifolium, 102;
caeruleum, 102, 151;
dasyphyllum, 102, 108,

144; divergens, 103;
douglasi, 103; ewersii,
101, 108; glaucum, 164;
gormani, 103;
hispanicum, 102, 108;
ibericum, 101;
kamtschaticum, 101, 158;
lydium, 101; nevii, 102,
136, 164; obtusatum, 103;
oregonum, 102, 103;
pilosum, 102, 170;
pulchellum, 102, 136;
purdyi, 103; reflexum,
101, 158; r. Minus, 102;
rupestre, 101, 158;
sarmentosum, 101;
sediforme, 100, 158;
sempervivoides, 102;
sexangulare, 101;
sieboldii, 107, 110, 121,
170; spathulifolium, 108,
158; s. purdyi, 103;
spectabile, 100;
spurium, 100;
stenopetalum
'Douglasii,' 103;
stoloniferum, 101;
telephoides, 136;
ternatum, 136, 164

Seedlings: transplanting,
128; watering, 128

Seeds: biennial plants, 129;
rcommended varieties,
129-30; rock plants
from, 123-29; winter,
124

Sempervivum:
arachoideum, 103, 108;
braunii, 103; funckii, 103;
globiferum, 103; pittoni,
104; rubicundum, 103;
tectorum, 104; triste, 103

Shade: plants for, 7, 134-40

Sheep laurel, 115

Shinleaf, 138

Shortia galacifolia, 138, 160

Showy Lady's Slipper, 137

Silene: acaulis, 167, 170;
alpestris, 164; dioica,

169; hookeri, 166, 170;
maritima, 164;
pennsylvanica, 109, 138,
166, 170; schafta, 110,
119, 168, 170; sieboldi,
168; virginica, 136

Silver jonquil, 27

Sisyrinchium
anguistifolium, 151

Snowdrop, 16, 47-48

Snowflake, 48

Snow lily, 55

Socrates iris, 70

Soil: acid, plants for, 137-
38, 160; ordinary, plants
for, 134-37

Soldanella alpina, 136

Solomon's seal, false, 136

Souvenir de Sale
(dianthus), 82

Spanish bluebell, 146

Speckled clintonia, 137

Sphagnum moss, 126

Spielia marilandica, 136

Spiraea: crispifolia, 114;
decumbens, 114

Spleenwort, ebony, 139

Spotted wintergreen, 137

Spruce, Norway, 112

Squirrel corn, 134

St. Johns wort, fairy, 157

Stachys: byzantina, 107;
lanata, 107

Star flower, 136

Star of Bethlehem, 52, 134

Stonecrop, 99, 136

Stones, in rock gardens,
107-9, 173-74

Striped squill, 51

Sunny gardens, plants for,
6

Swamp laurel, 115

Swamp pink, 138

Swedish juniper, 112

Sweet violet, 66

Sweet William, Wild, 88

Sweet woodruf, 134, 162

Symphyandra hoffmanii,
136